The New Neighborhood Senior Center

The New Neighborhood Senior Center

· ·

Redefining Social and Service Roles for the Baby Boom Generation

JOYCE WEIL

Rutgers University Press

New Brunswick, New Jersey, and London

Library of Congress Cataloging-in-Publication Data
Weil, Joyce.
    The new neighborhood senior center : redefining social and service roles for the baby
    boom generation / Joyce Weil.
        pages   cm
    Includes bibliographical references and index.
    ISBN 978-0-8135-6295-7 (hardback) — ISBN 978-0-8135-6294-0 (pbk.) — ISBN
    978-0-8135-6296-4 (e-book)
    1. Senior centers—New York (State) 2. Senior centers—United States. 3. Baby boom
    generation—Service for—New York (State) 4. Baby boom generation—Service
    for—United States. 5. Older people—Services for—New York (State) 6. Older
    people—Services for—United States. I. Title.
    HV1455.2.U62N78 2014
    362.6'309747—dc23   2014004943

A British Cataloging-in-Publication record for this book is available from the British Library.

Visit our website: http://rutgerspress.rutgers.edu

Manufactured in the United States of America

For Tanta Elena

Contents

Tables

Preface

As I write this preface in March 2014, after the body of the book has been written, senior centers remain in the midst of great change. The reauthorization of the Older Americans Act (OAA), delayed over 2011–2013, has not yet happened but appears to be gaining renewed momentum. Senior nutrition program funding—a mainstay of centers—remains dependent on states' funding reserves yet has had to endure a recent political impasse that briefly shut down the federal government. Still, despite delays and cuts, the OAA holds great promise to expand the group of older persons reached by centers. Also, centers can now "modernize"—whatever that may come to mean.

I did not begin to study a senior center to talk about meta–policy changes. This work started in 2008 as a simple summer project; I wanted to examine how senior centers might affect older persons' lives. I hoped to interview center participants and see how a group of elders in Queens, New York, viewed their senior citizens' center (as they were still called at the time). What some may think of as a quaint setting with bingo playing and "little old ladies" eating a group meal was definitely not the case. Yes, I cannot lie, there was bingo, and congregate meals were served, but a fuller picture of the world of the center truly opened up to me. It became so much larger than the four walls with the check-in and sign-in sheets, meal tickets, and holiday parties. As the center, like many others in New York City, began to close, or be shuttered, as this process is often described, a new world of politics and infrastructure with players and agents presented itself to me. I became an observer of a larger process, and the scope of my ethnography expanded.

This book gave me the space to explore, from many vantage points, facets of what a senior center is and where centers currently sit in our society. I wanted to understand how projections about the (almost mythological) baby boomers were affecting the real, lived situation of persons sixty-five and older.

I desired to explore how the setting of New York City and social class were also actors on the stage of the decision-making process about centers' futures.

As I wrote the final chapter, the city's innovative center models were in their fledgling stages. Vermont senator Bernie Sanders's 2011–2013 reauthorization of the Older Americans Act was under way, but with much debate, sequestration, and the federal shutdown, it was delayed. This reauthorization has the power to expand the population targeted by centers, while the modernization component will, hopefully, set more research and evidence-based plans in motion.

I wanted to learn what happens when working-class elders lose a center (a sense of space and a familiar social and service-provision setting) and where the displaced center members would go. How did all the pieces—the center participants, staff, community members, Department for the Aging (DFTA)—come together? I was intrigued to learn how and why all efforts to keep the center from closing failed in the end. What social capital and which social ties worked? What social capital and which ties were missing? And were other underlying events and processes at work?

During these past three years, I have felt as though I was at the precipice of the imminent changes in the senior center movement and kept thinking, Are these proposed changes more than semantic ones? Will baby boomers really differ? What image of a boomer are we planning for? Do existing centers really need to be "fixed"? Why are we constructing "currently old" centergoers and seeing their needs as different from, or even less than, those of baby boomers? Would new center models be a momentous improvement?

This book travels down many paths to reconstruct the life and closure of one center as a case to open up a window and broaden the scope in order to investigate these larger issues.

For me as a native New Yorker, born and raised in Queens, and a sociologist and gerontologist, it was very meaningful to combine all my roles and interests in the process of writing this book. By exploring this shuttering issue on many levels (individual through policy), I truly realized that there were no easy villains; large-scale change is a complicated process. I gained perspective as an author.

Handling an ethnographic case study, providing pseudonyms to elder participants, moving into policy issues, and interviewing and obtaining consent from experts took time and tact. So did protecting the identity of the center while describing its participants in detail. In some chapters, I walked the line of using press accounts without identifying the community. Getting access to multiple field settings and a main site, the center, through many staff changes, taught me patience and persistence, especially when—unknown to me at the time—larger changes were in the offing.

The entire work for this book spans 2008–2013, six years of data collecting and analysis. Being embedded in this center during parts of the closure process and being able to widen the focus to policy makes this book unique in its approach to center closure and modernization. I was also fortunate to talk to many key figures in the aging network in New York City and add their observations to my own. I used local media coverage of the center closures and innovative centers, as well, including the closure list, released internally at a City Council meeting and leaked in a newspaper blog. And I included evidence of larger policies, such as the Older Americans Act and the Affordable Care Act, since their changes directly relate to senior centers' functions.

I would like readers to be aware of the structure of the book, specifically the changing scope of the chapters. The general format here is that chapters begin with an ethnographic or narrower focus on the center, the people connected with it and its neighborhood, then move on to address issues on a larger scale, bringing in social policy. After giving an overview of the neighborhood and senior center in the Introduction, I set the stage in chapter 1 for the center's role and theories of why senior centers work. Chapters 2 and 4 are ethnographic and focus at the level of the center, the extended case study for the book. Chapter 3 moves the scale up to include city, state, and national debates about what senior centers should be, who should fund them, and whom they should serve. Then chapters 5 and 6 apply multidisciplinary theories to the events described in prior chapters. Chapter 7 looks at the local and national trends of changing centers to meet baby boomers turning sixty-five years of age. Chapter 8 concludes on the largest level, analyzing federal policies and giving suggestions for center sustainability in the nation as a whole.

Acknowledgments

I am grateful to many people who have supported my work. First, I would like to thank all the attendees of the now-closed senior center, the directors and staff, and neighboring centers and community members for letting me into their world and sharing their time and thoughts with me. It is their stories I have tried to describe, authentically, to readers. The work was enriched by my interviews with leaders in the senior center field in New York City: Lilliam Barrios-Paoli, of the Department for the Aging; Paola Miceli, of the Queens Borough President's Office, Igal Jellinek and Bobbie Sackman, of the Council of Senior Centers and Services in New York City; and Catherine Thurston, of Services and Advocacy for GLBT Elders (SAGE). Interviews with additional pseudonymous center directors and conversations with local reporters, along with their articles, helped flesh out the story.

Peter Mickulas, editor, Rutgers University Press, must be thanked for his constant support for this work and for appreciating the value of studying aging and the place of senior centers in local neighborhoods. My two reviewers at the press—Meika Loe and the anonymous reviewer—provided an excellent critique and offered new directions for my work. I would also like to thank Joy Stoffers, Marilyn Campbell, and Romaine Perin; their prepress and copyediting skills helped make this book a reality. Thanks are also due to Rachel Nishan at Twin Oaks Indexing for her earnest work and excellent attention to detail. My colleague and dear friend Natalie Byfield must be mentioned for helping me think through so many of the ideas in this work and taking me back to a more sociological stance. Diditi Mitra shared her clarity of thought and support. She reassured me that the process mattered and that things would get done.

My fellow gerontology faculty members at the University of Northern Colorado, Susan Collins and Robbyn Wacker, were always ready to lend a gerontology ear and be a sounding board for applying sometimes nongerontological concepts and theories to a work about older people. I feel particularly fortunate to have Susan, a fellow gerontologist, just down the hall.

I must thank Stephen Luttmann for his help in creating an original Derrida-inspired title for this book "Decentered: The Politics of Rebranding Neighborhood Senior Centers to Meet the Needs of Baby Boomers." I owe Sarah Cornella, a stellar graduate assistant at the University of Northern Colorado, a debt of gratitude for her help in organizing materials and patiently fact-checking items for "the center book" many times over. In addition, she created the Atlas.ti database for the Older Americans Act and Affordable Care Act policy materials for chapter 8. Eric Teman also provided great assistance. His combined doctorates in philosophy and law were most helpful for working through the many stops and starts of the Older Americans Act. I am thankful to all my colleagues and graduate students at the University of Northern Colorado for their exchange of ideas and the university for some summer funding support given to this work.

Two sets of parents kindly lent support to this project: Philip and Brenda Lefkowitz and Rosemary and Lawrence Weil. My spouse, David Lefkowitz, served as a supporter, but more important, often as first-line editor of this book. Drawing on his many years of work as a writer, performer, and editor, he taught me the importance of keeping to the truth while creating a good story for the reader.

The New Neighborhood
Senior Center

Introduction

● ●

Shuttered

> My dear, it is horrible. Even though our center was promised so much money, none of it came in. We had to suspend our programs and do not know if we will be able to open up again. Our seniors took it so hard, and we are so sad.
> —Associate director of the senior center, personal e-mail, August 2010

It's a typical hot summer in 2010 in Queens, New York, in a working-class neighborhood. This is a place where people sit out on the stoops of their brick row houses, and neighbors know each other well. It is a true "community" made up of many immigrant groups where Spanish, Italian, Polish, Romanian, and other assorted Eastern European languages can be overheard in what seems like a simultaneous conversation. Children play "on the block" on tree-lined streets, while city buses, baby carriages, strollers, and shopping carts noisily roll by. People are heading "down the Avenue" to shop for everything from clothes to food or just to socialize with friends and neighbors. But over the past few weeks of this particular summer, conversations among some community members have changed. There is something different about this summer. Older community residents are becoming increasingly upset because a senior citizens' center that has been in the neighborhood for as long as they can remember is on the verge of being closed.

Friends passing, meeting on the streets in the community, local supermarkets, and coffee shops weigh their options of where to go if and when the center closes. "We could go to Palumbo's, but they're too cliquey there."[1] Another center option would work, but they saw it as "already too crowded" with "not enough space in the basement for the people already going there." Mary, who is in her eighties, picked up daily and taken to and from the center by the center's van driver, laments the center's closure and the loss of her daily van trip.[2] She cries as she calls her friend and nearby neighbor Anita. "What am I gonna do? . . . and where will I go every day?" The friends then debate whether it's true, whether their center, "open for such a long time—almost forty years" will actually close its doors and remain closed "forever."[3] Mary thinks she may need to move in with her daughter in a neighboring community if her transportation to the center stops. But she is not too thrilled with this option. She likes living alone, in her own home, where she is independent but also close to family.

Karen, seventy-seven years old, legally blind and commuting by city bus to the center, considers her options. If she moves to a new center, she'll have to learn to navigate around the entire place again, not to mention planning a new bus route and "training new bus drivers." After the events of September 11, 2001, the attack against the World Trade Center in New York City, Karen experienced posttraumatic stress disorder, depression, and a newly diagnosed chronic condition. Her counselor recommended that she get out and "mingle with other people." In this center five years later, Karen finds her niche. She forms close friendships with other members. She serves as a greeter to new members and develops a bookmobile and reading program with large-print texts for all in the center and neighborhood. The experience also helps her own recovery. When I arrive at the center in 2008, it is Karen who is the first person to give me a complete tour of the facility. She leads me in and out of each room and floor of the center, noting how each setting has changed, been renovated, or removed from active use. Karen explains her methods of circumnavigation to me while critiquing the activities and programs run in each room.

Life at the center has its own flow and cast of attendees. The women who attend the center on a daily basis are referred to as the "regular members" and feel a sense of identity by "running" this center and serving on its board. These women, like Victoria, a seventy-four-year-old widow with five children and eight grandchildren and a member of the center's board, have a group of "regulars" to eat with every day. They pride themselves on their level of voluntary, unpaid participation in the center as they help organize trips and dances, work with local college "kids," and teach grammar school pen pals "to write letters in English," or give "the ladies in the kitchen (as mothers) the chance to get 'Workfare'" (referring to the employment policy requirements of persons receiving public assistance).

Lily, whose adult son and two teenage grandchildren have recently moved in with her, takes personal satisfaction in being an active part of the center— "something my mom didn't believe in." She has reinstated the Know Your Numbers group, a weekly meeting where people choose a disease or chronic condition (recent topics include diabetes and high blood pressure) and then "have conversations about good values" for that particular condition.

The center is not just a place for women; men are involved, too. Men like Jack, a seventy-six-year-old divorcé and ex-marine who "taught discipline" and "pays for the ladies' meals." He tells me he hangs around so the women can "have a man to dance with." Joe, at sixty-two, the self-proclaimed "baby of the group," likes to bartend at the center's weekend dances. He really only attends "to help his brother out" because his brother "needs the meals" and "doesn't cook for himself."

There are the so-called bingo or menu members, who see the center as a place to attend a specific social function (such as a dance) or a game (like bingo) or to have a meal (depending upon the menu for that day). They do not feel invested in the center's daily functioning, nor does the center play a pivotal role in their lives. These members view key services and activities much differently from the regular members and use them much less frequently. As Maria, eighty-two, who lives alone, drives, and feels she "lost her husband too soon," explains, she frequently goes to the center, mostly to attend dances. She and her husband used to go "only like Friday nights; we used to come with another couple. He was a Harvest Moon ballroom dancer; he taught me." After his death, she continued to attend the dances: "I can do anything; I am a dancer. I *love* to dance. I *love* to dance." Maria plays bingo "just to pass the time, but I'm not crazy about it." Maria mentions that she prefers to drive her friends to the movies rather than attend classes or other activities at the center.

And some, like Anita and Arlene, women in their seventies—one a recent widow of a few months and the other still married—visit the center for occasional meals, for dances, or to take some food from the food bank. They choose not to attend like the regulars or the bingo or menu members, those persons who attend the center for only a specific event or two. These women have spouses who either will not attend or choose other activities at their churches, or they prefer watching TV to going to the center. They meet with friends at coffee shops and ethnically based social and religious clubs in the area.

There are also the newly arrived Eastern European immigrant elders. According to more frequent centergoers, these newer immigrant groups "don't stay for activities or events." As the regulars explain, the newcomers are in charge of dropping off, picking up, and babysitting their grandchildren after school, while their own grown children work several jobs "to support the family, like our own parents did."

I will use the accounts of different groups of elders and the role of this neighborhood center in their lives to illustrate the key issues of this book. On the level of this particular center, I address questions such as the following: How did a vibrant senior citizens' center in a working-class neighborhood, in existence for well over thirty years and with dedicated leadership, political support, and active, engaged members—and not on the New York City Department for the Aging's (DFTA's) leaked closure list—end up being closed?[4] How did it lose its contract with DFTA? How was the closure of neighborhood centers depicted in local media accounts (with headlines such as "Seniors Win Big" [heralding the prevention of closure] and "Seniors Screwed: Red Tape Forces Temporary Closure of the Center" [once the closure process began])? What are the roles of social class and neighborhood context in the closing of senior centers?

Then, the lens will shift. The closure of the one center in this book will be placed in a larger context as more centers shutter and closures become more commonplace. That leads to addressing several questions of a larger scope: What does the closure and rebranding of senior centers say about the future of centers and the center movement in the United States? What changes in social policies are needed to support or supplement senior centers or the functions they serve?

Centers in New York City are at a particularly high risk, with closures imminent, or completed, for many. Changes began in 2008 when New York City mayor Michael Bloomberg initiated the All Ages Project, conceived to modernize centers and convert them into Healthy Aging Centers, based on a wellness approach (New York City Department of Aging 2008b, 2). Helping enact this project was then–commissioner of the DFTA Edwin Méndez-Santiago, who further developed this modernization concept. (The effects of the All Ages Project and modernization will be discussed further in chapter 3.)

Another element affecting centers would be changes in social policy and funding allocations, for example, as called for by the Older Americans Act (OAA). First authorized by Congress in 1965 as a way to provide services needed for older persons to remain at home in their communities, the OAA allocates center funding, specifically through its Title XX. The OAA has been reauthorized eleven times since its founding, but the last reauthorization (due in 2011) is now still under way. Although Congress did allocate senior center funding during the 2012–13 fiscal period, funding remains uncertain.

New York City centers have also faced edicts from the City Council and borough officials, changing quality markers, and "innovative" identity-based center models. Further, closure lists have undergone revision, with predictions of centers slated for termination ranging from 50 to 105 (Lucadamo 2011). In 2011, researchers in the field of centers wrote about the current critical state of senior centers, finding that "in 2010, New York State reduced New York City senior citizen center funding by 30%, resulting in elimination of approximately 15%, or 30 of the city's more than 300 senior centers."[5]

Herein lies the paradox. American society is experiencing a marked rise in the sixty-five-and-older population because of decreasing mortality rates and the first members of the baby boom generation turning sixty-five in 2011 (Federal Interagency Forum on Aging-Related Statistics 2010; United States Census 2009). As people age, they increasingly prefer to rely on community-based services, such as those provided by senior centers, to age in place (Rosel 2003; Sabia 2008). With the coming-of-age of the oldest groups of baby boomers, issues have been raised about the needs of house-rich, cash-poor boomers juxtaposed with the current group of frail, more socially isolated, and poorer members at the neighborhood center. But if the need for neighborhood centers exists, especially in areas of lower socioeconomic status, why are such centers closing? And how did we get here?

Currently, senior centers are attempting to adapt to rapidly changing demographics—changes in attendees' income, rural and urban shifts, variations in food preferences and healthy lifestyle options, and increasing ethnic and racial diversity. Centers are also faced with issues of how to tempt baby boomers and other older persons who are often resistant toward participating—which means addressing the needs of a diverse clientele. Some suggest that even the name *senior citizens' center* needs to be changed or the entity itself "rebranded" (Fitzpatrick and McCabe 2008; Van Ryzin 2010).[6] The relevance of past approaches and activities for engaging this emerging heterogeneous group of older persons has been called into question.

Aging in Place in Unequal Places

Historically, senior centers in the United States have served as sites for those sixty-five and older to age in place by gathering socially in a home away from home.[7] Aging in place is the ability of an older person to live independently in his or her own community and is dependent upon available social networks and resources. Aging in place also sets the stage for the function of senior centers within communities. A center assists in aging in place by increasing or replacing social networks and being a site for resource information and exchange. Senior centers emerged to meet the call of the Older Americans Act, passed in 1965, to serve as a focal point to bring community-based services, such as congregate meals and social activities, to elders based on a model of continuum of care.[8] In the late 1970s, Area Agencies on Aging were placed in charge of coordinating services, while the 1980s brought a decline in center funding. According to the reauthorization of the Older Americans Act in 2006, a multipurpose senior center is a "community facility for the organization and provision of a broad spectrum of services, which shall include provision of health (including mental health), social, nutritional, and educational services and the provision of facilities for recreational activities for older individuals" (United States Congress 1965). Further, such centers provide valued daily routines, which help seniors feel useful and productive (Lund and Engelsrud 2008). Centers have been found to provide positive social contact, to create lasting social networks, and to offer instrumental help (such as help with paying bills or shopping). They guard against loneliness and ward off isolation to build meaningful social identities and improve both mental and physical health.[9]

But all centers and communities are not created equally. Some neighborhoods do not allow their older residents to age in place. In discussing more urban neighborhoods, Andrew Scharlach suggests that these particular neighborhoods have undergone "infrastructure deterioration" with fewer and fewer places for elders to gather with friends and neighbors. He suggests that some elders may even be left without a bench where they can sit with friends and meet with others. These elders live in "Peter Pan" housing (not adapted to elders' needs) with limited access to public transportation (Scharlach 2009, 5–8).

The center is even more crucial in providing services to elders in poor neighborhoods or those in which the composition of residents is undergoing changes, because older persons' social world and access to a wider range of resources is seen as more limited. For poor elders, the social world centers around the home and nearby services. Victoria Burns, Jean-Pierre Lavoie, and Damaris Rose (2011) report that according to Véronique Billette and Jean-Pierre Lavoie's model, elders in poor neighborhoods often experience a combination of exclusions. For example, the exclusion of poor elders differs from that of middle-class elders and that of those with higher incomes. Elders may experience symbolic exclusion, making them seem invisible or viewed only by negative stereotypes within a neighborhood. There is identity exclusion, which makes marginalized "old age" seem the dominant identity category. Sociopolitical exclusion removes elders from political engagement, while institutional exclusion separates elders from resources. And finally, there can be an exclusion of significant social ties or territorial exclusion. Here, older persons would be left to live in unsafe or less-desirable places. Burns and colleagues see the removal of services and institutions as the equivalent of placing older residents under "house arrest" (9).

To counteract the effects of neighborhood change, neighborhoods need to be "age friendly" and meet the needs of elders more fully in the latter's physical environments. To understand the functions of the center used as an extended case study for this book, let's look at geographic setting and local resources.[10]

Table 1

Selected Characteristics by Census Tract,
Community District, Borough, and City Levels

Variable	Census Tract[a]	Community District[b]	Queens[c]	NYC[d]
Age-related characteristics				
Median age	33.2	38.1	37.4	35.6
% 65 years and older	8.4	13.7	13.1	12.1
Households with a person 65+	20.4	27.7	15.8	14.7
Households with a person 62+	29.1	—	26.9	23.9
Living alone 65+	3.8	4.2	9.5	10.2
Grandchildren living with 65+	10.9	28.1	22.8	31.2
Race/ethnicity (%)				
White	49.3	87.2	45.1	45.4
African American	4.5	1.7	19.2	25.1
Asian	9.2	6.5	21.4	11.7
Hispanic	58.4	33	26.3	27.4
Language other than English at home (%)	73.9	52.9	54.4	47.1
Foreign born (%)	47.8	36.5	47.1	39.5
Europe	32.0	40.1	49.1	39.8
Latin America	44.9	48.3	14.4	17.4
Asia	22.3	34.2	49.0	52.1
Africa	0.6	15.0	34.1	25.7
Other	—	2.3	2.1	3.8
Educational level (%)				
High school graduates (or equiv.)	27.7	36.6	29.4	26.0
Some college (no degree)	14.0	15.8	14.4	13.7
Associate's degree	5.9	6.6	7.1	6.2
Bachelor's degree	8.4	13.2	18.7	19.6
Graduate degree	5.1	7.2	10.1	13.5
Income and poverty				
Per capital income (2009 inflation dollars)	$13,534	$24,488	$25,268	$30,634
Median household income (2009 inflation dollars)	$38,345	$60,583	$54,870	$50,173

(continued)

Table 1

Selected Characteristics by Census Tract, Community District, Borough, and City Levels (*continued*)

Variable	Census Tract[a]	Community District[b]	Queens[c]	NYC[d]
Income and poverty				
Below poverty, all individuals (%)	16.8	12.1	12.1	14.2
Below poverty level, 65+ (%)	20.0	10.1	12.8	—
Social Security Income	17.5	27.0	26.2	23.7
Social Security Supplemental Income	4.3	3.4	4.2	6.3
Housing characteristics (%)				
Renters	79.8	57.3	53.6	66.1
Homeowners	20.2	42.7	46.4	33.9
Median house value	$172,500	$566,300	$470,500	—
Median rent	$736	$1,384	$1,136	$1,029
Homeowners 65+	26.4	—	46.4	55.7
Unemployment rate (%)	6.3	6.4	5.0	5.2
Occupational status/category (%)				
Managers	17.2	24.6	30.9	37.5
Service industry	21.6	21.8	22.6	21.4
Sales/office workers	27.4	28.2	26.5	25.0
Construction	9.6	13.3	9.0	6.8
Production/ transportation	24.2	12.0	11.0	9.2
Class of worker				
Private/wage salaried	81.0	79	79.3	78.3
Government	14.3	16.2	14.6	5.1
Self-employed	4.1	4.5	5.9	6.5
Unpaid, family work	0.7	0.2	0.2	0.1
Commute time to work (minutes)	37.1	—	42	39.2
Use public transportation (%)	50.7	50	50.7	54.7

[*] Noninflation estimates
[a] United States Census (2010); New York City Department of City Planning (2011b)
[b] United States Census (2009)
[c] New York City Department of Health and Mental Hygiene (2006)
[d] United States Census (2009)

Understanding the Geography of Place:
"My Neighborhood, Not My Borough"

Centers do not exist in a vacuum. Just as with other institutions, they are tied to a sense of place. In New York City, place is complex, to say the least, so before we can talk about the neighborhood or the larger community surrounding the center, let us get a sense of how the borough compares to the city as a whole and the distinctive features of the borough of Queens.[11]

Queens is not just the largest of the five boroughs that constitute New York City. It is much more than one big urban agglomerate that many label an outer (Rodwin and Gusmano 2006) or forgotten (Steinberg 2011) borough. It is a series of unique neighborhoods that border one another yet are distinct, each with its own character, history, and flavor. Ask Queens residents where they are from, and you will hear the neighborhood name, not the borough's (Freudenheim 2006). This sense of a locally centered place is even reflected in the organization of the Queens postal system; addresses on mail sent to Queens show a neighborhood name, the state, then the zip code—not borough, state, and zip code (Copquin 2007). Queens has been called "the largest, most diverse, foreign-born borough" of New York City (Wilson 2009, 41).

The local neighborhood where the center discussed in this book was situated is a community of immigrants and is solidly working class.[12] From its origins in the mid-1800s, this neighborhood has consisted of immigrants. Originally, the area was farmlands tended by German migrants. A huge, pre–World War I building push between 1908 and 1914 created "Matthews flats" and Paul Stier buildings. The community is one of the largest federal districts in the United States, with 2,980 landmark buildings ranging from private family homes to multifamily row houses built with Kreischer brick from Staten Island. In a 2006 guidebook, *Queens: What to Do, Where to Go (and How Not to Get Lost) in New York's Undiscovered Borough*, Ellen Freudenheim reprints a passage from a 1939 Works Progress Administration guide describing the neighborhood as an "old-fashioned, respectable German community [of] . . . comfortable brownstones with neat stoops and polished brass" (239). These homes were occupied by Germans, Gottscheers (individuals from what is now Kočevje, Slovenia, once part of the Austro-Hungarian Empire [Bencin 1996]), Hungarians, Romanians, and Italians.

In 1965, changes in immigration laws led to an increase in Latin and Asian groups and an overall increase in foreign-born residents in this neighborhood (Copquin 2007, xviii). This majority-minority transition, in which new groups of non-white immigrants join communities of existing European groups, was happening in several other Queens communities at the time (Sanjek 2000). Later, Geraldine Grant, a researcher at Queens College, conducted a project, "New Immigrants and Ethnicity," to address issues of ethnic tension around her college. Grant found that "ethnic groups self-segregate[d] by residence and association" but that many commonalties existed across the groups' experiences. For example, in terms of social class, many ethnic groups entered the workforce as unskilled laborers (1981b, 24).

Class played a role in the geographic division of the neighborhood. Before the 1970s, the neighborhood was an extension of its Brooklyn counterpart or a borderland between two boroughs. Its name was often hyphenated with its Brooklyn counterpart but is now divided into two distinct zip codes. The Queens portion, heavily steeped in manufacturing plants and knitting mills, consists mostly of working- and lower-middle-class families. Its Brooklyn equivalent is a mix of poor and working-class persons.

According to the most recent American Community Survey data, from 2010, the community housing the center now has a greater concentration of persons (60 percent) self-identified as Hispanic (of any race). Mirroring the diversity of the borough, in the area almost three-quarters of residents speak a language other than English in their homes. One of every two people in the neighborhood is foreign born. In socioeconomic status, people in this neighborhood have lower educational levels and post–high school degree completion rates than those of the district, borough, and city. Poverty is at a higher level in the district than either the borough or the city. Renters are more common than homeowners. The neighborhood has a higher unemployment rate than the borough and city—with more individuals in labor- and transportation-related occupations (factory, construction and bus- or truck-driving jobs).

Centergoers travel to the center from the surrounding, or catchment, area, the *community district*, a U.S. Census term for an area made up of several neighborhoods, directly adjacent to the center. In the community district, almost one-third of households contain a person sixty-five years of age or older; this percentage is greater than in the borough or city (New York City Department of City Planning 2008). According to DFTA's 2011 *Profile of Older New Yorkers,* four in ten elders are foreign born. Spanish and Italian are listed as the two languages most commonly spoken by older persons. The poverty rate for residents sixty-five or older in this census tract is about 10 percent, though the New York Academy of Medicine has it as closer to 20 percent (Finkelstein et al. 2008). In the community district overall, the percentage of persons receiving income support from Temporary Assistance for Needy Families (TANF), Supplemental Security Income (SSI), and Medicaid tripled from 10 percent to almost 30 percent between 2000 and 2010 (New York City Department of City Planning 2011).

Describing the lived experience for elders in this district, the community district's needs statement for fiscal year 2012 cites the following as issues of concern for the area: illegal apartments, speeding, sewer repair, subway station repair, critical firehouse repair, park management, crowded schools, illegal commercial dumping, and post-9/11 relief for workers. There is a call for more building inspectors to address illegal dwellings' code violations. The needs statement also calls for an increase in low-cost healthcare services, following the closure of two local hospitals. And residents of the district are under- or uninsured at greater rates than those of the city (New York City Department of Health and Mental Hygiene 2006).

For service needs related to aging, the New York City Department of City Planning's community district needs statement for 2011 highlights, given the district's aging population, the increased need for more meals-on-wheels delivery and congregate meals, more Alzheimer's day care, and increased nursing home capacity. The New York City Department of Health and Mental Hygiene's *Community Health Profile* for 2006 finds that those sixty-five and over in the district are at a greater risk of falling, with one in four hospital admissions related to falls. According to the New York City Department for the Aging's *Profile of Older New Yorkers* (2010), individuals sixty or older in the community district have ten times more impaired mobility and self-care than elders citywide.

The Center as a Case Study of Larger Structural Issues

In this book, I use my ethnographic work at a working-class senior center in Queens, New York, in three ways. First, the ethnography is an extended case used to describe both the functioning and the closure process of a center.

Second, the ethnographic work becomes a backdrop to lead into the examination of the role of social structure. The term *social structure* refers here to the relationship between neighborhood organizations, governmental officials, and social policies in shaping senior centers. Social structure is examined not only through its impact on the daily lives of older individuals attending the center but also as it affects changes at the level of the center as an institution within the neighborhood, the local community, the city, and beyond. Using an extended case-based analysis over time allows a nuanced analysis of social structure within a specific temporal, local, neighborhood-based setting. The analysis can focus closely on the perceptions of individuals and the influence of larger social organizations while broadening the lens to address social policies and institutional roles. My approach is like that of the Chicago school ethnographic style with a focus on both the individual and society and centered in a city setting.

Third, the book traces the effects of political, social, and economic institutions, organizations, spatial identity, and neighborhood processes involved in the decision to shutter this senior center once featured as a "best center in Queens" by a local newspaper, in 2002, and lauded as a "vitality center" by the

Department for the Aging, in 2006. The case, dealing with a center that was not on DFTA's fifty-center closure list, functions as entrée into the larger social policy, legislative, and ideological issues at play. The case can be seen as a way to introduce the state of the contemporary center movement and changes occurring in many centers and settings.

Theoretical Framework

In examining a contemporary working-class senior center's closure process, I tie together disparate literature from many disciplines. The theoretical discussion begins with essential gerontological literature about aging in place, theories of life course and the state (Elder 1994; Mayer and Schoepflin 1989), and cumulative advantage/disadvantage inequalities across the life course (Dannefer 2003). To continue to address larger, societal elements in the process, I draw upon sociological theory and incorporate Mario Luis Small's work in reframing social capital, agency, and organizational embeddedness for the poor and working class. Small's work builds upon that of Gubrium (1988), and later Gubrium and Holstein (1993, 2012), which established organizational embeddedness as a way of examining the influence of context or setting in the interpretation of behaviors. The organization or institution in which an event occurs strongly influences its interpretation, so the analysis of actions is linked to the place in which they occur. Small's ideas are used in the book to draw in the work of several classical social capital and social-tie theorists, such as Pierre Bourdieu, John Field, James Coleman, and Ronald Burt.

When I analyze social capital and ties, I create a framework that looks at three levels: the micro (at the center participant level), meso (at the local organizational level), and macro (at the level of the state). Glen H. Elder Jr.'s life course theory, which looks at problems related to "the impact of changing societies on developing lives" (1994, 5), will serve as model to show the impact of the closure of the center, as an institution, upon the lives of centergoers. The life course perspective provides historical context to an individual's life. It evaluates the timing of events as normative or nonnormative for a particular age and sees the individual's experiences in relationship to the person's greater social world. This perspective also values agency of individuals in shaping their own life course. Karl Urlich Mayer and Urs Schoepflin add a focus on a sense of place in the life course perspective. They suggest that one's life course does not "occur in a stateless social structure" (1989, 189). Rather, as Mayer and Schoepflin suggest, linkages between the state and one's individual life course are often overlooked. While it is often difficult to measure the direct impact of the state upon an individual's life course, social policies, care provision, and other public assistance and benefits programs are concrete examples of the effect of the state upon individuals' lives.

Additional urban anthropological literature then ties Steven Gregory's observations (in his 1998 book, *Black Corona*) about the politics of place to the neighborhood level and person-environment fit. I use literature on urban sociology and planning studies to illustrate spatial dynamics, "authenticity of place," and the politics of public space usage by social class (Whyte 1988, [1980] 2000; Zukin 1995, 2009, 2011). Last, I draw on relevant literature about the role of social class, displacement, and age in the gentrification process (Nyden et al. 2006; Petrovic 2007; Slater 2008) and empowerment of older persons as part of social movements (Giugni et al. 1999; Haber 2009; McAdam and Tarrow 2010; Meyer 2003).

Beyond Cumulative Advantage/Disadvantage Theory

In gerontology, cumulative advantage/disadvantage (CAD) theory has been used to show the effects of inequality across the life course. The theory examines how inequalities beginning early in one's life can be used to map disadvantages, influence an individual's ability to address adversity, and support the accumulation of risk across the life course. Early circumstances can limit a person's options in life, or inequalities can ebb and flow throughout life and illustrate the way individuals may or may not be resilient. Work on cumulative disadvantage has been focused at the intra-individual level and at the longitudinal level with gerontological studies examining the way membership in a larger cohort also affects one's life chances. The incorporation of larger structural and institutional forces in CAD work is often missing or without empirical evidence.

Cumulative disadvantage does not occur within "a social vacuum" (Dannefer 2003, S332), so the impact of larger structural institutions cannot be ignored, nor can the influence that temporal and local contexts (such as neighborhoods) have on the daily lived experience of older individuals. CAD is a function of "collectivities" and must integrate into social systems in the process. One cannot forget the role that structural arrangements play in state-created institutions and in market systems, thus creating differential opportunities. Recently, to reflect the influence of social structure in perpetuating disadvantage more than advantage for elders, researchers Kenneth Ferraro, Tetyana Pylypiv Shippee, and Markus Schafer (2009) suggested that CAD be named the more apt cumulative inequality theory. This push to include social class in the study of aging comes out of the need to address criticism that class is "remarkably absent in scholarship and policy-making on aging" (Settersten and Trauten 2009, 459–460). In a 2009 metareview, Karl Ulrich Mayer suggests that the direct, immediate institutional role in perpetuating disadvantage receives lesser investigation in contemporary studies in the United States. The inclusion of institutional components in the study of cumulative disadvantage, he finds, is more common in European analyses.

Gerontology has looked at intra-individual and intracohort differences, but much less attention is paid to the local structural changes occurring in particular organizations or institutions serving older persons. Changes in local institutions must also be taken into account to complete the full picture and scope of the issues that exist in perpetuating inequality. Recent sociological work, such as this book, can provide additional contexts to further address the call to make CAD (and cumulative inequality theory, for that matter) more than what Mayer calls "a metaphor."[13]

An Organizational Embeddedness Perspective

The work of Small can serve as a bridge to examine the effects of individual and institutional differences experienced by elders. He examines the accumulation of inequality across the life course while taking into account the relationship of social class and CAD or inequality theories. In his multimethod examination of centers in different social-class settings, Small (2009, 185) examines social capital (or the amount of resources generated from belonging to a particular social network) building among perceived disadvantaged groups to learn which organizational structures allow specific class groups to build better capital. He explores the way capital is embedded in particular institutional structures rather than focusing only on social capital at an individual level. Looking at the role of organizational ties (or the relationship of one organization with another or with an agency or institution) is essential because, according to Small, these ties arise from "the highly bureaucratic nature of contemporary society, where exchanging goods and resources constitute much of what businesses, government agencies, and nonprofit organizations do" (185).[14]

As Small states, "Not all centers broker social and organizational ties in equal measure . . . so that social capital is directly tied to institutional practices of an organization that a person routinely participates in" (177). Small suggests we change the way we look at an organization's function or purpose so the senior center does more than feed and provide services for seniors. He sees the need for the multiple exchange of "extra" information to call attention to larger network dynamics often ignored in the study of social inequality.

Like cumulative disadvantage or inequality theories, organizationally embedded ties can become a form of negative social capital. Small stresses the conflict of the individual versus the collective versus third-party organizations. He finds that these embedded relationships can also include "institutional coercion, by which people are forced, for the good of the organization and its members, to forgo at least some rudimentary rights, such as the right to refuse to represent the organization or the right to privacy about contact information" (188).

Small finds that one must account for neighborhood effects in the promotion of CAD. He postulates that "people in poor neighborhoods do not always do worse" in building capital, but the neighborhood's level of advantage or dis-advantage is very closely tied to the group's ability to use the capital generated (195–196). In other words, poor neighborhoods are not, by definition, lack-ing in social capital. Senior centers, as organizations, can play a pivotal role in either facilitating or disassembling social capital building.

Adding Neighborhood and Political Dimensions to Theories of CAD

In order to add neighborhood and political dimensions to theories of CAD and inequality, I will use Steven Gregory's volume *Black Corona* (1998). His work on the cumulative inequalities of race, class, and place in a Queens neigh-borhood challenges the labeling of a group as merely "disempowered" based on social position alone.[15] In part, Gregory followed the struggle of a commu-nity of working-class African Americans to maintain youth programs and to keep a monorail from being built over the Corona community. Gregory found that the struggle of individuals and groups was closely tied to power dynam-ics of actors in local organizations and not just the agency of individuals. "In contrast, their adversaries—sometimes the state, sometimes the capital, and often a complex amalgam of the two—worked to undermine this empower-ing political identity by employing practices of divide and conquer which con-stituted and braced disabling and power-evasive constructions of racial, class, and spatial identity" (1998, 251–252).

Addressing spatial dynamics, neighborhood change, and the politics of public space by class, I will bring in Sharon Zukin's concept of "authenticity," or the traditional neighborhood feel of a place. Authentic places, such as cities, have a personality of their own, with historical buildings, a mix of residents who feel they belong to that community, and mom-and-pop stores. Zukin sug-gests that cities are being reshaped by politicians and realtors to remove the urban poor and minority groups—including elders. She writes about the con-sequences of neighborhoods' converting from being filled with older home-owners to being populated by hipsters. Examples include the transformation of Williamsburg, Brooklyn, and the recent Harlem renaissance.[16]

I will also broaden the sense of neighborhood to look at social class, dis-placement, and age in the gentrification process. Gentrification has additional negative impact for elders. Elders experiencing rapid rent increases have less lead time to seek out federal rent-reduction programs. As they live through the gentrification of their community, they experience the loss of businesses, decreased access to services, and unsafe physical conditions. In some cases, landlords may steeply increase rent or turn off utilities to encourage elders to move. Elder homeowners may be reported for code violations or back taxes so they will sell their homes. Elders may also remain invisible in the gentrification process—not spoken about at all. When rents rise and new stores move in, elders may not be able to afford to shop at them. Past ties and social supports leave, and residents who had earlier filled these roles are no longer a part of the elder's social network. Ana Petrovic cites Mindy Fullilove's "root shock" concept when referring to elders moving out of the neighborhood as "the traumatic stress reaction to the loss of some or all of one's emotional ecosystem" (2007, 17). Tom Slater quotes a local community activist who sees gentrification as "something of a ghost—trivialized by the mainstream media, ignored by government, distorted in academia . . . or obfuscated by policymakers. . . . Because the 'audience' for gentrification is always the poor, people of colour, immigrants, working class seniors . . . the realities of gentrification are usually 'invisible' to those who shape the public's understanding of the issues" (2008, 217).

In addition to examining the ill effects of lower social class and age upon elder-community living, I will discuss the empowerment of older persons and their role in social movements. The call for elders to be empowered, in reaction to the baby boomers, is highly contested. David Haber (2009) makes a call for all gerontologists to become activists on behalf of elders. He also has some suggestions for ways elders can become empowered. In relation to senior centers, he suggests elders use proposed changes in senior centers as rallying tools. So the impact of making senior centers community centers, making centers intergenerational, and having name changes must all be addressed by older persons themselves. In Haber's view, these elder-led movements will improve conditions for all. The way social movements are conducted is changing, but their impact upon social policy remains. David Meyer suggests that "other sorts of social movements grow when the promise of success arises" and that "by politicizing communities, connecting people, and promoting personal loyalties, social movements build an infrastructure not only of subsequent movements, but of a democratic society more generally" (2003, 32, 35).

Description of the Extended Case Study and Ethnographic Methods

This book employs an extended case method, a process attributed to Max Gluckman and Jaap van Velsen and later developed for use in sociology by Michael Burawoy (1998). In the extended case study method, one study is used to connect the elements of a microsetting to larger, or macro, issues. As Mercer Sullivan suggests, the goal of this method is "to situate a given case in the widest relevant social field for an understanding of that case . . . not to abstract the minimum number of cases, but, rather to situate the individual case in as much richness of detail as possible within the wide social fields that structure the process unfolding within that case" (2002, 256). The extended case study method examines an issue across multiple levels of societal structure (individuals, organizations, institutions). Also, as theorists like Pierre Bourdieu suggest, this method assigns all elements of the social structure roles as actors in the field. All actors have their own agency (or ability to influence events) and have relationships to other elements in the field with power dynamics in play.

The extended case study method entails community-based ethnographic work—ethnography being a systematic study of people as they live in their own setting. Ethnographic data are collected through formal and informal interviewing, participant observation, field notes, memos/journaling, and artifacts or materials in the field setting. The overall goal of ethnographic work is to understand the complex social worlds of individuals from their own points of view and narratives.

Ethnographic work has a strong history in aging research. Since the late 1970s there has been an ongoing call for the combination of gerontology, anthropology, and sociology, along with other social sciences, to create ethnographies of aging/old age (Gubrium 1988, 1992; Gubrium and Sankar 1994; Keith 1979; Rowles and Manning 2011). J. Neil Henderson (1994) wrote about the benefits of the "targeted ethnographic survey." He described what we see today as a common ethnographic approach, using all social interactions as data and ethnography's nature to allow for "midcourse correction" or being responsive to the direction the study takes.[17]

Although it is difficult to mention every ethnographic study of older people, to give a sense of the scope, here are several seminal ethnographies of aging in a community setting by date.[18] Beginning in the 1970s, Jerry Jacobs wrote *Fun City: An Ethnographic Study of a Retirement Community* (1974). Barbara Myerhoff's *Number Our Days* (1979) described the life of elders attending a senior citizen's center in California, and Arlie Hochschild's *The Unexpected Community* (1973) detailed the lives of elders, mostly older widows, in a low-income housing complex. Graham Rowles's *Prisoners of Space* (1978) focused on the meaning of neighborhood space and neighborhood changes that long-time residents experienced over time. The 1980s brought several urban ethnographies of aging. J. Kevin Eckert published *The Unseen Elderly* (1980) about elders living in single room occupancy hotels (SROs). Maria Vesperi's *City of Green Benches* (1985) and Janice Smithers's *Determined Survivors* (1985) focused on how poor elders live day to day. Frida Furman wrote about the many ways older women saw themselves in a beauty shop in *Facing the Mirror* (1997). J. Kevin Eckert and colleagues provided a look at assisted living in *Inside Assisted Living* (2009) in the early 2000s. Philip Stafford's *Elderburbia* (2009) visited several aging-in-place and elder-friendly communities in the United States. Samantha Solimeo's *With Shaking Hands* (2009) described those living with Parkinson's disease and the availability of community resources. Both Christine Milligan's *There's No Place Like Home* (2009) and

Eric Klinenberg's *Heat Wave* (2002) detailed the position of elders "stuck in place" in communities during different hard times. More recently, Meika Loe's *Aging Our Way* (2011) focused on the lived lives and social ties of the oldest old aging in place.

Ethnographic work provides rich descriptions of the individuals and field setting from the individuals' points of view. Thus, ethnographic work also includes self-reflectivity on the part of the researcher. When selecting a site in which to conduct ethnographic research, it is recommended that one use personal experience in the selection process—because this experience lets the researcher use his or her own knowledge of the culture for context and reference. This sense of context is important when researchers interpret their participant observation in the field. An ideal setting would also be a site that has not been excessively studied and that is comfortable for the researcher. The setting should be one allowing access to the researcher and where the researcher's presence will not be obtrusive (Angrosino 2007).

I chose the center site as the primary setting for this book because it met the feasibility, level of interest, and need/significance criteria. This center had a rich mix of people, programs, and processes. It was a familiar setting where I had established relationships and trust. The extended case study in this book includes data that were collected from four time intervals, during 2008 to 2013. The work included ethnography, participant observation, field notes/journaling, and collection of artifacts. The center's closure was not the original focus of the study, and the ethnographic work began with key informants two years before its demise.

The original purpose of the study at the center of this book was to explore the way older individuals view the role of the center and what the center means to them in their own lives. But often in ethnographic work, experiences arise when you are in the field over time.[19] Therefore, the research focus extended to include the process of shuttering, or closing, of the center as it unfolded before my eyes. The work was expanded beyond the walls of the center to include nonattendees, community activists, local reporters, politicians, and agency heads. Participants were followed as they did or did not find new centers to attend. New center models were visited and social policies examined. The case at the heart of this extended study is not intended to represent all centers. The center study, interviews with experts, and media accounts are used to understand the case of centers in working-class communities and to understand the needs and effects of the changes to senior centers. I will use the extended case study to provide information for social policy—addressing next steps to take with the context of the history of centers in mind.

My use of ethnography to explore the process of reviewing social policy in the later chapters of this book stems from a long tradition of ethnographers' writing about policy and older persons. Shulemit Reinharz described the way qualitative research can be used as a form of process evaluation to inform policy. She attests that in a "culture of evaluation" of older people, qualitative research can keep the "program evaluator honest"—keeping the actual, and often less heard, voice of elders studied recorded (1994, 264–274). Janice Graham suggests that ethnographic work "humanizes" policy recommendations, giving policymakers a way to see the people who are the target of the planned legislation (2010, 188). Ethnographers of aging have looked at different effects that home care policies in the United States and the United Kingdom have had upon elders (Gubrium and Sankar 1990). Reinharz mentions how several ethnographic studies, previously discussed, have been used to generate policy. Hochschild's work has affected housing for widows, and Jacobs's work has had an impact on medical and leisure options in retirement communities. Myeroff's study relates to macroreligious rituals, and Eckert's work supports keeping SROs for poor elder residents.

Entering the Field, for the First Time

Before beginning the study in 2008, I had several meetings with the center director at the time. We initially met after many phone calls and e-mails, so I could get a formal letter of permission allowing me to do research at the center. During our meetings, the director was very supportive. Her support enhanced my credibility, making the study participants comfortable being interviewed. I did note, however, that she expressed great consternation about the center's grants, funding, and future. She was concerned that making the center more multiservice, in nature, would not suit her seniors.

Following Institutional Review Board approval, my initial interviews were generated by key informants, such as the director, mentioned above, or associate director. These were people liked and respected by persons attending the senior center. The associate director, always referring to the elders in the center as "like family," was the one who walked me down from her office to the main room of the center and introduced me to the first interviewee. A purposive sample was used to meet the regular members or initial key informants. Since they all identified as regular centergoers, they could provide me with a lay of the land, so to speak. All subsequent interviews of centergoers were suggested via snowball sampling, with each individual recommending another to be interviewed. When I first met people who could be in my study, I explained to them that I wanted to learn how they viewed the center and what role, if any, the center played in their daily life. I asked them what they liked and disliked about the center and the activities they participated in to understand the center from their point of view. I wanted to learn about the center and if it had a role in health, wellness, and social support. All interviews of center members were conducted privately at the center. Those not attending the center were interviewed in their homes or local restaurants or coffee shops in the community. For the nonelders interviewed, key figures were identified from the community, media accounts, and websites for governmental bodies and agencies. All interviews were digitally audiotaped and transcribed verbatim. Field notes and observational data were handwritten.

Returning Many Times

Elder Interviews, Wave One: The "Regular" Members. To understand the way frequent centergoers used the center, I conducted six in-depth interviews with women, aged seventy and older, who attended the senior citizens' center from June through September 2008. Data collected in this first-time interval included the "regular," or frequent, attendees, such as those members who were active as center volunteers and in center board activities. They attended the center at least four days a week and participated in center events other than meals (at least three days a week). This group included a center member who also had a part-time, paid position in the center but participated in other center activities and met the "regular member" classification.

Interviews consisted of basic demographic/background questions (e.g., living arrangements, overall health, and life satisfaction) and continued with broad, open-ended questions. The interview schedule included questions recording levels of participation in, and choice of, activities, for example: "Tell me about some of the social activities you participate in . . . [prompt: meeting neighbors/friends/family, classes, religious services, movies, card games, volunteer work, or other events]"; "How often do you participate in . . . ?"; "How would you say these events relate to the way you feel or your sense of well-being? Or what does participating in these activities do for you?"; and "What do you like/dislike about participating in these activities?"

Elder Interviews, Wave Two: The "Bingo" and "Menu" Members. In December 2009, I returned to the center to follow up with the people I had initially interviewed and to begin interviewing a wider variety of attendees identified in earlier interviews as "menu" and "bingo" members. These were center members who were less frequent attendees (fewer than three days a week) and focused their participation around specific center activities. The "bingo/menu member" classification arose from interviews with those regularly attending the center. As I was told, bingo/menu members are the "people who just come and eat and go home" or people who shop around the local centers for the best meal or best activity for that particular day, which is not being "center loyal" or having a "home center." This December visit also brought a change in directors (one "pulled from a local ethnic organization") and changes and reductions in center staff. Some of the regulars felt this director was "doing pretty fine"; one noted, "I see the director down there [in the dining room]." During this visit, I had made the observation in my field notes that the center was also undergoing a renewed wave of construction.

Elder Interviews, Wave Three: Rare Visitors and Nonattendees. The third group of interviewees, contacted in summer of 2010, rarely or never visited the center but frequented coffee shops or restaurants in the area. They lived in the same area as center attendees but chose other activities in the community. They may have attended the center once or twice in the past but chose not to attend regularly.

Elder Interviews, Wave Four: Locating Members and Branching Out to New Centers, Agency Leaders, and Elected Officials. As the scope of the study expanded outward, so did the individuals included in it. In the winter of 2012–2013, key figures, such as in the local media, agency heads, activists, elected officials, and others prominent in the senior center academic community in New York City, were also interviewed. This last wave of interviewees differs from those with the elders in that these individuals may have chosen to identify themselves by name or by title only—whereas the elders are always referred to by pseudonyms. These expert or leader interviews began in April 2012 with Catherine Thurston, the senior director for programs at Services and Advocacy for Gay, Lesbian, Bisexual, and Transgender Elders (SAGE) in New York City. They continued on to include Lilliam Barrios-Paoli, commissioner of DFTA; Paola Miceli, director of health, human services, and senior services, Office of the Queens Borough President; Igal Jellinek, Council of Senior Centers and Services of New York City' executive director; Bobbie Sackman, CSCS director of public policy; local media; and center directors. After the center was closed, the site was expanded to find places where members of the closed center subsequently went for meals and activities. This later follow-up gave me a chance to see how the elders fared during this transition.

Concurrent Observation and Collection of Materials. Materials produced by the center itself, such as monthly calendars, programs for events, menus, fliers, and news clippings about the center, were also collected as part of the process. The ethnography also included a concurrent collection of media accounts, local and national papers, and the Internet. Media accounts included fifty-one articles in the *Times News Weekly* from January 4, 2007, to February 9, 2012, as well as from national organizations, social policies, and proposed center legislation (e.g. reauthorization of the Older Americans Act) during this period.

"Teaching Me Something about Being Old": Self-Reflection about My Experience in the Field

The ethnographic experience of being out in the field, as part of the research process, calls for a great deal of self-refection on the part of the researcher. Since researchers act as the data collection instrument, they may be questioned about their choice of setting or persons interviewed and asked about their theoretical or personal biases. Contemporary ethnographers (especially those conducting urban ethnography or ethnographies of activism) also work under an additional premise of greater self-reflexivity, or an ongoing practice by which researchers evaluate their own role in the study throughout the entire research process.

For me, just as the doors of the center opened to reveal larger issues and policies, the more I explored the issue of senior centers and talked to people, the more I understood there would be no quick and easy solutions or suggestions as a magic fix. At first, with my thinking about the halcyon days of this center as a place filled with dances and music, through the lens of my childhood memories, I wanted to see how one center of many may have been "wronged." Of course, this was a center for which I held particular affection; but as I spoke with others in the field (experts, stakeholders), I continually saw new and different center models while my own views were enriched. I can see the need for new centers for some and the need for neighborhood centers for others. It makes sense to me to really link all centers and the resources they have to be of service to older persons. Maybe the center network can maintain this variety and embrace difference, so that everyone's aunt, uncle, grandmother, grandfather, and other elder family members, just as mine did, can find one where they can dance and enjoy a sense of belonging to a place.

Organization of the Book

Chapter 1 provides background on the "senior citizens' center" movement. This chapter begins with an overview of the history of senior centers in the United States with a special focus on those in New York City. Trends in aging and the contemporary picture of aging in the United States are introduced.

In chapter 2 the scope of the book switches to look in depth at one particular working-class center in Queens, New York. The discussion then moves to this center, as a case study, giving a picture of what daily life is like for those attending a center and how the center, its activities and its social relationships, shape the way attendees see themselves. It follows the "good times" of the center and the roles and functions it played in the lives of attendees in its heyday.

In chapter 3 the lens shifts again as events of the center move beyond the attendees and building itself and looks at the larger, structural forces at play in the center-closure process. The center is used as a backdrop to showcase wider local, regional, and national political debates and economic struggles concerning the treatment of centers and viability of funding and options to keeping existing centers in place. The struggle of this one center is placed into the context of the struggle of all centers as part of a larger interconnected network of institutions for older persons in the process of undergoing great change.

In chapter 4 the discussion then moves on to cover the leaner times of the center as it struggles to stay open and, ultimately, is closed by the Department for the Aging. This chapter incorporates narratives of the centergoers, center staff, individuals in the community, local civic leaders, political figures, key people in the local senior movement (including nonprofit organizations), and journalists providing media coverage of the center; its closing and other events; and interviews with those in the NYC Department for the Aging (DFTA). This chapter reconstructs the time line and series of events that led to the closure of the center.

Mario Luis Small's work in *Unanticipated Gains: Origins of Network Inequality in Everyday Life* (2009) provides the theoretical backdrop for chapter 5. It focuses on the way centergoers' efforts to gather social, political, and economic capital to save the center were halted. I look at how social capital generated by the center participants moved forward or stopped in its tracks. My framework of analyzing social capital and social ties at three levels (micro, meso, and macro) intends to capture the complexity of capital and tie-building. By looking at how social ties are brokered, I will examine why centergoers' efforts could not keep the center open. The center was "sunk," or as reporters quoted it, "screwed"—despite network affiliations, promised political and financial support, and its absence from the NYC Department for the Aging's leaked fifty-center-closure list.

Not only do networks matter, but the location and specific neighbor characteristics affect which centers remain open and which close. The age, race/ethnicity, immigration status, and socioeconomic status, along with the history of the neighborhood in the borough, are analyzed in chapter 6 using a framework like that of Steven Gregory's case study *Black Corona: Race and the Politics of Place in an Urban Community* (1998). The idea that poor elders are marginalized and seen as vulnerable will be compared to the actions of elders throughout this shuttering process. I will examine the cost of displacement from one's familiar setting using Mindy Fullilove's "root shock" concept (as suggested for elders in Petrovic 2007). Parallels between the process of gentrification and recent changes in center closures are made to address the dilemma of what happens when centers disappear. The loss of one's senior center is framed as a loss of "authenticity," as suggested by Zukin. Processes of authenticity loss and root shock (versus being "stuck in place") are balanced with a discussion of elder empowerment and social movements.

If existing neighborhood center models do not work, what other models are out there both locally (and "innovatively") in New York City? And what about current models that are cited by national organizations and external reviewers, such as those highlighted in the New York Academy of Medicine report *NYC Senior Centers: Visioning the Future* (2010) or its *Age-Friendly NYC: Enhancing Our City's Livability for Older New Yorkers* (2009). A push is under way for centers that are based on membership in an identity group—such as for gay, lesbian, bisexual, and transgendered (GLBT) elders, for those with visual and hearing impairment, and for individuals of South Asian ethnicity. In chapter 7, I review many models cited as using best practices. I also evaluate center characteristics, such as the charter center model and strategic partnerships, including those for lifelong learning. Since a one-size-fits-all model will not work in meeting the needs of a very diverse group of aging persons, I make predictions about how multiple center models can exist and be tailored to the needs of a local community. I place the changes in center models in the context of boomer cohort-olatry (or what Harry "Rick" Moody [2008a] describes as the obsessive focus on the baby boomers without much regard for any structural forces other than their birth cohort). I will explore the ways attitudes held about this group shape center policy.

In chapter 8, the discussion is broadened to consider how social policies and legislation, such as the reauthorized Older Americans Act and the current Affordable Care Act's Community First Choice rule and Independence at Home demonstration projects, can be used to sustain centers on a larger, national scale. Here, I place current elder policy debates in the historical context of social policies and "entitlements" for older persons that have been developed. I employ concepts of the political economy of aging and the moral economy to further analyze the ideologies behind current policy debates. The chapter closes with my praxis, or linking of theory to practice, and some suggestion for senior centers as they move forward.

In the Appendixes, I pick up on themes of self-reflexivity (suggested by Pierre Bourdieu) begun in the Introduction. This final section talks about my role as a researcher and my reflections about the field and field setting.

1

The History of
Senior Centers

· ·

The Rise of the Center
Movement and How Centers
Form Spatial Identity

> Dot: We're unhappy when we can't get
> here; it's like a drug. . . . It makes us feel
> better. That's the truth . . .
> Pam: A lot better! (Both laugh.)
> —A conversation between two center-
> goers in their eighties as they enter the
> senior center, Queens, New York,
> June 2008

Senior centers mean different things to different people. Some were formed to supplement social services, some for pure socialization, and some to meet the need for a variety of services. The first center, the William Hodson Center, was founded in the Bronx, New York, in 1943 by a group of individuals concerned for the needs of older persons they encountered in their work in the public sector.[1] In 1949, a center in Menlo Park, California, was created, though this one was more geared toward social activities and recreation for a more afflu-ent group of older persons. Between that time and the mid-1960s, when the

Older Americans Act was passed and senior center–based national organizations were formed, there were about three hundred centers nationwide. Centers were formally created in the 1960s in the United States out of a combined impetus from a White House Conference on Aging in 1961 and the passage of the Older Americans Act in 1965.

With legislation and national organizations promoting senior centers in place, the number of centers grew to accommodate the mandate of providing supportive services, including recreation activities and nutrition services, such as congregate meals (National Health Policy Forum 2009). In the 1970s, the Public Works Act and changes to the Social Security Act benefited center construction, as did a call for nonprofit organizations to receive funding to create "multiservice centers"—centers mixing both referrals for services and social aspects. In the late 1970s and early 1980s, the Area Agencies on Aging ("triple As," as they are called) organized provision of services under the Older Americans Act, and senior centers were moved back to Title III. By the end of the 1980s, between eight thousand and ten thousand centers were in existence. Centers, both "senior" and "multiservice" varieties, were seen as the focal point model for a multitude of goods and services.

Reauthorization amendments of the Older Americans Act in 1992 and the delayed reauthorization in 2000 did not provide any substantially new provisions for senior centers; they maintained the status quo and provided a clear definition of a multipurpose senior center. The 2006 amendment supported the senior center policies of prior ones but added a call for aging in place and community-based programs and services. An estimated eleven thousand to fifteen thousand centers exist in the United States today (National Council on Aging and National Institute of Senior Centers 2011). Senator Bernie Sanders's proposed reauthorization of the Older Americans Act—the Older Americans Act Amendments of 2012, S. 2037—calls for the "modernization" of existing centers to appeal to a broader base of older persons, the implementation of evidence-based practices, and competitive grant funding allocated to accredited centers (United States Congress 2011).

Senior Centers as a Site of Identity Construction

Senior centers are sites where older individuals build meaningful social identities with identity-supporting friendships (Grenier 2005; Hurd 1999). These center-based social networks may replace lost networks. Studies of those attending senior centers found participants often talk about their health, social activities, and overall lives with others. In conversations, individuals may acknowledge changes in their health but see these changes as a way to understand themselves, in part, and who they are at a particular point in their lives. Centergoers may use their experiences to express feelings about changes that accompany aging and see these changes as either natural or nonnormative (Counihan 2008). Despite more negative evaluations of others, older individuals may use their narratives to review and evaluate their health status and activity level; these assessments are key components of their identity or who they are in their current lives (Lund and Englesrund 2008). Using a temporal social-comparison method, older persons may reflect upon their past selves to give meaning to the way they see themselves and their statuses in the present day (Henchoz et al. 2008). Aging in place, at least for Swedish elders, is seen to affect one's assessment of well-being on four levels: "lack of well-being, well-being so far, well-being despite it all, and well-being" (Oswald et al. 2011).

Studies have also found that centers can offer some negative experiences for older persons. Early work by Hurd (1999) found older women distancing themselves from other women at the same center by making distinctions between those who are "old" and themselves (who are "not old"). The women saw the center as a place where loss and failing health were the focus. Later work by Lund and Engelsrud (2008) found that some individuals at senior centers felt that those who were older or frailer were viewed as "threats" or reminders of conditions they may one day face. Center members, like those in Hurd's work, found the center was viewed as the most appropriate option for only the "disabled" and "old." Salari, Brown, and Eaton (2006) found centers to be generating conflicts over territory and ownership of physical space and fostering social cliques (especially in activity and meal seating).

The (Missing) Role of Senior Centers in Contemporary Literature

After the passage of the Older Americans Act in 1965 and until the 1990s, the senior center was a prominent focus in academic literature. Studies debated the benefits of various conceptual models (Taietz 1976; Wagner 1995), community collaboration and links to services (Krout 1989), urban/rural differences in center populations and activities (Krout 1987; Yearwood and Dressel 1983), national indicators of participation (Krout et al. 1990), the efficacy of intergenerational models (Aday et al. 1991), the role of the center in the lives of minority elders (Miller et al. 1996; Ralston 1991), and quantitative differences between center attendees and nonattendees (Miner et al. 1993).

From the late 1990s until the present, the focus of research shifted. The center was more often used as a site of research, not as the main focus of the research itself. Studies used the center as a place to recruit individuals for work about aggressive behaviors (Cohen-Mansfield and Werner 1998), falls and risk management (Baker et al. 2007), health-and-wellness programs (Kuczmarski and Cotugna 2009), and comparisons for a recreational park model for adolescents (Cohen et al. 2009) and as a recruiting site for a correspondence bias study (Stanley and Blanchard-Fields 2010). Yet a few exceptions that focus on the center itself do exist. Examples are Jan Walker, Carol Brisbee, Russell Porter, and Joanne Flanders's (2004) quantitative study concerning reasons for declining center attendance and Jacqueline Eaton and Sonia Salari's (2005) qualitative study about the technological learning needs of center attendees. In 2012, James Laditka, Sarah Laditka, and Katherine Lowe reviewed programs about cognitive health promotion at 181 accredited senior centers. Other contemporary studies focusing on regional and center-based differences have examined contemporary center use from attendees' perspectives (Ashida and Heaney 2008; Cohen et al. 2009; Fitzpatrick et al. 2005; Pardasani 2010). Centers have been seen as broad in their appeal, welcoming all, or designed around the interests of specific groups (Wacker and Roberto 2014). Work done on the Health Indicators Project, begun in 2006 as a collaboration of Hunter College faculty, the Mayor's Office, and the city's Department for the Aging (DFTA), was specifically designed to collect absent health and social indicators for center attendees in fifty-six centers in the five boroughs of New York City. In the case of this research, the center was both the central focus of the study and the site where the data were collected (see Friedman et al. 2012 for additional details).[2]

To highlight the state of contemporary research on centers in a metareview of senior center literature, Teresa Dal Santo states, "In light of all of the accomplishments senior centers have made in servicing older adults, it was disappointing to uncover such a small number of studies documenting their important service, and the quality of research was disheartening" (2009, 10). A recent analysis of national center models (with a low response rate) suggests six new models of centers based on the National Institute of Senior Centers: community centers (for all ages), wellness centers (for those fifty and older), lifelong learning centers (for those fifty and older, currently working), continuum of care/transitions (equivalents of neighborhood centers, for more frail elders), entrepreneurial centers (that make use of work skills after retirement) and café programs (meal based). Interestingly, the majority of these models would not identify as senior centers (Pardasani and Thompson 2012).

With the current influx of baby boomers, much of the literature centers on ways to rebrand or update centers to meet the needs of the boomer groups whose battle cry is thought to be "I'd never be caught dead at a senior center." Coupled with the rebranding trends are new and evolving theories about how best to age in one's own community. To illustrate the changes in thinking about centers and their users and the current theoretical developments, the following sections will describe those currently sixty-five and older (perceived as seniors) and those newly or imminently turning sixty-five (baby boomers). I will review the various models of aging in community and theoretical paradigm shifts associated with the boom. In the final section, I will use the state of New York City senior centers as an example to tie in the legislative/policy changes, the preparation for the boomers and perceived changes, the paradigm shift in ways of thinking about center models, and DFTA's changes in the way senior centers are organized, evaluated, and funded.

Emerging Trends in Aging: The Contemporary Picture of Aging in the United States

With the rise of the baby boomers, a distinction is often made between boomers and those who are "old." The boomer cohort has been the subject of heated debates labeling them as "entitled" or the "worst generation."[3] This "gray wave," with its "active agers," requires its own Boomer Bonds (or set of informal contracts by agencies to meet the needs of the baby boomer group, in terms of mobility and access, housing, supports systems, community engagement and education, safety and security, and community design for active aging).[4] But it is important to differentiate between the two groups: those currently sixty-five and older (seniors) and the boomers who have just begun reaching the sixty-five-years-of-age marker in 2011. We must move beyond labels and baby boomer cohort-olatry.[5]

So, What Are People Sixty or Sixty-five Years of Age and Older Currently Like?

According to a 2012 telephone survey conducted by the National Council on Aging, United Healthcare Foundation, and *USA Today*, called "The United States of Aging," on 2,250 persons sixty years of age and older living in five regions of the United States, you would be "positive about your current quality of life and optimistic about future health and happiness." You would feel you have "purpose and passion about your present and future" and be "confident in your ability to stay in your current home with only a few making modifications." You would feel certain in your ability to maintain exercise/physical fitness levels in the presence of any chronic conditions. Despite the need for improvements to do so, you would be "largely satisfied to live in your own communities" (Berland 2012, 2).

In 2011, one in eight people in the United States is sixty-five or older, with these numbers expected to double by 2030. Your life expectancy is increasing, and on average, at sixty-five years old in 2010 or 2011, you can expect to live an additional nineteen years.[6] You may be at the tail end of the Good Warriors or Greatest Generation (born 1908–1928) like those who may have fought in World War II, been born in the United States, and solidly blue collar and unionized. You could also be a member of the Lucky Few (born 1929–1945) the first generation to be smaller than the previous one and see mostly peacetime in your early lives.

In either case, if you are a bit older than sixty-five, you would most likely be an older woman, as older women outnumber older men. If you are an older woman, you are more likely to be unmarried and have a decline in physical functioning (which differs from the general trend of an improvement in physical functioning) and live alone in the community (Administration on Aging 2012b). Between 20 and 24 percent of this age group is non-White (Federal Interagency Forum on Aging-Related Statistics 2010). About 10 percent of your peers would be living below the poverty level (Administration on Aging 2012b).

If you head a household, you would own that home and, with your peers, account for about 5 percent of the workforce. Social Security would be the primary source of income (Federal Interagency Forum on Aging-Related Statistics 2010). You would receive Medicare for your hospital coverage and report some difficult walking (Administration on Aging 2012b) and receive a combination of paid/formal and unpaid/informal care for difficulties you may be having. One in four of your peers would report exercising regularly. More often than not, your chronic conditions would include some combination of heart disease, high blood pressure, diabetes, cancer, and arthritis (Hung et al. 2011), and you would report your health status as good overall (Federal Interagency Forum on Aging-Related Statistics 2010). You would spend one-fourth of your time doing leisure activities, most often watching television.

And What Are Initial Waves of Baby Boomers Like?

In 2030, you will account for 20 percent of the total population. The boomers will have both elder and child care at once with siblings to help or hinder that care (Fingerman et al. 2012; Rogerson and Kim 2012). Your peers will have higher rates of education and divorce or nonmarriage than in the past and be more racially and ethnically diverse (Frey 2010). You'll have a higher job status and fewer children than those in prior generations. But you may be financially unprepared for retirement, because of market changes and single incomes, and reliant upon Social Security (much like current elders) or continue to work longer (Baker and Rosnick 2010). Just as with contemporary elders, you may not be prepared to address your own long-term care needs (Finkelstein et al. 2012). You are seen as being very charitable, giving more than past generations, but your ability to be charitable has been affected by the recession (Frankel 2012). And despite any negative aspects of aging, you will be "upbeat" about your future (Reaney 2012) and use medical technology, such as apps for your phone or virtual health monitoring (Baum 2012). Even Internet channels, such as PBS's Next Avenue (http://www.nextavenue.org/)—"where grown-ups keep growing"—are created for you (Tillotson 2012).

Boomers may distance themselves from older persons by not wanting to be labeled as "old" and seek more "active aging" options (Roth et al. 2012). You may use a senior discount but refrain from calling it "senior" (Tuttle 2012) and face a shortage of in-home healthcare workers (Seewer 2012). You will have more varied ideas of what brings meaning to life, and these expectations will extend into your patterns of leisure. Leisure will be used as a means of self-expression and competition (Sperazza and Banerjee 2010). As a boomer, you may favor more holistic health options and those medical facilities tailored to the needs of your group (for example, those with Wi-Fi availability; Jaworski 2011). One in six boomers will move to another state after retiring, and this number is decreasing (Hannon 2012). If you are a member of a later boomer cohort, you will use more strict evaluation criteria when assessing your overall health than past cohorts. You will have lower levels of disability but higher rates of some chronic conditions, such as heart disease (Martin et al. 2010). You will be both civically engaged and politically active and see drug use as more normative than past generations (Duncan et al. 2010).

Marketers and consumer ratings groups will love the boomers, some labeling you "marketing's most valuable generation" (MVG), "too valuable to ignore," and the "most marketing-friendly generation in U.S. history" (Nielson and BoomAgers 2012, 2–6). You will be sought after by Hollywood as a demographic of moviegoers and also featured on the big screen (McClintock 2012).

How Centers Work and Fit with Existing Theories

Changes in theoretical trends parallel age-based demographic changes in society. Current theoretical developments about the experiences of elders living in their own communities (aging in place) can be divided into four broad categories: first, those rooted in a sense of immediate place (that is, an older person's attachment to his or her home) and, second, how well an older person is matched to his or her neighborhood setting. The third focus is on the effect of an older person's life course on his or her current community-based resources, and, last, there is the move to person-centered housing.

Let us begin by reviewing aging in place in general. *Aging in place* and *age-friendly communities or cities*, are two terms that are bandied about in academic circles and dominant culture. *Aging in place* was the first of the terms to evolve and is discussed in several contexts. Aging in place is viewed in terms of the way being in one's own community supports elders' continued psychosocial development. Aging in place is also seen as an outgrowth of housing/mobility preferences. Some liken the trend to the increase in homeownership post–World War II and the move to suburban settings (Callahan 1992). Using the term *aging in place* meant seeing the aging person in the context of his or her home and larger social environment. So aging was both person based and place based.

Aging in place and attachment to one's home or community reinforce the idea that older persons may be best served by aging within their own communities in their own homes, as opposed to being placed in institutional care.[7]

In the United States, part of the aging-in-place movement for elders can be attributed to changes in the 1999 Olmstead Act. Although the focus of a portion of the act was to keep persons with disabilities in their community setting with services, not in institutional segregation, the legislation fostered the community-based ideas for older persons.

On a global scale, the World Health Organization (WHO) defines age-friendly cities as those that encourage "active ageing by optimizing opportunities for health, participation and security in order to enhance quality of life as people age. In practical terms, an age-friendly city adapts its structure and services to be accessible to and inclusive of older people with varying needs and capacities" (2007, 1). WHO has surveyed thirty-three cities globally and created a framework of eight topic areas grouped around physical, social, and built environments. These elements include predictable items, such as access to services and transportation, but also pay attention to open space available.

Additionally, aging in place can be viewed through the lens of service provision and services needed to achieve this principle. Aging in place is also a way to draw in more structural societal elements to the study of the life course. Graham Rowles's (1978) concentric-circle model places home at the center of the aging-in-place continuum (from home, surveillance zone, neighborhood to community). In *Prisoners of Space? Exploring the Geographical Experience of Older People,* Rowles examined the ways elders held physical, social, and emotional attachment to place in older age. He found that being in the same place provided a setting where one could affix one's autobiography, but he also warned against romanticizing the notion of aging in place. Along with Rowles, Barry Fogel (1992) described how a home was more than a place but aided in identity construction (how older people see themselves). The home could be the "one constant in an emotional world threatened by losses" (Rowles 1993, 1).

Robert Rubenstein (1989) described why the home is crucial to elders. He suggested that it allows an individual to create a daily social routine (social-centered processes). Home lets elders keep a mental inventory of all their things/possessions (accounting), display personal touches and tokens (personal referents), and truly bond/love their immediate home environments (extension and embodiment). Then, using a body-centered process, an elder can adjust home stimuli (of intensity of activity, sights and sounds, from television volume to color choices, called *entexturing*). Elders may also keep needed items close at hand (environmental centralization). This "control center" can be empowering—literally, allowing elders to maintain control of their immediate social world (Lawton 1990). Jane Kroger and Vivienne Adair (2008) suggested that the home is a sort of portal. The home ties an individual to parts of his or her past. Objects in the home reinforce elders' past social status. The idea that aging in place supports attachment or "staying put" was supported by Janine Wiles and colleagues' work with elders in New Zealand (2012, 364). Additionally, aging in place supports identity development of elders by maintaining social roles based on seeing oneself as independent and autonomous.

Taking aging in place out of the home setting, M. Powell Lawton and Lucille Nahemow's ecological (1973) models describe the fit of a person to his or her environment. Lawton (1982) suggested that this theory of person-environment fit proposes that we all are aging in the dimension of place. In this theory, the match between one's competencies (abilities) and one's environmental presses (or limitations imposed by one's surroundings) determines the satisfaction one feels. Tied to theories of person-environment fit is Lawton's environmental-docility hypothesis: elders of marginal/lower status, or who are more vulnerable, have an increased dependence upon neighbor and place. There is also the environmental proactivity hypothesis: the more competent an elder is, the more social resources are needed to maintain his or her satisfaction.

Phyllis Myers's *Aging in Place: Strategies to Help the Elderly Stay in Revitalizing Neighborhoods* (1982) described programs involved in neighborhood revitalization that would benefit elders aging in place. In a small survey of midwestern elders about independent/ retirement living preference, 89 percent of community-dwelling persons wanted to remain in place (see Merrill and Hunt 1990). This preference of aging in place raised concerns among retirement housing administrators about meeting housing needs in the 1990s.

Eva Kahana and colleagues (2003) suggested that there are four factors crucially related to neighborhood satisfaction: physical amenities (such as the look of the neighborhood), resource amenities (such as shopping and transportation), level of safety, and amount of stimulation and peacefulness (according to an older person's taste). Joseph Sabia's empirical study "There's No Place Like Home" (2008) suggested that positively aging in place is better achieved in neighborhoods with greater home values and more community ties among residents. Other independent work showed an elder's assessment of his or her neighborhood relates to quality of life (Oswald et al. 2011).

Aging in place can also have negative aspects. In the realm of legal issues related to housing as a component of aging in place, Jon Pynoos and colleagues (2008) found that private homes and dwellings in public housing (such as those in the U.S. Department of Housing and Urban Development's Section 202 Supportive Housing for the Elderly Program) were often not adapted for elders. Most failed to meet the requirements of the 1999 Olmstead Act and of the 1988 fair housing laws, such as the residential component of the Americans with Disabilities Act. The researchers suggest that cohousing and other options better suit aging in place. Work done by Stephen Golant (2008), and Fenyang Tang and Joseph Pickard (2008) found older women (75+), of lower socioeconomic status and education, living with chronic health conditions or poor activities of daily living (ADLs) do not generally benefit from aging in place. Relocation may be a more viable option for this group. Unfortunately, other options may not be discussed, so a gap in knowledge of resources exists.

Senior centers provide aging-in-place resources for at-risk elders. Tang and Pickard (2008) looked at knowledge of aging in place, while Tang and Yeongjung Lee (2010) looked at service utilization and perceived needs of those aging in place. They found that vulnerable elders (seventy-five or older with chronic conditions) were less likely to predict what they needed to age in place as compared with less vulnerable elders. When services were used, the order of use was first, senior centers; then the visiting nurse; then in-home care or transportation services. Tang and Lee (2011) found that social networks can help link an elder to services and help with decision making. Social supporters can help elders see that home and community-based services are a form of instrumental support to aid in staying at home.

Emerging Theories: Biographical Structuration of the Life Course and Elder-Centered Care

Twists on two theories address one's ability to age in place. The first, "biographical structuration," furthers ideas of the life course and where one ends up in life. The second, a shift to elder-centered care, ties personal living preferences to class-based options. Social gerontology and sociology and other social sciences have long valued the influence of the life course perspective. This perspective, as originally conceived by Elder (1974) and his peers, sought to include the combined impact of being part of a cohort experiencing similar life events and history, earlier life events, and the role of social institutions and policies upon one's experience of aging throughout one's life span. The life course perspective incorporates intra-individual variation in an individual's life course, and the process is affected by key developmental markers such as turning points and life transitions.

Elder's life course perspective has four key principles. The first is the need to include historical time and place when examining a person's life, meaning that the time in which one is born and the events one experiences as part of an age cohort shape one's life. The second concept relates to the timing of life events, that is, the sequences of expected roles or events in a society. Events happening in the normative age-graded patterns have different effects from those that are out of sequence. The principle is centered around the linking of one's life to the lives of other people in their social world throughout life. The fourth principle incorporates the element of human agency, or the way different people make choices in their lives based on their available options (which alter one's life course). The life course perspective provides historical context to an individual's life. It evaluates the timing of events as normative or nonnormative for a particular age and sees the individual's experiences in relation to the person's greater social world. This perspective also values agency of individuals in shaping their own life course.

At a panel, "What's in a Name? Perspectives on the Sociology of Age, Aging, and the Life Course," held in mid-August 2012, some leaders in the field of sociology debated whether the use of the term *life course* accurately reflects the current state of thought about age and aging. As such, cumulative advantage/disadvantage theory has lent itself to the study of life course so that the role of social structure and institutional impact upon individuals' lives has become the focus of study (Dannefer 2012). Theories of cumulative advantage/disadvantage have become theories of cumulative inequality (Ferraro et al. 2009).

Yet in March 2012, the editor of the *Journals of Gerontology: Social and Psychological Sciences* created a special symposium within the issue, "(Re)considering the Life Course as a Key Concept in Social Gerontology," to examine developments and remaining issues about research on the life course perspective. Several key figures, Duane Alwin, Dale Dannefer, Jon Hendricks, and Angela O'Rand, were asked to address shortcomings and needed future directions in life course research. Key themes from their discourse included the need to expand a view of cultural generations in addition to period and cohort effects, the need to include a personal sense of time, the addition of geographic place and socioeconomic strata, and the role of individual agency in relation to accepting or discounting norms (Hendricks 2012). Dannefer's title expresses his view of what is needed: "Enriching the Tapestry: Expanding the Scope of Life Course Concepts" (2012). Angela O'Rand (2012) adds in concepts of fellow researchers and explains the need to examine an individual's "compensatory mechanisms" to overcome cumulative inequality.

As the first theoretical shift, Marcus Schafer, Kenneth Ferraro, and Sarah Mustillo (2011) suggest that we weigh "early adversity" with human agency in later life—naming this process "biographical structuration." Their term "refers to the constraining influence of a person's past for his or her present and future life chances. . . . It is through the human capacities of memory and narration that biographical details from across life are woven together and remain consequential for the present and future. This interpretive phenomenon adds another dimension to the concept of structure in the life course. Situated choice, in other words, is biographically structured, reflecting both one's social location and lived experiences" (17).

The second shift in theory refers to the focus of care or way we think about working with an elder. In the past, care was centered on rhythms that favored staff, but there is a movement to make care, mostly in long-term care settings such as skilled nursing care facilities, be directed by the older individual, often thought of as a consumer. Person-centered care, once "patient-centered care," as its name implies, stems from a healthcare-based model. *Crossing the Quality Chasm: A New Health System for the 21st Century*, by the Committee on Quality of Health Care in America, Institute of Medicine (2001) promoted "patient-centered" care as the core of quality improvement in healthcare (with "care [being] customized according to patient needs and values" and "the patient [as] the source of control"). Common person-centered principles include respect, self-determination, and individuality (Love and Kelly 2011).

Organizations such as the Robert Wood Johnson Foundation, AARP, and the Centers for Medicare and Medicaid favor this model, as do governmental programs such as Cash and Counseling, in which the money follows the person. Although some argue that the adoption of person-centered care lags behind the theory, many cultural change movements toward person-centered care currently advocate for change (Koren 2010). For example, we now have nonprofits, such as the Consumer Consortium Advancing Person-Centered Living (CCAL), promoting consumer advocacy and informed consumers embracing the organization's philosophy of "nothing about me without me." Organizations are changing the person-centered care component to reflect the aging-in-place, person-centered-living (PCL) idea. According to CCAL's website, PCL fights against the "loss of humanity" for those aging or disabled. The older person directs his or her lifestyle, and "if support is needed, supports are centered on personal preferences and values that stress dignity, choice, self-determination, respect, privacy, and individuality. PCL means being kind, respectful, and sensitive to those being served and honoring their right to make their own choices" (CCAL n.d.).

With the move to focus on the individual (as a person, not an object) came the focus on matching the physical, or built, environment, to fit older persons as they change over time. This path of study is called *environmental gerontology* or, later, an Ecological Systems model. Lawton and Nahemow (1973) theorized the match between elders and their environment as their Person-Environment Fit model. Research has focused on the immediate home environment and less on larger infrastructural levels, with limited continuation of changes/adaptation over life or on more physical outcomes, such as falls, and has limited advancement from its earliest theories (Kendig 2003). Researchers suggest that environmental gerontology, from the 1990s to 2000s, focused on "private home environments, planned environments, and residential decisions" (Wahl and Weisman 2003, 622–623; see also Gitlin 2003; Golant 2003). Neil Harris and John Grootjans (2012) suggest that there are actually four domains that need to be in balance in a model that matches person and environment. These domains include attention to the physical built/natural environment, the social environment (relationships and meeting places), governance of the self and environments, and active living. The researchers further suggest that three levels, personal, communal, and societal, must be considered within each domain.

Along the person-centered continuum of care, we see the "greening" of housing: elder-centered community-based or cohousing models, such as the Green House Project (built on Eden Principles), cohousing, and expansion of the visitability concept for all elders. Green Houses, according to a metareview of literature and panel of experts, in work by Sheryl Zimmerman and Lauren Cohen, have the following "essential elements": "Physical structure (small size, no more than 12 rooms), Private rooms and bathrooms; Access to the outdoors; Dining (non-institutional, residential-style kitchen); Staffing (consistent assignment, universal role within self-managed teams, clinical staffing—RN, NP, and PA—nearby); Elder case mix (diverse—acute/chronic, physical/cognitive impairment, private pay/Medicaid and stable); Elder-centered care (not according to fixed schedules); and Engagement (normalized rather than organized activities)" (2010, 719).

Cohousing picks up on the Green House trend and focuses on the mix of persons living together and dividing tasks for a continuous period of time, aging in place together. Cohousing models in the United States began in the late 1990s, picking up on models set forth in the Netherlands. Unlike naturally occurring retirement communities (NORCs), cohousing communities are intentional or planned with certain design elements. As Anne Glass (2009) suggests, cohousing is based on community and communal management/leadership. There is attention to shared common areas with private housing. The first elder-based cohousing was named ElderSpirit by founding members. The group then formed Trailview Development Corporation to oversee the building of the community in 1999. It is a "center that would provide a spiritual setting for older adults . . . an ElderSpirit Center, resonating with traditional associations of 'elder' with wisdom, leadership, dignity, and ritual."[8] These cohousing communities have a mix of renters and homeowners, a common house, and a spirit house with parking at a distance from the homes.

The idea of making single-family homes have "visitability" was suggested by Eleanor Smith, an advocate, and her Concrete Change group in 1982 (Heavens 2002). Although legislation covered commercial and multifamily residence in terms of accessibility, Smith felt that private homes were less accessible. She suggested three basic changes to make these homes "visitable" by all. Single-family homes should have a zero-step entry door, at least thirty-two-inch-wide interior doors, and a half bathroom on the first floor. So theoretical and demographic trends indicate that we are moving toward community-based living with services that are elder and baby boomer friendly and accessible by all. The next section will describe center changes in New York City to see how they fare against current trends. This focus will set the stage for the Queens-based center case, which begins chapter 2.

A Brief History of Senior Centers in New York City:
Center Changes Parallel Changes in Theory and Trends

Little substantive information about senior citizens' centers is available from
before the late 2000s. In New York City, 256 to 329 centers serve 225,000 older
adults annually.[9] A metareview of center types and services found centers to
have distinct styles ranging from solely recreational and food service provision
in traditional, community-based settings to larger, multipurpose senior centers serving multiple communities. Program and service offerings were in five
major categories: nutrition, health and fitness, recreational, volunteer opportunities, and social services (National Health Policy Forum 2009). Findings
from work done with New York City senior citizens' center stakeholders
found five traditional functions suggested as a critical core: providing social
engagement opportunities, offering public services/benefits, supplying links
to community resources, presenting nutrition services, and promoting both
positive physical and mental health behaviors.

I have compiled data from a series of New York City Mayor's Management
Reports, 1997–2011 in table 2.[10] The 1997–2000 listings of briefs by DFTA
mostly charted the increase in older persons using the Senior Citizens Rent
Increase Exemption (SCRIE) and training of Senior Citizens Referral and
Entitlement Eligibility Network (SCREEN) workers in 1997. DFTA chroni-
cled the incorporation of a bilingual Interactive Voice Response (IVR) System
and the New York State Tax Relief (STAR) program in 1998. Later reports
noted grants received for Alzheimer's research (1999), the expansion of Provider Data Systems (PDS) in 1998 to track service usage, and a twenty-four-
hour senior helpline in 2000.

In 2001, the format of the report was greatly expanded, with senior centers
prominently featured. The mayor and City Council had provided $3.15 mil-
lion to create nine senior centers. Of the six that were awarded contacts, two
were operational in 2001 (the remaining four needed more extensive work).
Three were in process. In 2001, a report assessing decline in center use around
congregate meals was contracted with New York–based universities but
delayed. Preliminary 2000 results indicated that meal participation was influenced by center location, quality, food choices and presentation, and degree of
understanding of center regulations. There were new standards and training
and four million dollars allocated for physical improvements. In 2001, DFTA
completed half a report about forty centers: 98 percent participated in meals
and 94 percent were somewhat or very satisfied with senior center services. In
2002, senior center use (in terms of meals) was stated to have dropped over the
past five years, but the creation of four new centers kept lunch numbers up.
Lunches declined in 2003, and the number of centers well utilized (at 90 percent capacity for the lunch meal) decreased to 69 percent. It is here we find

Table 2

Senior Center Characteristics, 1998–2011

Characteristic	FY 1998	FY 1999	FY 2000	FY 2001	FY 2002	FY 2003	FY 2004	FY 2005	FY 2006	FY 2007	FY 2008	FY 2009	FY 2010	FY 2011
Number of centers	n/a	n/a	n/a	n/a	336	336	329	329	325	329	329	304	259	256
% Change of center loss	n/a	n/a	n/a	n/a	n/a	n/a	-2.1%	n/a	-1.2%	+1.2%	n/a	-7.6%	-14.8%	-1.2%
Percent of centers operating at 90%+ capacity	n/a	n/a	74%	76%	81%	69%	n/a	n/a	58%	56%	55%	52%	51%	·
Citywide senior center utilization rate*	n/a	n/a	n/a	n/a	n/a	n/a	n/a	n/a	n/a	n/a	n/a	n/a	n/a	88%
Number of contractors	n/a	n/a	n/a	n/a	600+	600+	600+	600+	600+	600+	900+	900	800	700
% Change in number of contractors	n/a	n/a	n/a	n/a	n/a	n/a	n/a	n/a	n/a	n/a	50%	n/a	-11.1%	-12.5%
Meals served per year (millions)	n/a	n/a	n/a	n/a	12.5	12.5	12.2	12.4	12.4	12.4	12.6	12.6	10.5	10
Meals served per day (at senior centers only)	31,607	30,540	29,524	29,240	29,354	28,856	28,010	28,655	28,510	28,038	28,518	27,951	27,046	25,107
DFTA expenditures (millions)	184	192	215	237	231	237	229	231	268	272	299	290	282	277

SOURCE: Compiled by the author from the New York City Mayor's Management Reports, 1997–2011.

*In 2011, the percentage of centers operating at 90%+ capacity indicator was replaced by the new measure of citywide senior center utilization rate.

the warning "During Fiscal 2004 DFTA will work with underutilized senior centers to explore possible reasons for declining usage and develop plans to address underutilization" (New York City Mayor's Office 2003, 61). In 2004, "the number of meals served to seniors decreased for the second year in a row," center lunches decreasing, "while home-delivered meals increased" (New York City Mayor's Office 2005, 59). In 2004, highly utilized centers were defined as those with 90 percent or more lunches served (Stephens and Kwah 2009). They stressed the role of the director (in addition to good sponsorship) in creating a sense of community at a center. The concept was that the first meal gets them in, but the social environment makes them stay, or "gets them hooked."

In 2005, "due in part to DFTA's diligence in holding its contractors accountable for adhering to contractual service levels, utilization of senior centers increased during Fiscal 2005" (New York City Mayor's Office 2006, 59). In 2007, "the percent of senior centers that are utilized at a minimum of 90% capacity declined by 2 percentage points. As part of DFTA's broad initiative to modernize services for older adults in New York City, a workgroup will redesign the senior center model with health and wellness components" (New York City Mayor's Office 2007, 43). A 2007 commissioner's letter described the counterintuitive state of center utilization of meals. Poverty was increasing for New York City elders, yet then–commissioner of DFTA Edwin Méndez-Santiago stated that congregate meal usage and the percentage of centers meeting 90 percent meal capacity had been declining since 1998. The letter stressed that through a DFTA-commissioned study, the meal turnaround was possible with a few recommended steps.

As mentioned in the introduction to the present volume, in early 2008, Méndez-Santiago created a modernization program to address Mayor Bloomberg's All Ages Project, to convert centers into Healthy Aging Centers based on a "wellness approach." In late 2008, with the unexpected resignation of Méndez-Santiago, Bloomberg named Lilliam Barrios-Paoli as the new commissioner for DFTA.[11] At the time, three hundred or so senior centers in New York City were seen by officials as serving only a small percentage of older New Yorkers. With this in mind, Barrios-Paoli's task for 2009 was to "overhaul the operations of the city's 329 senior centers" (Chan and Chen 2008). In December 2008, the modernization plan was temporarily halted because of backlash from the City Council and Speaker Christine Quinn (Barbaro 2008). In 2008, a little over half (56 percent) of senior centers met the 90 percent utilization goal.

In 2009, a reworking of service provision based on requests for proposals was under way. Age-Friendly NYC, a partnership between DFTA and the New York Academy of Medicine, cited many existing centers as "less than optimal facilities" that were noncompliant with the Americans with Disabilities

Act or unable to host core services (New York Academy of Medicine 2009, 88). DFTA offered one-time funding assistance for relocation, higher rents, and maintenance to increase center appeal. In 2009, 44 percent of the 329 senior centers were characterized as "substantially underutilized and . . . losing popularity in New York City" (Haber 2009, 288). On April 30, 2009, the City Council announced the closure of fifty centers following the orders of the commissioner of the DFTA, based on "fewest meals, fewest hours, and most management/maintenance problems." Centers were to be notified by July 1, 2010; DFTA would not release their names until Bloomberg's final approval. Individual centers speculated about closures in the media. Closures by borough were said to be nine in the Bronx, eleven in Brooklyn; sixteen in Manhattan, ten in Queens, and four in Staten Island. On May 10, a *New York Times City Room* blog article leaked the list of fifty shuttered centers, having received it from someone who had attended the meeting of the City Council.

In 2010, "due to budget cuts," the number of senior centers across the city was reduced to 259. Of the remaining centers, 51 percent were operating at a minimum of 90 percent capacity "of their projected number of congregate lunch meals" (Stephens and Kwah 2009, 164), a decline of 1 percentage point compared with the same period the previous year (45). In 2012, with the number of centers reduced, 88 percent met the utilization criteria.

In July 2012, DFTA released a report based on census data for the older population of New York City. Brooklyn and Queens have the largest numbers of persons sixty years of age and older (about 30 percent each) but have slow growth rates of this population when compared with those of the entire city, where about 17 percent of the population is sixty or older. The report also mentioned the need to identify the "young elderly," who have service needs different from those of older elders.

As part of a 2011–2012 initiative, an announcement on NYC DFTA's "Innovative Centers" webpage reads, "Through its competitive procurement process, DFTA selected eight community-based organizations to develop innovative senior centers with contract start dates in January, 2012." There would be five borough-based centers: BronxWorks (in the Bronx); Lenox Hill Neighborhood House and the YM/YWHA of Washington Heights and Inwood (in Manhattan); Selfhelp Community Services and Services Now for Adult Persons (in Queens); and the Jewish Community Center of Staten Island (in Staten Island). Two of the centers would serve citywide populations: Services and Advocacy for Gay, Lesbian, Bisexual and Transgender Elders (SAGE) and Visions/Service for the Blind and Visually Impaired.

The Visions Center at Selis Manor officially opened on January 3, 2012, followed by the SAGE Center, on March 1, 2012. In summer 2012, a call to all older New Yorkers was posted on DFTA's website, advertising the changes in centers and its center-based programs. The full text reads:

If you have the preconception that senior centers are not for you, pay a visit to your local center and judge for yourself! Not only are senior centers a home away from home for many older New Yorkers, they offer an exciting variety of activities. Chances are, whatever's on the agenda on any particular day, the center will be bustling. What's more, should you need information about senior benefits or services for seniors in your community, the center's friendly staff will be glad to help you. And if you just want to relax with good friends over a game of cards or cup of coffee, well, pull up a chair! Being with friends is the best part of attending a center! . . .

Looking for free exercise classes, a walking club, a discussion group where you can talk about the issues that concern you as a senior, a blood pressure monitoring program? Join a center that offers one or more of DFTA's Health Promotion Programs. (NYC DFTA n.d.)

While the change to center models in New York City was happening, neighborhood centers were chugging on their way to keep pace with these changes. In the next chapter, we will take a step back and look at the case of a working-class neighborhood senior center in its heyday.

2

The Case of the Center before Shuttering

• •

The Daily Life of the Center

> It gives you a reason to get up in the morning. It forces you to get up, get dressed, and get out.
> —Vera, in her eighties, in the center's vestibule, with her red shopping cart that she affectionately calls her "Mercedes-Benz," 2009

Enter the center, circa 2008.

The senior center is one of five in the community district.[1] It is on a block easily accessible to transportation and shopping. There is a city bus stop on one side of the building and access to a grocery store and drugstore chains down the other side of the street. It is an older commercial brick building, the tallest building in the immediate area, with a few benches outside and main access at street level. A sign on the brick front announces meal program times and contact information. An American flag hangs outside the building.

The center is the only tenant of the building, and it occupies three floors. The main floor houses staff offices, which are fair sized and retrofitted into the older building's structure. The offices of the social worker, bookkeeper, and program staff have glass doors, and all offices, even the director's, have frequent visitors—with centergoers wanting to chat or bring in some local baked goods. These staff offices truly have a welcoming, open-door policy. For example, when I have an appointment with staff in their offices, centergoers, bearing treats such as Italian cannolis or Polish pączki from local European pastry shops, often stop by.

A newly installed video surveillance camera system (in one of the staff member's offices) monitors all rooms in the center. The upper floors, accessible by both stairs and elevator, house an exercise/dance room, a computer room, a member-created library, and a food pantry. The exercise room is sparse but holds a pool table, a television set up for exercise videotapes, and space enough for dancing. The computer room resembles the layout of all computer labs, with two rows of computers lining the walls. Here elders are often found just e-mailing or surfing the Net. The library consists of several bookshelves of donated and large-print books available for loan to all members. When the elevator doors open to the food pantry, you are likely to be greeted by an elder with a shopping cart, picking up donated canned goods and fresh-baked bread, also donated by a local bakery.

The basement is the main hub of activity, where meals are served for those buying a meal ticket, guests are invited to speak, and members play tabletop games. After going to the ticket seller and getting a ticket, you would proceed to rectangular tables set up on each side of the room. The tables face an electronic bingo board and a main table set up for speakers and presentations. Behind the tables, you hear cooks talking and pans clanging in the center's kitchen. Off to the side of the dining tables on this basement floor, where fewer elders sit, is a member-created table where new and used items donated by members are sold to help raise money for the center.

Although attendees congregate outside the center, they typically enter through the front door each morning and sign in at the front desk (I was told, "Keeping track of attendance is important") while taking time to chat with the person at the door, calling herself a "hat-check girl" who "mans the coat closet." (When I spent time sitting at the door, I met the most people, sometimes all at once.) Then, individuals, alone or with others, make their way downstairs to the main room. A pre-meal snack of coffee and bread is served for a fee; then members get their meal ticket for lunch and make their way to their usual tables, where they meet up with others in their long-standing group of friends. Prior to the meal, guest speakers present topics (the last, a talk by a nutritionist promoting the benefits of eating cabbage, was graciously endured by centergoers) or games are played. Some members do exercise or work on the computers upstairs, but most stay in the main room—this is where the action is; it is the heart of the center. Although typical, this pattern does change depending on that day's scheduled activities and on the days when bus trips or special-themed dances and parties occur. A room or activity filled one day will be vacant the next, when there are field trips, such as one to a local movie theater.

The center's printed monthly newsletter, created by the associate director, offers columns such as Meet Our Members; birthday greetings for that month's "birthday babies" of both centergoers and staff; a section devoted to centergoers' "grandpets and other furry friends'" photos; announcements of upcoming trips, parties, and celebrations; the ongoing activity schedule; a thank you to local businesses that have recently donated to the food pantry; and a list of everyone in the center "family": the board of directors, advisory board, and center staff and "all our beloved members and volunteers." Filling in a blank space in one of the issues on the menu pages is the following inscription from the center staff: "Dear Members, We just want to take a second to let you know that we cherish every moment you are with us. Your presence is never taken for granted. To please you is our desire. To serve you is our privilege. Thank you, Center Staff."

Each newsletter includes boilerplate text describing the ten main services the center provides: case assistance, entitlement screening and processing, completion of forms for clients, congregate meals, daily education and recreational programs, health promotion with blood pressure monitoring and stress management, round-trip transportation, functioning as a cooling center on high-temperature summer days, and a biweekly community food-pantry program. The center is open seven days a week and offers breakfast two days a week, congregate meals six days a week, and soup to go two days a week. On average, the center serves 3,240 meals a month.[2]

Monthly center newsletters announce the activity options for attendees: bingo (four times a week), morning news and conversation (three times a week), billiards (three times a week), puzzle time (twice a week), ballroom dancing (twice a week). Other options are offered only once a week: Eldercise, yoga, stay-well aerobics, morning stretch, blood pressure screening, open pool table, and social dancing with a disc jockey. Recent examples of speakers, presentations, and events include holiday-themed parties (Hawaiian vacation, New Year's), a defensive-driving course, pen pals from a local elementary school, a breast cancer presentation from a nonprofit group, a Medigap speaker, a cooking demonstration, and a monthly birthday celebration. Typical trips include visits to museums and religious institutions and a garden luncheon. The center even receives two particular distinctions. It is featured as a 2002 Best of Queens senior center by a local newspaper and receives a Star Award for its Meals on Wheels program. (In 2006, two years before I formally began my study, the center was highlighted as a spotlight program in a DFTA newsletter for the work of its director and its novel, privately funded programs. The newsletter called the facility a "vitality center" and ended the write-up with "Let there be no doubt: there's a new kind of senior center being developed all over the City by centers like [this one].")

Now that you have an idea of what the center was like when flourishing, I want to describe how centergoers saw the center. What was center life like for the most frequent attendees (or regulars, as they would call themselves)? How did the less frequent (the bingo or menu) members and nonattendees at a senior citizens' multiservice center in New York City see the role of the center and its activities in their daily lives? Well, in 2008, after some correspondence with the director, I received a letter inviting me to "interview women [and men] 65 years and over at the Senior Center" and was thanked "for my interest in the process of exploring how social class, social support, physical health and well-being relates to older [persons] living in the community." I got to know the center as attendees, staff, neighbors, and those in the community viewed it. Through these groups' own words and observations, I learned about the array of activities and social relationships at the center and in the community. The picture painted is one of what daily center life was like in the good times, before its closure.

The majority of elders interviewed for this study were women (70 percent) with an average age of seventy-five years (SD = 4.5). Most individuals self-identified as white (89 percent); 45 percent were homemakers, 30 percent did work as a clerk, teacher's aide, or office worker, 10 percent were in managerial roles, and 15 percent were in professions requiring certification. About 71 percent rented their apartments or homes. Half were widowed (50 percent) and lived alone or with a spouse (43.5 percent for each). The individuals lived within a few blocks of the center and traveled to the center on foot (50 percent), by carpooling (32 percent), on public transportation (14 percent), or in the center van (4 percent). For additional descriptive characteristics, see table 3; for a detailed description of methodology, see appendix B.

Let's Meet the Attendees: Regular, Bingo, and Menu Members and Nonmembers

The Regular Members

As their self-assigned moniker implies, the "regulars" are indeed that. They report doing regular center activities: volunteering at the center (83.3 percent), going on trips and outings (66.7 percent), attending center parties (50 percent), and running a thrift table or helping prepare coffee and a snack or meals (each 33 percent). Sixteen percent engage in each of the following activities: playing bingo, watching movies, participating in discussion groups, attending a self-defense class, dancing, visiting the bookmobile, joining a Bible study group, and doing puzzles.

Table 3
Characteristics of All Participants (as percentages unless noted)

Characteristic	Participants (n = 29)	Regular (n = 20)	Menu/Bingo (n = 5)	Nonattendees (n = 4)
Mean age (SD)	75.4 (4.5)	77.3 (3.3)	70.2 (5.1)	73.7 (1.0)
Gender				
Female	69.2	70.6	60	75
Male	30.8	29.4	40	25
Days per week	4.4 (1.9)	5.3 (1.0)	3.4 (0.9)	n/a
Years in attendance	8.8 (2.3)	11.4 (9.4)	7.0 (4.7)	n/a
Length of interview (average minutes)	62 (25.4)	56.6 (29.4)	61.2 (2.7)	83.7 (16.0)
Marital status				
Widowed	50.0	40	80	25
Married	33.3	40	0	75
Divorced	4.2	0	20	0
Never married	12.5	20	0	0
Race				
White, non-Hispanic	88.9	100	60	100
Hispanic	3.7	0	20	0
Black	7.4	0	20	0
Living arrangements				
Alone	43.5	35.7	60	50
With spouse/ significant other only	43.5	50	20	50
With spouse & adult children	4.3	0	20	0
With spouse, children & grandchildren	4.3	7.1	0	0
With adult children/ grandchildren	0	0	0	
With other relatives	4.3	7.1	0	
Transportation to center				
Drive/carpool	31.8	33.3	40	n/a
Walk	50	46.7	40	n/a
Bus/public transportation	13.6	13.3	20	n/a
Center van	4.5	6.7	0	n/a
Occupation				
Homemaker	45	50	40	0

(continued)

Table 3
Characteristics of All Participants (as percentages unless noted) (*continued*)

Characteristic	Participants (n = 29)	Regular (n = 20)	Menu/Bingo (n = 5)	Nonattendees (n = 4)
Occupation				
Entry level (teacher's aide, clerk, civil servant)	30	50	40	0
Midlevel (insurance agent, telephone company manager)	10	0	20	25
Professional level (registered nurse)	15	0	0	75
Home ownership				
Rent	71.4	97.1	80	0
Own	28.6	8.3	20	100

The overarching theme for this group is that the center is a place where individuals meet with friends and make new ones. The center is a site for social interaction and to do meaningful work. It was a place where one can apply one's efforts to make older individuals feel better and to foster well-being. At the peak of the center's days, individuals' interactions with me range from conversing about their everyday lives to kidding around to having frank discussions about the economic role the center plays in their lives. In these early days of my study, the regular members feel they need to educate me about the ways of the center and also be engaging. They often comment to me, "It seems like you are having a good time, too." At first, they seem to want to meet my perceived expectations for social desirability and sometimes marginalize their roles as interviewees. Common comments and questions are "Is this what you wanted to know?" "I'm taking too much of your time," "I have nothing to contribute," and "That's all I have to say." Some even ask if I would become a member, and as I spend time with the regulars, I come to learn more about the way the center is seen in relation to their lives.

Seven specific themes arise from analysis of the regulars' transcribed interview text: (1) health problems are expected but do not greatly affect participation in the center's activities; (2) being with others at the center provides emotional support; (3) being an active member is a crucial part of quality of life and identity; (4) social interaction with others at the center is pleasurable and helps with instrumental tasks, such as transportation, meal preparation, and financial matters; (5) choice and agency in selecting (or not selecting) one's activities at the center are essential; (6) social interaction with others at the center wards off mental decline; and (7) individuals see themselves as helpers of others at the center and not helpless or vulnerable.

Health Problems Are Expected but Do Not Greatly Affect Participation in the Center's Activities. When asked about current health conditions and how they affect their activity choices, the participants initially mention conditions such as heart problems (angina or high blood pressure), diabetes, osteoporosis, emphysema, arthritis, vision issues (such as cataracts and macular degeneration), hip and joint issues, and general difficulty with mobility. After naming these conditions, the individuals are quick to point out that although the problems may have been many, they do not greatly influence their ability to navigate their social world. Lily, seventy-three, a regular for eleven years, has an adult son who came to live with her "temporarily" and lives two and a half blocks from the center. She states, "Us seniors, we all have something—there's no such thing as a healthy senior. . . . As long as I can do what I do, I'm going to. There may be a time I won't be able to. I have a very severe heart condition, I'm a diabetic, I just had a hip replacement, I'm gonna have my knee done in December. But as long as I can do things, I will do it. . . . I come here because I am not a stay-at-home. . . . Even if I don't feel well, I come. . . . Well, basically we all have our problems. Take a medical encyclopedia of medicine and read out a disease, and ask; somebody has it."

Victoria, seventy-four, who holds a prominent position on the center's board and organizes many activities and trips, echoed Lily: "[Despite my health conditions] . . . I *make* myself go out. Sometimes four, sometimes five times. It depends on what I have to do; like today, I have to grocery shop. And I'm doing a dinner dance for next week, a party where I sell a lot of tickets. . . . I know everybody." When asked about quality of life, Karen, seventy-seven, legally blind, and involved in starting up the center's library, states, "Well, let's be honest. I would rather have my eyesight. Going back and forth to Brooklyn . . ." But then she continues on to discuss the activities she either organized or participates in at the center.

Being with Others at the Center Provides Emotional Support. When asked why they come to the center, the regular participants continually raise the idea that being at the center with others makes them feel better. Cara, eighty, the most recently widowed of the group, drives a carpool for other members and rents out apartments in her house. She remarks, "I come anyway [when feeling stressed]. I don't think about it. . . . That's life. You have to come and talk; if you're in the house by yourself, you're alone." Lily adds, "Well, it's a place for seniors to come to . . . because a lot of them live alone. We do have activities here, and they can socialize."

Being an Active Member Is a Crucial Part of Quality of Life and Identity. When asked about the activities they enjoy, the participants stress that they are not the type of individuals to "just sit around." Instead, they all have a lot of work to do and feel they are integral to the success of the center. Angela, seventy-six married, heavily identifies with a spiritual calling and mission. She states, "Well, I'm always busy; I'm always doing something. I don't like to sit down. I, I have to keep on going. I'm sitting now, but you know what I'm saying. I like to be doing something. This afternoon, I'm meeting an individual who has a problem. Oh, the Lord knows me. I have groups, individual groups that come to the house." (She has a cane by her side during the interview but never mentions it.) The other individuals mention their activities. Lily begins: "I come here, I do the meals for the homebound, I do the bread for the table, I do silverware, I am a volunteer, I do the coffee, I help upstairs with the food bank, I sit at the front desk." She smiles. "I am also a big pain in the neck." Victoria talks about the activities she is in charge of: "I am the president [of a group within the center]. And I do a lot of activities. I run the dinner dances, I do this [the thrift table], run bus trips, make money for the center. . . . I *always* get a full bus." Karen reflects upon many activities that she takes part in at the center:

> I started [helping with] Meals on Wheels. And then we were having a plant sale, so I got involved with that. . . . And then I got the garden. I was doing the garden in the driveway. Then we had the library, but it was so-so. But a lot of the authors I know, so I can recommend what, how, and where. I do the bookmobile on Thursday. And then we started with the thrift table, so I help out on that. We used to have a rummage table twice a year. We do very well on it. I think in a five-month period, we had nine hundred and some-odd dollars. Plus, you get to talk to the people. Now, the last couple of days, I'm working on the Hawaii party. I keep myself busy. If there's something I can do, I'll put a hand in and do it—because I can't just sit here and wait for my lunch, and eat my lunch and leave.

Social Interaction with Others at the Center Is Pleasurable and Helps with Instrumental Tasks, Such As Transportation, Meal Preparation, and Financial Matters. The participants note that being with others at the center can be a source of pleasure and also provides tangible, instrumental help with meeting one's daily needs for subsistence. Commenting that social interaction is pleasurable, the individuals relate the following narrative, according to Karen: "Well, on Monday, we went and ordered the cake from Stop n' Shop." In a jesting tone, she went on, "I go grubbing with my dark glasses and my cane, and we got a twenty-five-dollar gift certificate to buy snacks for the p-party." She laughs. "And, oh—being a senior can be a lot of fun! Plus, I'm selling raffle tickets for the 50/50 on Sunday." Cara adds, "Any group you come into, you either decide, 'Okay, I just want this out of it, or this is all I'll give, or whatever.' So it's basically how you deal with the group is what you get out of it." On a level of daily subsistence, the individuals raise the issue of instrumental help. A good example is Karen's account:

I'm sure there are many people that need food. I mean, that's the sad part with this economy. There are many people that, really, maybe before wouldn't have needed food but now . . . we have a limited amount we can give. So we have people on the waiting list. But basically, the centers have a lot to offer of all kinds. They have the case workers who can help people who have no family close by with problems with the landlords. The windows are broken or the stove doesn't work. Or they, they are getting hassled or whatever. Or the landlord wants to raise the rent, and that they don't have the right to. Or some of the seniors depending on their financials, they can get breaks on rent. The city would pay so much on Con Edison bills. They could get a break on any utilities. Depending, they can get this help; the caseworkers here know all the forms and whatever.

Choice and Agency in Selecting One's Activities at the Center Are Essential. When asked what kind of activities they like to participate in, the participants stress the importance of self-selection of tasks as opposed to being forced to do activities that did not meet their interests. The individuals also stress the types of roles one could choose from as a center attendee and the value assigned to each of these roles—even though an individual might not fully participate in all the activities he or she discusses. You may notice that all the individuals stress what they would do, sometimes more so than what they actually do at the center. Lily's narrative illustrates the do-what-you-like theme, as mentioned by the individuals: "Well, we have a pool table upstairs. We have computers. They can watch TV. We have all the exercises here. Monday and Friday . . . exercises . . . discussion groups. We come in and discuss health problems. Like today they have exercises upstairs. They have self-defense and ballroom dancing. On Friday, they do dancing from one to three. And we have a lot of activities." According to Karen, "This center has a lot to offer. And you're not forced to take it. If you don't wanna do the classes—you don't have to. And if you just wanna come in and do lunch, nobody bothers you or pushes you. We try when we see a new face, somebody will go over and talk to them and say, 'Haven't seen you before.' You know, the usual talking. And then you'll explain about lunch. Or you'll say, 'Would you like to be a member? You're not committed to being a member of our center.'" Victoria discusses the daily offerings:

> We have bingo Monday, Tuesday, Thursday; we do today, too, but prize bingo, not money. After lunch you are lucky if you have fifteen people here . . . 'cause the other place has dancing. You go where you feel. . . . Like me, before I became a volunteer, I used to go to [another center] on Monday. I'd come here on Tuesday. I'd play bingo. I used to follow the bingo; I'd go to [another center] on Friday. . . . A lot of people do it. A lot of people follow the dancing. Like Tuesday/Thursday there's dancing at [another center]. . . . You go over there on a Tuesday, the place is

mobbed. On Friday we have dancing. Like if I come Friday, I'll have lunch, then I'll leave. Oh, yeah, I don't dance; I got a bad hip, I can't dance.

Lily describes other activities and groups at the center:

I like conversations; [another centergoer] and I do a project. I take a topic—diabetes and heart condition—she takes high blood pressure and cholesterol. And we try to get people interested in it. . . . It's called Know Your Numbers. We took a test on it and got a certificate on it that we taught a group here. But it's up to the individual. Some just come, eat their lunch, and go; others stay and do stuff like that. It's up to the individual. But I believe that as a senior center they should enjoy it. They really should enjoy it, but like I said, a lot of people just come and eat and go home.

Victoria is the first to suggest that "some people come in and have lunch. And just lunch. They are 'menu' members, I call them. 'Cause, if we're having something good, say, roast beef, they're here. But if [another center] has something better, or is having free lunch, they go there. Seniors are very fortunate. . . . We've got three centers right here." Some of Karen's statements describe additional "nonregular" member types: "But those are the 'menu' members. Then we've got the 'bingo' members. Sometimes they overlap. But like, we have bingo on Monday, Tuesday, and Thursday. Like, we have bingo today, but it's not for money. It's for dish detergent, for Tide, for gifts. But on Tuesday and Thursday, you'll see how we have the bingo crowd for lunch. Like, once a month we have bingo on a Saturday for six dollars. But [another center] has it on another Saturday, so that they're in conflict."

Social Interaction with Others at the Center Wards Off Mental Decline. Some of the participants address the way social interaction through center participation is a way to keep oneself mentally healthy. Karen states that after becoming depressed after September 11, 2001, "it was more or less kick myself in the butt and say, 'You ain't gonna do it [stay at home] no more, you gotta do something else.' There's so many activities. Basically, if you wanna sit in a corner and be a grouch, you sit in the corner and grouch. And there's so many other things available. Some days you feel good and you participate. Other days, some people play cards for a little while. Some people play bingo. There's enough to mentally stimulate you, if you want. And if you don't want, there's nothing anybody can do." In part in jest, Victoria raises another issue: "You gotta get out of the house. It's a proven fact; if you look at the four walls, you get Alzheimer's." She winks.

Individuals See Themselves As Helpers of Others at the Center and Not Helpless or Vulnerable. Just as the participants see themselves as active rather than passive in their roles, they also view themselves as givers of help to others and not the docile recipients of help. Angela, stressing the fact that in addition to being a "full member" she is a paid employee, adds, "I love my job here, I really do. I love the people. You know, we were taught a long time ago—you love the person. You love the sinner but not the sin." Victoria, in her role on the board, reflects, "Basically, the center runs on volunteers. The jobs, you know, [imagine] if they had to pay somebody to serve coffee or make the bread. . . . We have our meetings; we address issues with the director or the assistant director. We adjust things." I ask, "So you're like a sounding board?" She replies, "No, sometimes we have a little bit of power, and it helps a little bit. If we get enough complaints, they'll do something about it." I then ask for an example, and Victoria offers, "For a while there, they were giving us cups of milk, and we didn't want it. We carried on so much; we went back to getting little containers. 'Cause most of them take it home, they don't drink it here." Karen adds that the individuals at the center help a wide variety of others: "Now this group comes in with the mentally challenged young people. They volunteer. We get the students from [a local university], too. And yesterday we had the young Mormons. They come in—they give out the bread, the milk, the juice. They put the meals on the table. Then they eat lunch. And then they'll make up the dessert for tomorrow or make up the bread for tomorrow. Very pleasant young men . . . We do have the ones who get welfare. And they have to work so many hours, you know, for their requirement."

"We're Not *Regulars*": Themes from the Bingo and Menu Members

People in this group see the center as a place to attend a specific social function (such as a dance), play a game (like bingo), or have a meal (depending upon the menu options for that day). They use the center as a place of entertainment or meal provision but do not feel invested in its daily functioning, nor did the center play a pivotal role in their lives. These bingo and menu members see the role and function of key services and activities much differently from, and use them with much less frequency than, the regular members. In terms of the activities and events that these members participate in, they report the following: 100 percent participate in the meal option and play bingo or attend a dance (each 60 percent). They tend to discuss only nutritional services (such as congregate meals) and the function of providing social engagement (be it limited and lacking, as they suggest). For this group, three main themes emerge: (1) social events are the only draw—other activities are not of interest, (2) the activities offered at the center now are not as good as those in the past, and (3) the people attending the center now are different from in the past.

Social Events Are the Only Draw—Other Activities Are Not of Interest. Maria, eighty-two, lives alone, drives her own car, and feels she "lost her husband too soon." She frequently goes to the center, as she states, mostly to attend dances. She and her husband used to go "only like Friday nights; we used to come with another couple; he was a Harvest Moon ballroom dancer; he taught me." She attends dances after his death. "I can do anything; I am a dancer. I *love* to dance. I *love* to dance." Maria does play bingo "just to pass the time, but I'm not crazy about it." Maria mentions that she prefers to drive her friends to the movies than attending classes or other activities at the center.

Jack, seventy-six years old and divorced after forty years, attends the center for meals but strongly states that he "eats right" and is very selective about center food: "I don't eat any processed food; that stuff will kill you." He says he prefers to go to dances and pays for meals for several "ladies" at the center who cannot afford to pay for their own meals. Jack comments about his dancing: "I dance with the ladies here—they love it—they need someone to dance with. . . . I was a marine."

The Activities Offered at the Center Are Not As Good As Those in the Past. I sit with a group of women, Teresa, Joanie, and Linda, who are preparing their cards for bingo. They talk about old times and about the center past and present. Teresa explains to me, "Things ain't the way they used to be. . . . Like for us old-timers . . . we don't go on vacation [trips] anymore. . . . They stopped." Maria adds that they once had a great dance instructor. "She is a marvelous person, and I love her so much. She helped you in a lot of ways," but things are different now since "she is gone."

Joe, sixty-two, is somewhat younger than others in the group (as he says, "I'm only sixty-two. I'm a baby"). He is the only baby boomer in the group and has close ties to the center because his deceased wife once ran this particular center. He now sells insurance and sees his center attendance as a social outlet. It is important for him to tell me that he goes to the center only as a "companion, to help my brother, the person that was sitting there" and when his wife was alive, he had begun to help with parties. Joe states, "I used to go to the Sunday parties. I still do it. I do only it for her [in memory of his deceased wife]." He comments on other changes, noting, "Now even the exercises are on tape," and that "it would be great to get the bands back for the dances and not a DJ." He also would like to have someone start a conversational group. Joe tries to come to the center for the Sunday bingo game and remarks on the way the quality of prizes has changed: "Some people come and say, 'I'm not a bingo person. I would rather go to Vegas where I can make some money.' Not for nothing; here I'll win a bottle of Ajax and have someone come up to me and screaming at me because they won a bottle of Ajax. I say, please leave me alone—*it's ridiculous!*"

The People Attending the Center Now Are Different from in the Past. As a group of women are getting the microphone ready for bingo, one of them, Joanie, speaks about differences in the relationship between the staff and the elders, in her view. She states that she used to babysit, and she is upset that "one past director let me bring the kids in, and the others would not let me bring the kids to the center." Joanie says that there is not consistent enforcement of the rules and that the "rules were broken by others," which is "not fair." Linda echoed this, adding, "Even the people ain't the way they used to be" and noting that some of the more recent immigrants to the community "come for the food bank but don't stay or eat meals since they have to watch their grandkids while the parents are working—as part of their culture."

"The Center's Not My Cup of Tea": Themes from Nonattendees

When compared with regular and bingo and menu members, the nonattendees tend to have higher levels of education, to have professional status, and to be married. For this group of nonattendees, three central themes emerge about their reasons for nonattendance and the omission of center activities from their daily lives. In terms of the outside activities and events that nonattendees participate in, they all report some of the following: other organizational attendance, outside ethnic/social group attendance, and TV viewing. This group find none of the key activities and functions of centers to be applicable to them; the services of the center are seen as best for "other seniors that needed more help than them." Activities and events outside the center have greater value for this group. The three themes that emerge are (1) other social activities or organizations are more important than attending the center; (2) conditions at the center make it less appealing for new people to attend; and (3) there are benefits of center membership—for others, not for these nonattendees.

Other Social Activities or Organizations Are More Important Than Attending the Center. Anita, seventy-three, a nonattendee, recently widowed within the month, and a former telephone company worker, clearly states her reason for not joining the center: "I do not go to the senior center because I have other things that keep me busy!" For the first twenty minutes, she speaks about the many clubs she belongs to and her role in each. After detailing her past club participation, Anita speaks of her religious work. She belongs to an interfaith group of women who visit different religious institutions each month. As she states, "Well, in general I belong to the church. I'm on the church council; I belong to the choir. I belong to an organization that meets the first Monday of the month. We meet at different churches, and we'll just socialize a little bit and things like that." Anita then asks that I pause the tape so she can read her church's mission statement to me. According to Anita, her church work ties in nicely with her role in other related organizations. For example, she says, "You know, I have to write up a lot of cards and birthday cards or anniversary cards, maybe even letters. I wrote birthday cards for my German organization, every month, and I would write the cards—up to ten a month. I have the sayings that I put in there and mail them away. Plus my own, I send birthdays and anniversaries and things."

Arlene, seventy-three, a married noncentergoer and a former registered nurse, talks about the important role of religious institutions in her life: "I just go to church on Sundays; I don't belong to any organizations. I just go to mass on Sundays, being I'm Catholic. I belonged to the Sacred Heart League. We met once a month. . . . We would go to church, mass and then after mass, we'd go for cake and coffee, and then there would be promoters. I wasn't a promoter, so then I would go home. The promoters ran the card parties that they had and things like that. I was just a member." Arlene explains that her "family ties" are another reason for not eating at the center: "I don't go to lunch because, I mean, I have a husband; he doesn't want to go to the center. So for me to go and eat lunch . . . it's you know, if my husband would go, then we'd both go together, it'd be okay." Scout, sixty-nine years, offers me a litany of preferred roles he holds in local volunteer organizations. He serves on many nonprofit boards, is active within the community, and has started several community groups in the neighborhood.

Both Anita and Arlene mention that television viewing is preferable to center attendance. Anita remarks, "Television relaxes your mind, and you can just watch what you want and keep on going." Arlene adds that she enjoys television as well:

A nice movie on TV for two hours like on weekends. I watch the movies when my regular programs are off, my soap opera. I like to watch the different programs. Some of them, they remind you of things that happen in your lifetime . . . and there are things that could happen to you or should happen to you or would've happened to you.

If you want to watch something more real, something more fictional, you've got a variety. . . . I mean, if you watch them all the years I've been watching them, forty years, you know that they can't be married, this one woman married ten times and things like that, and some of the things are ridiculous but I mean it is, uh, you know it's not the way things really are—but it's just something that draws your interest. When I watch the news, a lot of the times it's very depressing—but I watch it anyway because you gotta know what's going on in the world.

Conditions at the Center Make It Less Appealing for New People to Attend. Anita feels that negative group dynamics are a major roadblock to her attending the center. She states, "I went a few times early on and then, but I don't go now. . . . You've got to sit in certain places, everybody has their clique, and I'm not a cliquey person. Everybody sits where they want, but if you come every day, they have their own little gathering with 'the group.'" Arlene echoes Anita's feelings about the way groups work at the center: "I don't live far from the center, but the thing of it is, I don't want to go there alone, and my other friends don't go to the centers either that are my age.... Ah, I don't know, I guess it'd be all right, you get a table, you probably get to know the people. I know a lot of my friends, they introduce themselves, or they'll say, 'Sit here.' . . . Or you could go and say, 'Is anybody sitting here? Or, is this table filled?' . . . but I don't know I just don't, I never started; maybe if I started I would continue going, but I just never got started."

Arlene says she used to go to the center "on occasion" (two or three times a year), eight years ago, with an older relative who has since died. Arlene, attending "only as a guest," explains:

> [Her relative] had about six, seven friends that would all get together, and so I got introduced to them, and we would go to different things around the holidays, and I would go with them. So, I knew her friends that went to the center with her because I would go on all the trips with her from different organizations that used to pick 'em up at the center.
>
> They got older; they're seventeen years older than me . . . in their nineties—ninety-two, ninety-four—so they're all gone. That's who I used to know from the center. Well, I didn't continue it; I just I don't know, it seemed like they were drawing new people coming in, and the old people that I knew were different and, I just, and I didn't want to socialize with them. I just dropped out, and I just never got back in.

Arlene highlights two types of activities that have either become stagnant or changed, in her opinion, and not for the better; she notes repeated gambling trips to Atlantic City and the lessening of the center's involvement in government programs. "I went to Atlantic City when they were running them once a month; they were running them years back maybe about six, seven, eight years ago I went. I just stopped going because I've been there so many times. I'm not a gambler, and to walk up and down the boardwalk sometimes you get a seat sometimes you don't. I've been in and out all the souvenir stores, so I've been there so many times, it's not a novelty to me anymore." Discussing lost government programs, Arlene comments, "They used to just give out free food and commodities, cheese and canned food and things like that. They had surpluses, and they were giving them to the senior centers to distribute to senior citizens, and I used to go there and get the cheese and stuff like that. They used to give you a five-pound American cheese. I used to go up there for that with my Medicare card; you had to have it to show you're a senior. I only went when they gave that out."

There Are Benefits of Center Membership—for Others, Not for These Nonattendees.

Daisy, who lives within close walking distance from the center, speaks about the meals being a benefit for those who cannot afford food elsewhere. But for Daisy herself, the quality of the meals is not appealing. They are too processed and high in fat: "Seniors had picked the menu. So that's why they had things like what I was telling you. Like the two frankfurters with macaroni. With baked beans. And you'd have a starch—a pudding or something for dessert. It was just horrible in those days." Anita feels that the center is important for others, in "keeping Access-a-Ride [a transportation service] for people that cannot walk for themselves, or have heart trouble, or with their legs; they pick up people."

Arlene tells me about the other perceived potential benefits of the center: "I know I should be involved in a lot more things at my age 'cause I know a lot of people that are my age that are into everything. When you talk to them, they work at the church, they volunteer at a hospital doing things, or in their centers. The senior centers, they're doing a lot. I guess I could go one day and try it and, if I like it, and I meet people there that are nice and friendly—then, maybe I would go twice. I could find out what days they're there, and then I would go. Maybe once in a while, when they're going to be there, I could go, too."

One Center, Multiple Uses and Functions

An ethnographic approach goes beyond the count or frequency of activities older individuals report doing at the center. It goes deeper than naming tasks individuals report they do and looks at what elders get out of what they do (or do not do) at the center. Findings provide a more extensive assessment of life at the center. Activities, whether mentioned or completed, are a vehicle to understanding why individuals attend or fail to attend the center and what the center means in their daily lives. Seeing activities at the center from the point of view of the participants allows the researcher to take a less preconceived view of the center's role as participants articulate their views.

For the regular members, being seen as active in many capacities within the center is a large part of their identities, the way they define who they are. For these members, the center activities, especially in board and voluntary roles, were seen as more important than their health limitations. My findings about actively involved regulars challenges the work of Van den Hoonaard (2005), who found a marginalization of the widow's role and lack of power and agency among the older individuals who were studied. Individuals at this center are aware of the exchange value of civic engagement and volunteer roles (National Council on Aging 2012d).

The regulars also find that the center provides emotional support through friendships and camaraderie. These engagements are a source of enjoyable interaction and practical assistance, which help ward off mental decline and distress. The strength of social support networks and exchange described by my center members was seen by Buck Rosenberg (2013) in Australian senior centers. Earlier, Ronald Aday, Gayle Kehoe, and Lori Farney (2006) found that friendship support was a common feature in women's center experience. In their work, almost 90 percent of center attendee women had what they identified as "close center friendships" and provided help to center friends inside and outside the center itself. The emotional support from these friendships increased women's life satisfaction and feelings of independence while decreasing levels of loneliness. In terms of the effects of social engagement, research by Hyun-Shik Kim and colleagues (2011) found that elders participating in senior centers in Korea reported better mental and physical health than nonattendees.

Regulars at the center in my study feel that choice of activities is essential even if they often share accounts of what others do at the center rather than what types of activities they favor themselves or participate in. Regular members here are quite similar to typical New York center members, in being women and widowed and with moderate-to-low income and some physical limitations in activities of daily living (ADLs) and instrumental activities of daily living (IADLs) (Krout et al. 1990; Miner et al. 1993; Pardasani 2010).

Regular members of this center view its role of providing instrumental help for members as important. Participants note that the center and staff provide help with utility bills, access to governmental programs, negotiating disputes with landlords, and food provision via the in-house food bank. Prior studies reveal that, although a meal provision is mentioned, centers are often thought of as sites of leisure (Counihan 2008).

The less frequently attending bingo or menu members find attending one or two social events or meals to be more important than regularly attending the center. Overall, they feel there is limited choice in the activities offered and that the activities are decreasing in value. The findings from the bingo and menu members support the work of Walker and colleagues (2004). Based on a study of center members and directors, they recommend that to attract members, centers need more music without dancing, variety in meals, exercise equipment for younger elder attendees, and increased marketing to counterbalance misperceptions about centers (for example, that centers are suitable for only the "very old," "poor," "vulnerable," and "frail"). These results also acknowledge the difficulty of matching activities to the needs of all center members. Cohen and colleagues (2009) found that improving the physical aspects of facilities does not necessarily increase center use but that extended hours for staff, marketing, and outreach are also needed. The issues raised by the bingo and menu members lends support to Eaton and Salari's (2005) finding that new technologies or other programs would help in increasing both attendance and participation because existing programs are seen as "old," "stale," and of low quality, as in the bingo prizes or existing exercise classes.

The nonattendees suggest that those attending the center are not supportive in encouraging new members to join and that current members actually inhibit their desire to attend. They do not care for the flavor and nutritional content of the meals. This group chooses attending events sponsored by religious organizations, seeing to family commitments, conducting public service, and even watching television over attending activities at the center. The nonattendees do, however, suggest that they might enjoy potential benefits if they become members—but only if current group dynamics and conditions at the center change. Nonattendees make a clear distinction between "us" (those who do not go to the center) and "them" (those who do attend, such as the "disabled," "frail," or "in need") as suggested by Hurd (1999) and Lund and Engelsrud (2008). Nonattendees often discuss the "cliquishness" of the center members and bring up "issues of territory" (seen in groups claiming ownership such as of places in the dining hall, as Sonia Salari, Barbara Brown, and Jacqueline Eaton [2006] suggest).

3

Reconstructing Shuttering in a Larger Social Context

• •

Political and Media Accounts

> Can you tell the mayor that we don't
> want [the center to become] a health
> club?
> —Question posed to me by Lily, a regular
> center attendee, in 2009

Backstory: The Changes to Centers at the City, State, and Federal Levels

Nothing remains static. Changes to senior centers in New York City at the center level happen within a broader historical, regional, and legislative context. Because the city's senior centers operate as nonprofits with 501(c)(3) status, both organizations and official legislation and policies are key players in the center change process. The NYC Department for the Aging (DFTA), the NYC Mayor's Office, and the Older Americans Act both create and influence official policy and legislation. Funding changes in larger institutions—such as DFTA; the Mayor's Office; and the City Council, in its discretionary funds—directly affect centers. Major nonprofit organizations both influence and analyze the effects of policy upon centers. These nonprofits include the Council of Senior Centers and Services of New York City (CSCS), the National Council on Aging, the National Institute of Senior Centers, and the New York Academy of Medicine. Additionally, media accounts closely follow and vent the public's feedback to changes in senior center policies at the local, national, and regional levels. Primary documents from these sources help construct a cohesive time line of senior center changes in New York City from a few years before my study (the early 2000s) until mid-2013, when my study ended.

Quiet on the Home Front: Before Modernization

In this chapter, I use information from organizations, legislation, and media to create a time line of city-based changes affecting senior centers in New York City. My time line begins in January 2004 with the removal of English as a second language (ESL) classes from DFTA's funding in senior centers (CSCS 2004a).[1] Many advocacy groups saw this as having a negative impact on centers with large immigrant populations. Later in 2004, in support of center services, the CSCS created a list of thirty ways older persons benefit from senior centers—including a center's core functions: education, recreation, cultural activities congregate meals, home-delivered meals, and case-management services. Centers were not much discussed between 2005 and 2007 with the main exception being the 2005 White House Conference on Aging's report, *The Booming Dynamics of Aging: From Awareness to Action.* It stressed the need to prepare for the aging population thirty years into the future by balancing policies and services to address all aging groups in multiple areas of life, from the workplace to spheres of activity that involve engaging and marketing to the baby boomer. Harry "Rick" Moody's commentary on the report, "The White House Conference on Aging in 2015: The Shape of Things to Come" (2006), addressed three essential areas he felt were overlooked in the 2005 conference: end-of-life decisions, lifelong learning, and drawing on the wisdom of elders.

Later in 2006, CSCS wrote about the predicted increase in the city's older population and the related changes this "age revolution" would bring to community-based services. At the end of 2007, CSCS reported on the key role of centers in New York City in addressing hunger in elders by providing both congregate meals and meals on wheels. Meanwhile, a "flash frozen" meal program was being pilot tested in the Bronx. The frozen meals, though controversial because not fresh, received a positive evaluation by the KMG research group, which evaluated them in 2007. At the end of that year, DFTA also issued a request for proposals (RFP) for centers' case management services.

"Modernization of Centers" Ideas Take Hold

In 2008 there was a resurgence in talk about centers and their usefulness in the lives of older persons. A later CSCS infographic, "How Age-Friendly Is NYC?" (CSCS n.d.a) would report that over the fiscal years 2008 to 2012, senior centers had experienced more than fifty-one million dollars in cuts. A January joint report from the mayor and DFTA commissioner, *Promoting Positive Aging 2005–2007* (New York City Department for the Aging 2008c), reviewed many programs during those years that "helped people age well through promoting healthy life style, maximizing independence, helping seniors meet basic needs, connecting to isolated seniors, supporting productive and meaningful aging, [and] celebrating aging and diversity." In a DFTA press release on January 22, 2008, then-commissioner Edwin Méndez-Santiago launched the "modernization effort" as part of his focus on the three "senior needs of today and tomorrow [case management, home-delivered meals, and senior centers]" (DFTA 2008b, 1). In a State Society on Aging of New York 2008 winter newsletter, Méndez-Santiago explained the origin of the modernization concept and changes in services. He wrote:

> Over the past several decades our old notions about aging have so dramatically altered that it is fair to say aging has been "re-imagined." Aging services, in contrast, have lagged behind this transformation. To serve today's elders, aging services also must be "re-imagined," or, to use the term applied by the Administration on Aging to the reauthorized Older American Act, "modernized." I believe a modernized system must devote significant resources to helping communities develop the opportunities, interventions and supports needed by their residents for healthy aging. In other words, we need to develop community-specific programs that support healthy aging-in-place and supplement the current menu of available aging services designed mainly to address vulnerabilities and deficits. We also need new service delivery models based on collaborative, cross-system and cross-disciplinary approaches. The days of working in a "silo" are gone. (2)

Méndez-Santiago further described his early vision of "modernized senior centers." They were to be a one-stop resource center for older persons' needs, adding in employment and more creative opportunities than what was then available. He called for a greater variety of services and delivery because the "new values of flexibility, adaptability, outcomes and results must replace the old prescriptions" (2).

Talk of Center Closures Begins

However, a January 2008 DFTA press release puts quite a different spin on the modernization plan. The press release heralded the conversion of current senior centers into "Healthy Aging Centers." It saw current centers as failing in their original mission to reduce elder hunger, so much so that, according to the press release, "nearly half of the Department's 325 centers throughout the five boroughs are underutilized, resulting in close to 1 million free meals going unserved annually" (2008b, 1–2).[2] Reacting to the health and wellness press release, on February 28, Assemblywoman Catherine Nolan of Queens released a statement on her official website. She commented on the loss of case managers, the possible loss of centers, and the ("too rapid") RPF process for meals and other services. Nolan wrote: "While I am intrigued by the streamlining goals of the DFTA Healthy Aging Centers proposal, I believe we should move forward with caution. As the number of seniors increases, it follows that more services not less is necessary. I do not want to lose any of the vital senior centers in my Queens community" (New York State Assembly 2008, 1).[3]

A March 12 Queens newspaper reported that Méndez-Santiago affirmed that centers would not close but that he needed the City Council's support for his modernization plan.[4] The article included community board and City Council questions about the proposed cuts and rumors of closures on the street. A potential City Council candidate was quoted: "The word is out to the senior population. They're all concerned about closing; it's a real concern." In the article, Méndez-Santiago took the approach that centers must change because current models do not work. He was quoted as stating, "In fiscal year 2007, 44 percent of DFTA-funded senior centers were underutilized, and 95 percent of those were determined to be 'chronically underutilized,' meaning that they have been underutilized for the past three-to-five years. One million meals go unserved annually due to underutilized centers." The reporter ended with an exchange between Méndez-Santiago and City Council president Helen Marshall: "'Clearly, something is not working,' said Méndez-Santiago." To which Marshall replied, "'Why can't we fix the centers [we have]?'"

Advocacy Groups and Politicians Weigh In on the Initial Modernization Plan

In a March 17 *Gotham Gazette* article online, Bobbie Sackman (2008) of CSCS expressed concern about DFTA's plan to undertake changing all centers in the system at once. Sackman was quoted: "It remains unclear how this will be accomplished and how many centers will exist under the plan." Using her experience working in centers, she talked about "inaccessibility": "If a senior center moves from one part of a community to another, it may become inaccessible to the 85-year-old who walked there. . . . The industry rule of thumb is that seniors will travel within a 10-block radius to get to a senior center." Sackman spoke of the utility of centers for new immigrants as culturally specific "welcoming havens." In terms of the proposed division of DFTA funding to the community-district, coupled with the closure of centers and lessening of transportation to centers, she predicted, "The shift would force senior centers to compete for the money as though from scratch. Because of this uncertain funding formula, much of what senior centers provide appears to be at risk, from transportation to social services to programs."

Yet another article, this time from the *New York Times*, "Its Appeal Slipping, the Senior Center Steps Livelier" (Gross 2008), heralded the decline of the neighborhood center, replaced by a café model that would appeal to boomers. The author quoted the then–deputy mayor, Linda Gibbs, who suggested that without drastic transformation, centers would become obsolete.[5]

> This is a time of ferment for the United States' 15,000 senior centers, many vestiges of the 1960s and '70s when federally financed meals for the elderly were a pillar of the Great Society. . . . Nutrition and companionship remain worthy goals for them but are no longer the draw they once were. . . . In NYC, with a network of 329 centers, almost half are underused, according to Deputy Mayor Gibbs. A plan by the administration of Mayor Bloomberg to make the city more user-friendly to the elderly includes modernizing the nation's largest system of senior centers, and including cafes, according to the mayor's office and DFTA. The 40-year-old model is not "serving the seniors of today or attracting the seniors of tomorrow," Ms. Gibbs said. . . . Experts predict that baby boomers will not walk in the door of outdated centers, which are often in church basements, reminiscent of high school cafeterias before the advent of food courts, with few activities besides bingo and transportation to the mall. (A14)

DFTA's modernization plan has had to reconcile with the New York State Office for the Aging. For example, its director, Michael Burgess, held a hearing to "ensure that senior centers retain access to essential supports during the aging services modernization initiative" in New York City, so that services would not be compromised during this transition. He wanted to ensure that "care for today" and "management for tomorrow" were both parts of the New York State Project 2015 plan, "Shaping Public Policy Preparing for Demographic Change."

A November 14 *New York Times* article, "Quinn Vehemently Denounces Bloomberg's Plans" (Chen and Santos 2008), included Quinn's famous quote that the mayor's plan for senior center closures belonged "in the garbage can." One month later, the *New York Times* ran a story about the mayor's announcement that Lilliam Barrios-Paoli would replace Méndez-Santiago as DFTA commissioner. Méndez-Santiago, said the article, left for "personal reasons." (Other news accounts suggested the impetus for this change was a sexual harassment lawsuit filed against him and not the center closures.)[6] On a professional networking website, Méndez-Santiago's gave his term as DFTA commissioner as from "January 2002–December 2008."[7] He described his role: "As Commissioner, I was able to revitalize the agency and develop new models of care while strengthening and modernizing the traditional services provided directly by the Department as well as the multiple services offered through hundreds of contracts with not-for-profit community partners. I was able to return DFTA to its advocacy mission and transcend its traditional service delivery role to promote the planning and implementation of programs across all city agencies to support longevity and establishment of NYC as an 'age-friendly' city."

On December 17, the *New York Times* quoted Mayor Bloomberg as saying he would "take another look" at the senior center plan. But the article concluded with Deputy Mayor Gibbs correcting the mayor: "[The plan] is an issue of discussion between stakeholders and the Council, and no decision has been made to change the schedule at this point. . . . It's clearly something that Lilliam and I will be talking about with all those stakeholders in the very near future." Two days later, another *New York Times* article, "Bloomberg Retreats on Overhaul of Senior Centers," reported that the "the administration said it would hold off on plans to consolidate up to $20 million in financing for the centers, [but] they planned to 're-evaluate' the overhaul." To provide justification for revamping the center system, there was a claim in the article that publicly funded centers were only "used by 2 percent of the city's elderly population" (Barbaro 2008).

In 2009, the group Transportation Alternative produced *Walk the Walk: Connecting Senior Pedestrian Safety to Seniors in NYC* and interviewed older persons at senior centers to help assess city walkability and dangerous routes. In March 30, 2009, the New York City Council released its *New York City Council Budget Report: Analysis of the Fiscal 2010 Preliminary Budget and Fiscal 2009 Preliminary Mayor's Management Report for the Department for the Aging*. Again, DFTA's Senior Center Modernization Plan was reviewed and heavily critiqued. The report expressed great concern over DFTA's November 2008 modernization plan to create "15–30 comprehensive wellness centers . . . to regionalize senior center services throughout the City" and select centers using RFPs. The report cautioned, "The current financial crisis called into question the City's ability to fund new larger centers, while maintaining all the neighborhood senior centers that provide vital core services, however, the Administration planned to move forward. This new plan would have forced current neighborhood senior centers to close, resulting in a loss of core services at remaining senior centers, leaving centers with unbalanced funding and programming. Furthermore, it would have given senior centers unclear information on how to address transportation issues or social-work services, among a number of other services seniors rely on" (1). The report was also wary of the so-called increase in funding for the center changes. The tone of the report suggested that although there was an increase of $23 million, "the majority of that figure did not represent new funding, but rather money that was allocated by the City Council and Borough Presidents. As a result, there would not have been enough money per region to retain the current number of senior centers. . . . [DFTA's own] RFP implied up to 85 local community senior centers would possibly close as a result of this process" (2).[8] Based on some serious concerns, the City Council's final "verdict" was to halt the RFP process for senior centers. Their recommendation reads as follows: "Although the Administration and the City Council agree on the overall vision of modernization, which intends to offer a comprehensive health and wellness approach promoting social, physical and mental wellness, it is for the reasons outlined above that the Council was successful in having this RFP rescinded" (2). And the contracts of the existing centers were extended for a year without the requirement of completing an RFP, at this point.

Predicting New Center Models for New York City

Late 2009 brought new terminology to the suggested new senior center models (with solid management and fund usage); they would be called "charter centers," suggested by Bobbie Sackman of CSCS in August 2009. These incentivized charter centers, it was proposed, would serve as guides for existing, struggling centers, with their creative programming and expertise shared. In that same month, the Office of the Mayor, the City Council, and the New York Academy of Medicine (NYAM) produced a press release, "Mayor Bloomberg, Speaker Quinn, and the New York Academy of Medicine Unveil Blueprint to Enhance City's Livability for Older New Yorkers," describing the plan as a "blueprint for promoting active aging focused on four areas: community and civic participation; housing; public spaces and transportation; and health and social services." This Age-Friendly NYC initiative was seen by DFTA as a way of making New York a World Health Organization Age-Friendly City. An initiative bundled in this plan would include innovation grants to create new models of service for fifty senior centers.

The Age-Friendly NYC initiative's Investment in Senior Centers section of the "Mayor Bloomberg, Speaker Quinn, and the New York Academy of Medicine Unveil Blueprint to Enhance City's Livability for Older New Yorkers" press release included commentary about changes in private and public funding sources for centers. Besides the usual language about matching centers to the needs of their attendees, the press release contained new language describing the "innovation grants for the creation of new models of service at 50 senior centers across the five boroughs. The 50 centers will offer staff autonomy, attract new talent and entrepreneurial energy and bring a real sense of innovation and competition to the entire senior services system" (2). But, according to the NYAM's plan, the age-friendly models would also have another level of responsibility: "They will also be held accountable for producing vibrant programs, high participation rates and better health outcomes for older New Yorkers . . . [and] become model centers of wellness offering innovative health programs" (2).

That August, the New York City Department of Culture announced a new artists-in-residence program at senior centers in all five boroughs. This program stemmed from the call for civic and community participation in the Age-Friendly NYC initiatives and the plan's more "active" aging focus. In October 2009, as part of a campaign to use existing transportation to improve older New Yorkers' access to fresh produce, Dr. Barrios-Paoli went with elders from the RAICES Senior Center to a farmers market in Brooklyn. During 2008–2009, about five hundred centergoers from forty-one senior centers and NORCS made seventy-four similar trips to farmers markets.

In December 2009, Robert Stephens and Helen Kwah, on behalf of DFTA, published an article assessing what makes congregate meal programs work at senior centers. According to their article, centers that met their meal quotas had a strong director, a strong sense of community, and sponsorship. Stephens and Kwah suggested that to improve their meal programs, center directors should know everyone's name and be a friend to the members, discourage reserved seats, and improve customer service. Successful directors would hire the best staff, evaluate ideas in an ongoing manner, and involve members in meal planning. They would keep the food as a restaurant would with good meal options. The best directors, it seems according to this article, run the center as a business and get the community to buy in. They would also not forget to heavily market their centers.

In February 2010, CSCS released the findings of its study *21st Century Senior Centers: Changing the Conversation; A Study of NYC's Senior Centers* (2010c), self-described as the "the largest study of its kind on senior centers," with thirty-six hundred older persons. The report and fourteen recommendations focused on senior centers' role in elder's lives, challenges of current centers, administrators' challenges (on many levels, such as members' needs, peers, community), and funding struggles. The recommendation for charter/innovative centers was supported here.

The Funding Cuts and Elder-Led Advocacy Begin

The City Council's *Hearing on the Mayor's Fiscal Year 2011 Preliminary Budget for the Department for the Aging*, of March 9, 2010, heralded the changes in state allocation from the federal government that would affect center closures and the (re-)modernization plan. While acknowledging federal funding to the state remained the same, the report explained the difference in the distribution of the Title XX monies to "save State dollars." For example:

> In previous fiscal years, this $103 million [in Title XX funding] was split between mandatory services (that is, adult protective services, child protective services, domestic violence, etc.) and discretionary services (that is, senior services etc). The Fiscal 2010–2011 State Executive Budget proposes that all Title XX funding be used to offset State and local Adult Protective and Domestic

Violence costs, thus saving the State $18 million. Therefore, all discretion-
ary funds for senior services would be eliminated. DFTA currently receives
$25.2 million in Title XX funding. They estimate the closure of senior centers if
they were to lose this funding in Fiscal 2011. (2010b)

Concurrently, on March 9, 2010, the City Council and elder advocacy
groups joined to create the "Save Our Centers" campaign with the mission to
mobilize seniors to stave off potential funding cuts affecting the closure of 110
senior centers in the city. The press release and accompanying video on City
Council Speaker Christine Quinn's website included commentary from many
in the aging network about the potential quarter cut in DFTA funding and
related eighty to one hundred closures resulting from the modernization plan.
With center members in attendance from senior centers all around the city,
centers were praised by many for their service and meal provision. Committee on Aging chairperson Jessica Lappin noted, putting the cuts in context,
that "these cuts would literally starve thousands of poor seniors." A New York
State AARP director lent a statement of support about AARP's membership's
desire to age in place and the role that centers play in the process.

During the rally, Speaker Quinn called centers "a lifeline, especially during this recession. We're urging everyone to call their state legislators and the
Governor's office to let them know these cuts are unacceptable. We won't
allow Albany to turn its back on our seniors." Manhattan Borough President
Scott Stringer added, "We are not going stand by while the senior centers
[elders] rely on are attacked." Bobbi Sackman, of CSCS, explained the tangible effects of the proposed cuts: "The tsunami of city and state cuts raining
down on senior centers and other services funded through the Department
for the Aging will close up to 110 senior centers and cripple the funding of the
remaining senior centers." CSCS also predicted a grim future of senior centers
being padlocked. Senior center workers and nonprofit organizations relayed
their feelings about the cuts during the press conference. Representatives from
Selfhelp Community Services, the UJA Federation of New York, and the
Federation of Protestant Welfare Agencies, along with many other groups,
spoke about the services neighborhood centers provided to seniors in multiple
areas and the great loss their members would experience if such closures went
through. All organizations in attendance urged elected officials to keep neighborhood centers open and funded. Curiously, in that same month, DFTA also
produced a press release about working with Microsoft to offer older persons
a virtual center option to be present via cyberspace and participate in center
activities and events (Microsoft 2010).

From March to September 2010, the Brookdale Demonstration Initiative in
Healthy Aging, sponsored by DFTA and the mayor at Hunter College, using
three years of data from older adults who participate at senior centers, released

toolkits to use their evidence-based practices and community-based health interventions. The initiative also evaluated the effectiveness of programs (such as falls prevention and diabetes care). Its evidence-based toolkits (for cancer, depression, falls, obesity, and heart diseases) were posted on their website so centers could try these tested interventions for themselves (see Fahs 2012).

The Unofficial "Hit List" of Closures Is Released

In April 2010, the City Council officially announced the closure of fifty centers per the commissioner of DFTA. Closures were based on "fewest meals, fewest hours, and most management/maintenance problems." Interestingly, these management and maintenance issues were new criteria. Centers were set to be notified by July 1, 2010. DFTA cautioned it would not release names until Mayor Bloomberg's final approval. Individual centers, however, did speculate wildly about closures; so did the news media. Closures by borough were thought to be nine in the Bronx, eleven in Brooklyn, sixteen in Manhattan, ten in Queens, and four in Staten Island. The *New York Times* article, by David Chen (2010a), was headlined "At Least 50 of City's Senior Centers Expected to Close to Save Money." While the centers' names were not released, the commissioner did describe the number of centers closed by criteria, noting that "32 centers serve fewer than 30 meals a day; the citywide average is 90; . . . 13 are now operating part-time—meaning that they are open less than five days a week, or are open less than five hours a day. Another seven part-time senior centers serving more than 30 meals will also be closed, as will another 11 plagued by substandard facilities or poor management, based on the city's assessment of their performance." Chen reported that the commissioner "said another 25 centers would be notified soon that they could be closed on July 1 if the city received less money from Albany than it currently anticipates."

Around the same time, CSCS released its *More with Less Is Impossible* (2010a) report. Findings of its survey of senior service providers in the community (including senior centers) revealed that they were doing just that—over half reported losing funding and having waiting lists for services with staff cutbacks. A CSCS action alert, on April 26, 2010, "The Shoe Drops," confirmed what was feared—by May 15, 2010, fifty centers facing closure would be receiving a letter from DFTA.

Chen's (2010b) May 10 *New York Times City Room* blog leaked the list of fifty centers to be shuttered. He outlined the closure numbers, according to the mayor: "In Manhattan, the number is 16. In Brooklyn, 11, and Queens, 10. In the Bronx, it's 9. And for Staten Island, it's 4." The mayor, wrote Chen, "formally announced that he planned to close 50 senior centers. He said that the centers had to be closed because of a budget shortfall that he blamed on Albany's inability to come up with extra money. Another 25 centers could be closed on July 1, too, if the city receives less money from Albany than it currently expects." The onslaught of closure reports in the media continued with the local Queens papers getting very borough specific. The *Queens Chronicle* had the headline "Ten Senior Centers in Queens May Close" and listed the centers by name: CCNS St. Mary's Senior Center in Long Island City, JASA Jackson Heights Senior Center, JASA Whitestone Senior Center, JASA Holliswood Senior Center, CCNS Woodhaven Senior Center, CCNS Wakefield Senior Center in Jamaica, JSPOA Conlon in Jamaica, JSPOA Foster Laurie Senior Center in St. Albans, and South Jamaica Senior Center.[9]

The Public Responds to Closure Possibilities in Person and Online

On May 12, 2010, the *New York Nonprofit Press* online's article "DFTA Lists 50 Senior Centers to Close June 30" (2010a) divided the DFTA fifty-center official-but-not-final closure list by reason: "Thirty-three of the centers serve fewer than thirty meals daily. Twenty of the centers operate on a part-time basis. Seventeen of the centers were identified as having 'poor Vendex ratings or chronic issues.'" Another wave of online pieces about the closures began. Stacey Torres, a doctoral student in sociology, wrote a critical piece about the closures, "Bloomberg Shuttering Lifesaving Senior Centers." She raised concern with the way "the Mayor blames cuts on 'Albany's irresponsibility'" and how the cuts would disproportionately affect the "core city services that serve the most vulnerable New Yorkers." Torres asked the reader to think about the real cost of saving this money and what the closing said about our larger societal priorities.

The next month, the *New York Nonprofit Press* online wrote about the proposed budget cuts for the fiscal year 2011 Bloomberg budget and the formation of an umbrella advocacy group, Don't Cut the Core Coalition. An executive director of a community organization claimed, "The cuts to these preventative, cost-effective services threaten to destabilize tens of thousands of NYC residents who rely on them and must be reversed to protect our community" (2010c).

On August 17 the *New York Nonprofit Press* website had the headline "Future Is Soon! DFTA Previews New Senior Center Model, New Contracting Process" (2010b). Its story covered the new innovative senior center concept and existing neighborhood center model distinctions. The article stated that the new models stemmed from the DFTA and NYAM partnership and the NYAM's report *NYC Senior Centers: Visioning the Future*. As previously noted, the NYAM study analyzed data from 281 full-time centers and 20 part-time centers with a variety of programs using multiple methods, such as surveys, focus groups, consultations with stakeholders and senior center directors, and literature review. Its key findings were that poverty is pervasive in the city's older adult population and was especially an issue for senior center users.

The older population was diverse, with a need for greater integration between senior centers and community resource. Centers' core functions could be met by a variety of delivery methods but must consult older adults about what happened at the center. New innovative/charter center models could meet the needs of neighborhood centers as the image of senior centers changed.

The *Nonprofit Press* article provided details about the new two-stage procurement process. The first, prequalification step ensured that the organization was capable of providing center services. Step 2 involved DFTA's working out a contract with approved venders. There could be competition for contracts among prequalified vendors. There were hearings and a "go live" date for this process scheduled for September 2010.

On November 16, the New York State Assembly's Standing Committees on Aging and Children and Families held a public hearing, "Senior Centers: Funding, Challenges, and Value to the Community." According to an online notice, its purpose was to "to evaluate the current sources of funding for senior centers, the challenges that senior centers face across the state, the effect of the cuts and restorations of funding in the 2010 state budget, and how senior centers provide value to their communities" (New York State Assembly 2010). The call asked participants to address issues of varied center funding sources by region, the effects of losses in the Older Americans Act (OAA), the impact of the cuts upon elders, other nonfunding challenges, ways to provide center services not in a center, and how centers helped to age in place. Around the same time, a fact sheet for the OAA 2011 Amendment created by U.S. Senator Bernie Sanders listed "modernized senior centers and community planning for an aging population" as one of the nine key areas of interest. In terms of the 2011 OAA reauthorization, the National Council on Aging (NCOA) and National Institute of Senior Centers (NISC) supported the ideas that centers must change to meet baby boomers' needs, and staff must be trained. However, they equally maintained that funding must also remain in place for multipurpose/neighborhood senior centers.

In March 2011, the *New York Nonprofit Press* released the DFTA closure list, in "DFTA Lists 105 Senior Centers to Be Closed." This online article reiterated the case of New York governor Andrew Cuomo's use of Title XX funding for non–senior center costs.[10] It included a familiar quote about the impact of center closures from Judith Kleve of Catholic Charities, who stated that without senior centers, "seniors will be forced to choose between food and paying for other expenses, such as, medicine and rent." A *NY1* blog story on the same day was headlined "105 Senior Centers Slated to Close" (2011b) and asked readers for feedback. The call for responses resulted in fifty comments. All were against center closures. The majority blamed bad political practices (of Mayor Bloomberg and Governor Cuomo, for example) and corruption as causes of the closures. A couple of writers felt that the closure threat was a political ploy ("The Bloomberg Administration must now be seen as having an open agenda—the outright destruction of vital public services in the interest of enforced obedience to the dictates of private wealth and power. This latest threat—the possible closure of more than 100 senior centers—is designed to demoralize the public and coerce subordination to a miserable social condition. Julie, Manhattan"). A few posts focused on the corporatization of New York City ("If these senior centers do indeed close, it is surely a signal of the beginning of the end of what is left of civilized society in NYC. How about these blood-sucking fat cat investment firms fork over the money to fund ALL of the senior centers in NYC? Just a small piece of the bloated bonuses these guys are giving themselves would do the job. That would be a good first step toward trying to repair their seriously tarnished image. Peace, Nick, Hell's K").

Some responders asked politicians to reflect upon their own aging and aging family members ("Note to Bloomberg: I hope the City treats your Mom this way too, like she doesn't count. You should be ashamed! Disgusted in Sunnyside, Liz"; and "Do elected officials realize that they will become old sometime? The closing of the Senior Centers will isolate certain seniors who really don't have any family and use the centers as their social networking place to go. Not everybody is on Twitter, Facebook etc. Mike, East Village").

Center directors and members also wrote in and expressed concerns with the selection process, calling the idea "despicable" and "throwing seniors under the bus." One blogger wrote, "Several years ago I spent six months working at Jamaica Service Program for Older Adults & it provided meals, outings, classes & companionship. Where and what will seniors do without these centers. As a native New Yorker I am ashamed of how politicians are trashing the quality of life in this city. Teri, Jackson Heights." One woman provided a testimonial about the impact that center participation had had on her mother, who had joined a center after being retired for almost ten years:

Let me tell you something. . . . (And I'm very passionate about this) . . . Belonging to the Sr. Citizen Center has breathed NEW LIFE into my mother. Before she began going there, she was very non-social, she didn't have much conversation for anyone at all, and she didn't have much interest in learning new things. NOW, she looks forward to going there. She's met new friends. She goes for breakfast sometimes, she goes for lunch daily and she plays games there, she is learning computer skills and she is just a whole new happy person! I'm grateful for the centers! . . . She's excited about telling me about her day . . . about the games she plays, the entertainment that was there, the prizes she won. . . . I'm sure that all of the seniors that go to the centers have a similar story. My mom worked nearly 40 years before retiring. She paid taxes each and every year just like the other seniors. . . . They deserve to have this service for the balance of their lives! THE AUTHORITIES CAN'T CLOSE THESE CENTERS! . . . THEY JUST CAN'T!

A second March 2011 *NY1* story was headlined "City Council Members Blast Proposed Senior Center Closures" (2011a). City Council members and older persons rallied together against the cuts. A CBS New York article covered their rally at City Hall to protest center budget cuts and gave momentum to the "new letter campaign featuring seniors sending snapshots of themselves with moving messages asking what they would do if their centers were closed" (2011).

The City Council Points the Finger at the State

Released on March 14, 2011, the City Council's *Hearing on the Mayor's Fiscal Year 2012 Preliminary Budget and the Fiscal Year 2011 Preliminary Mayor's Management Report* for the Department for the Aging contained more definitive information about the cut/reallocation of state Title XX monies. According to this City Council's report, the state would allow the federal Title XX monies to go to only mandated services, while they had customarily also been used to cover discretionary funding for the city's senior centers. This change in money usage would mean DFTA would not receive twenty-seven million dollars in discretionary funding for DFTA to support senior centers. The City Council restated the predicted losses by borough—Brooklyn, thirty-one; Bronx and Queens, twenty-two each; Manhattan, twenty-six; and Staten Island, four—and expressed its view of the bleak outcome. The report stated that the loss of funding "would severely cripple the City's senior center network, forcing DFTA to close 105 centers, or approximately 40 percent of the current system. . . . DFTA estimates that 7,800 seniors will be affected by the citywide closures, many of whom will be left without services entirely" (New York City Council 2011b, 8).

The council's report set the stage for dire results from the new mandatory-services-only rule: "It is reasonable to assume that this cut may cause a rise in the number of seniors on the public assistance rolls, preventable emergency situations, emergency room visits, hospitalizations, elder abuse reporting, long-term care placements, and preventable deaths. . . . Additionally, 23 aging services sponsors will no longer operate a DFTA senior center, and some may go out of business entirely, as a result of this cut" (New York City Council 2011b, 9). The report mentions the Program to Eliminate the Gap (PEG) in relation to senior center closures, as a way to fill in spending cuts made by the mayor. City Council restorations provided $1.6 million for this fiscal year's PEG program to keep open some of the centers fated to close.

On April 8, 2011, the *Council's Response to the Mayor's FY 2012 Preliminary Budget and Preliminary Management Report* (New York City Council 2011a) called for a halt to the budgetary plans. The council sought to save, not close, centers, although it noted that twenty-seven centers had been closed. It applauded the efforts of DFTA in keeping seven centers from closing and its own efforts to give funding to save an addition seventeen. But the report noted the perilous condition of the seventeen it had "saved": "Contracts for the 17 centers kept open by the Council have been delayed, with several centers still operating without contracts, while 2 centers have been unable to open at all." The council went on:

> Why these same centers were allowed to continue operating in the past despite these problems remains unclear. Having fought successfully to ensure that State Title XX funds would be available to fund senior center operations, the Council believes that no further senior centers should be threatened with closure for purely budgetary reasons. Management or maintenance issues should be addressed by the agency with center sponsors, and where justified, new, responsible sponsors should take over operations. The centers that are currently funded through so-called discretionary contracts should be fully funded with agency program contracts beginning in Fiscal 2012. (8)

The now defunct New York Beat website covered the elder backlash against center closures in its online article "NYC Seniors Come Together to Protest the Closing of Senior Centers" in February and June 2011. During that time, DFTA press releases from June to September 2011 highlighted three new programs. First, TimeBankNYC, a part of Age-Friendly NYC, let elders give or receive assistance with many services, from "arts, crafts, music and recreation to wellness or community service." Second, DFTA announced it had received National Endowment for the Arts funding to expand its program of artists-in-residence in senior centers. And, third, DFTA featured its Fall Prevention Initiative.

Innovative Centers Enters the Vocabulary

In an October 2011 press release, Mayor Bloomberg featured the eight providers offering "specialized programming" that were selected to develop the city's first innovative senior centers. According to the subheading of the press release, these eight were examples of "centers [being] the cornerstone of the city's age-friendly NYC." The eight chosen through the RFP processes were Lenox Hill and the YM/YWHA (in Manhattan); Bronxworks (in the Bronx); Selfhelp Ben Rosenthal and SNAP (in Queens); JCC (of Staten Island); and two citywide organizations, Visions and SAGE.

In September 2011, NCOA and NISC produced an issue brief, "Older Americans Act Reauthorization: Multipurpose Senior Centers for Positive Aging." Here, these two pro-center organizations sought to build on the existing strengths of multipurpose centers—including efforts to modernize. They saw these centers as strongholds of knowledge about congregate meal and Meals on Wheels programs. They posited that all centers could be a part of

Age-Friendly and other health initiatives. This is one of the first times multi-purpose centers were suggested as being able to aid in the "development and implementation of Aging and Disability Resource Centers (ADRCs), as well as clarify the importance of formal partnerships between aging and disability organizations in order to successfully implement an ADRC network" (1).

A December 8 *IBO* blog post aptly titled "Senior Centers Come, Senior Centers Go" (Salas and Turetsky 2011), likened the center closures selection to a sports game in need of a "scorecard" to track the changes. The authors explained:

> Against a backdrop of limited funding, the city has closed some senior centers and curtailed services and changed the status of others, yet also launched an initiative to create new senior centers. . . . The plan to close the more than four dozen centers was one of the most controversial parts of the Mayor's budget plan in the spring of 2010. In the end, 27 centers were shuttered and 24 were spared. . . . Despite the public funds, the 17 centers were cut loose from operating under the aegis of the DFTA. The department does not consider the 17 as part of the city's network of senior centers, which makes them ineligible for city funds to support transportation and food, two prime services for seniors. While these centers have been orphaned from the city's official network of senior centers, the Bloomberg Administration is moving ahead with its plan to create eight new centers under its Age-Friendly NYC initiative. Although the new innovative centers are likely to be spared from the city's budget pressures, other senior centers could find themselves "aging out" of the network.

The new year, 2012, brought the first innovative senior centers in the nation for blind and visually impaired older New Yorkers. Then, it being March, the City Council produced its *Hearing on the Mayor's Fiscal 2013 Preliminary Budget and the Fiscal 2012 Preliminary Mayor's Management Report for the Department for the Aging*. For 2013, the report predicted a twelve-million-dollar cut from the prior budget for centers. The City Council also warned about a funding paradox: while the council gave DFTA monies in the past fiscal year to cover over 20 percent of senior center and meal costs, the funding that was provided in 2012 would not be reallocated in the 2013 budget (2012, 2–5). The council's report featured many of the council's successes: providing DFTA with fourteen million dollars to "stabilize the system" and infrastructure of senior centers, having PEG monies to keep some centers on the closure list open, and seeking to offer over one million dollars to help maintain senior centers' physical structure (2012, 2–5).

In April 2012, the Office of the Mayor, together with the DFTA commissioner, heralded the opening of all of the first eight of the innovative centers. The "Innovative Eight," as I call them, get a lot of press coverage, such as the *ABC Eyewitness News* article "Innovative Senior Centers Offer More to the Elderly" (2012) calling for "forget[ting] the days of Bingo and cards." The article describes the way the "city is radically changing the way it provides for seniors. And the changes are paying off. . . . Participation is way up, system wide, with plenty of new faces." Then, there were ten. In August 2012, two more innovative centers in Brooklyn (Riverway and Surf Solomon) brought the final count to what I call the "Innovative Ten."

In September 2012, DFTA published its *NYC Department for the Aging Annual Plan Summary, April 1, 2013–March 31, 2014*, covering the OAA, New York State Community Services for the Elderly, and Expanded In-Home Services for the Elderly Programs. The *NYC Department for the Aging Annual Plan Summary* provided details about the relationship between the two senior center models, neighborhood and innovative (also called innovative senior centers, or ISCs), and credited NYAM's work on Age-Friendly NYC and *NYC Senior Centers: Visioning the Future* in helping to create "comprehensive senior congregate services" (2012, 22). According to DFTA, with the help of NYAM, its RFP application for the funding process for neighborhood and innovative centers was rolled out. A tally was given of contracts given to both center types. There were between 235 and 238 neighborhood centers, including six new service organizations. There were eight ISCs—with an additional two pending. The need for centers to have increased responsibility and the evaluation of all centers was a central theme. The 2012 DFTA plan emphasized the requirements for neighborhood centers: "All senior centers going forward will have a consistent set of services, including a minimum of 60 meals per day, an average daily attendance of 75 persons, and a required Health and Wellness component" (22). During this time period, there is also a pervasive theme in NCOA website articles: senior centers must change to meet the needs of boomers and shake that negative "cards and bingo" image (Van Ryzin 2010). The organization also touted the benefits of centers during September's national senior center month (NCOA 2012e).

In 2012, Age-Friendly NYC created a toolkit for creating age-friendly communities one at a time based on the findings of its 2007 report. During 2010–2011, three pilot age-friendly programs in East Harlem, the Upper West Side, and Bedford-Stuyvesant were begun, and the toolkit was created to help more neighborhoods get buy-in and perfect the community-building process when establishing more age-friendly communities. In October, DFTA announced it would have two hundred thousand dollars in funding for the ongoing, successful Seniors Partnering with Artists City Wide (SPARC) program. The program places artists-in-residence in senior centers as part of the Age-Friendly NYC Initiative. In the same month, the *Daily News* ran a story about Bronx/Pelham Parkway Houses as the fourth "Aging Improvement District," places that integrated all services that improved the lives of older persons (Samuels 2012).

In February 2012, the Administration on Aging released its list of topic themes it received when seeking public feedback about the OAA reauthorization. The role of senior centers as congregate meal providers was mentioned in the third-most-addressed topic. Later in the fall, "It Happens at My Senior Center" was announced as NCOA's theme for September 2012's national senior center month, using the "power of stories" of elders as a means of engagement.

In November, a newspaper in Manchester, United Kingdom, reported how the city's residents were using the Age-Friendly NYC principles to "stand up and help old folk" in England (Glendinning 2012). A winter 2012 issue of *Oculus*, devoted to the theme "Aging in Place: There's No Place Like Home," featured an article about improving built environments as part of Age-Friendly NYC. In "Designing Residences and Communities Where Aging New Yorkers Love to Hang Out," Jerry Maltz and Christine Hunter reviewed three age-friendly communities in Bedford-Stuyvesant, Harlem, and the Upper West Side and talked about how each community has developed an age-friendly elder model:

> Stores provide seating areas, allow use of their restrooms, and utilize large-font signage; libraries and museums develop programs; pools establish special hours and are adapted for disabilities with disabled changing areas and pool lifts; gyms organize exercise classes; the Apple Store offers technology classes; food markets sponsor cooking classes; and hospitals hold lectures about healthful eating. . . . School buses in their idle hours drive older adults to shopping areas; vouchers are provided for taxis; traffic lights are rescheduled to increase crossing times at intersections. Capital investments, such as new taxis and bus shelters, are designed with aging in mind. (28)

Also in November 2012, DFTA released a NORC concept paper before its RFP went out—exploring the roles of NORCs in NYC. On its website, DFTA displayed links to neighborhood center solicitation forms, the list of 234 centers receiving an award, and forms for prequalification to provide senior center services. As of that month, NCOA announced, there were over 120 NCOA-accredited senior centers. Only three centers in New York State are listed, with two in New York City. A NCOA senior center fact sheet (2012d) covered the predicament of the good work done by centers with few, and decreasing, resources. You see "the 11,000 senior centers serve 1 million older adults every day" with "over 60% having OAA endorsement for congregate meals and designated services." "These centers provide [research proven] measurable improvements in their physical, social, spiritual, emotional, mental, and economic well-being" (1–2). But, on the downside, NCOA's fact sheet describes the juggling act of maintaining these services with funding from approximately three to eight funding sources. At this time, NCOA also released a statement in support of Congress's fiscal year 2013 Health and Human Services education appropriation to defend current OAA funding levels.

Early 2013: Innovative and Neighborhood Centers Brace for a Future without OAA Reauthorization

The year 2013 brought with it CSCS's conference, "The Power of Aging: The Intersection of Health and Social Services." Igal Jellinek, the executive director, described the rapid increase of those sixty-five and older in New York City in need of senior center services: The conference program read: "The population of NYC's older adults is expected to grow 45% by 2030. The dramatic increase, coupled with the current needs of the 1.4 million seniors living within the five boroughs, will offer both challenges and opportunities to provide enhanced services to our elders throughout the continuum of care" (CSCS 2013, 2). He called for a "transformational" conference and forward focus: "While celebrating our skills and insights, the foundation of who we [in the senior center community] are, we must learn to design other paths. This means finding and working with partners in both the public and private sectors that need our skills. It also means moving outside our comfort zone into uncharted but exciting places and remaining true to our history of promoting the right to age with dignity and independence" (2).

In a January 18, 2013, phone interview with Dr. Barrios-Paoli, I asked about the future relationship between the closure of neighborhood centers and the ISCs, to which she replied:

> The neighborhood centers that we closed were not in the context of this [ISC effort]. We had a number of dramatic cuts that happened to our budget. And it had to do with the fiscal crisis that the country was going through and the city was going through and everybody went through. And essentially, it was in that context that we closed centers. And the centers that we closed—about fifty-three centers—had to do with centers that were serving fewer than thirty people. [There were] centers that had really bad planning issues, where they were getting flooded every time it rained. There were some centers that had no Certificate of Occupancy, that they were really problematic to have seniors there because they could be a deathtrap if there was a fire. . . . So there were issues of safety, there were issues of just not good management, there were issues of underutilization, but in any event, all the centers that we closed had serious issues. And they were not serving a large number of seniors. So, one thing really had nothing to do with the other in terms of the innovative centers and [neighborhood center] closures. The big change was that to create a new model, we did not have to sacrifice people in the old model.

Centers as a place of health service provision emerged as a thread in the center discourse. February 2013 saw investigation of centers' role in helping elders manage their health through programs such as a Matter of Balance and diabetes screenings. The possibilities of Medicare eligibility and reimbursement for these health-based programs were also on the radar. Picking up on the health-based theme, the Westside Senior-Supported Agriculture (fresh produce) Food Bag Program was set up in that month. In March NCOA published "Senior Centers Reach the Hard- to-Reach," highlighting the real benefit of centers to isolated seniors, with four programs showing success: telephone reassurance programs, intergeneration connections, activities for individuals with physical/cognitive impairments, and special meals and companionship.

Also in early 2013, the effects of Hurricane Sandy—which had hit the New York area hard the previous October—came into play. According to a 2012 CBS story, at its peak, Sandy left 2.2 million persons without electricity and affected all essential services (for example, access to clean water and food). Sandy affected voting and the New York City Marathon, and in its worst case, took the lives of forty people in the city. The severity of this act of nature raised some issues about the quality and availability of services for elders in the city. A *Wall Street Journal* article in February 2013 quoted NYAM as claiming that better programs and services for older persons during natural disasters (such as Sandy) would have alleviated much unnecessary suffering.

As part of NCOA's public policy priorities for the 113th congressional session, the organization endorsed the reauthorization of the OAA. In its list of reauthorization priorities was the need to "enhance nutrition assistance for food insecure seniors" calling attention indirectly to centers and their role in congregate and home-delivered meal provision. As of March 13, 2013, when this time line closed, NCOA was wary about the House's proposed fiscal year 2014 budget resolution, believing it "poses more harm to seniors programs" (in health care, social programs, and elder employment).

From neighborhood to innovative models and with foci ranging from health promotion to social activities, senior centers are obviously undergoing great changes in their very nature. At the same time, centers' funding streams, from city, state, and OAA sources, and their target groups (current seniors versus baby boomers) are up in the air. All these events are interwoven within the closure process for centers in New York City. It helps to keep these larger changes in senior center policies and politics in mind as the next chapter explores the way these changes, and others, affect the focal center of this book.

4

The Case of the Center
as It Is Shuttered

• •

Larger Changes Hit the Center

Senior Ctr. Saved from Shutdown
Seniors Screwed: Red Tape Forces
Temporary Closure of the Center
—Media headlines, summer 2010

Sometimes you can understand events only after they have happened, which allows you to put them in context. I began contact with the initial center director during my study in early 2008. After sending some general questions to the center's director about what I thought (at the time) would be a summer project, I was sent a formal letter of permission in May 2008 to "interview women 65 and older at the center" and was "thanked for my interest." What I didn't fully grasp at the time were the then-director's remarks about the tremendous difficulties in "finding funding" and her consternation about "grants, funding, and the future." During our time together, she focused on telling me how the elders were not too keen on having a center that was an intergenerational setting. The elders, she said, felt that in the past, the "kids" (teenagers in a trial intergenerational program at the center) "took over" the computer room, and the center was less "theirs" (center participants) than it was the "younger ones'" (the teenagers). My observational notes for our visits often reflect our discussions about "where funding would come from" and needing to write grant proposals to get funding with their frustration noted in the margins. Yet at the time, these remarks did not "stick" as I happily began my interview script with the elders.

The next change happened during one of my later times regaining access to the field in 2009. I had previously heard rumblings and learned there was a new executive director ("pulled from a local ethnic organization" as described by the centergoers) in early 2009. After repeated phone calls, I was let back into the center. However, this time getting access to the center felt more forced and seemed to take many more phone calls to reach the executive director. When I got to the center, in addition to the new director, there were some new staff that I had not met and some old staff had left. Despite these staff changes, I received my usual warm reception from the elders (being introduced by the new director to center-attendees—with the director saying, "She's part of the family"). Paradoxically, I had known many of the attendees much longer than the new executive director had at the time. So, this well-intentioned introduction brought a few winks and smiles from the crowd.

Those in attendance were quick to share their thoughts and opinions with me. From our discussions, I could see that some elders' impressions of the center were subtly changing, and personal narratives shifted. In the summer of 2010, several themes dominated the elders' thoughts. These centered around lack of security and staff unavailability. The staff changes became a dominant theme in the interviews, with some evaluating the new director as "doing pretty fine." This came from Joe, sixty-two, a recent widower and less frequent attendee, who continued, "I see [the director] down there [at the congregate meal setting]. The last couple of directors, they don't mingle like [a beloved past director] did." Karen, one of the people constantly working and doing something at the center, felt that the director "stayed up in the office" too much and was not with the people in the main room enough where meals were served. In a group conversation with steady bingo friends Ellen, June, and Linda, all widowed women in their seventies, I was told members could no longer get information about energy rebate programs, since "[the nice social worker] was fired," and the "old director—who helped everybody—chose to leave." I wanted to understand why and how people left, so I asked John, a regular member, about the center staff changes: "Did the past director choose to leave? What happened there?" John replied, "Yes, [the director left by choice] but [the social worker] was out-placed or outsourced or whatever, I don't know."

The building itself was also undergoing changes. A member, in passing, expressed concern about a renewed wave of construction and the changing physical environment: "They were working on something the other day . . . grouting. . . . At one point, they were gonna make senior apartments here. Or, senior housing, there are so many floors here . . . that could be used" (Jack, seventy-six, divorced, ex-marine and retired civil service worker). I was told that a lot of old buildings were being bought with the intention of being converted to "senior apartments." This idea of local institutions being converted to apartments for older persons may have come from a contentious story in a local paper about a proposal by a real estate developer to purchase a landmark local church, one mile away from the center. Using energy company incentives, the proposal was to add on to the historic church building, making an apartment complex for elders. The size of the building, with almost fifty apartments, was of concern to the local community and a point of discussion. During the same period, the center building owners also built solar panels that were prominently featured in a ribbon-cutting ceremony in a local paper. The centergoers were not certain of the utility of these panels, though.

Elders brought up the use of security cameras in the center and made a point of showing their locations to me. Karen tied the camera use to the staff changes; she reasoned, "There are cameras on the street, everywhere. Because you don't have as many people available in the building. The monitors are there—in the offices. If somebody falls or something, somebody can see it on the camera. Say, somebody came down here and started a disruption. They're chasing people, or whatever. You can't always get up, but they've got the camera. The camera is right over the clock." She pointed and smiled. "I can't see it, but that's where it is. I can't see the clock, but that's where it is." She laughed. Others suggested the cameras were more to "watch the staff than the seniors," but the camera discussion brought safety to light. Maria spoke to me at length about not feeling safe in the center or secure in her own home: "Over here I took self-defense, there is one guy here we call him the Big Bopper. A lot of times he don't ask you to dance, he just grabs your arm, so I grabbed his leg. . . . One time I was crossing the street and a guy grabbed me and I was ready to hit him, and he said, 'Lady, you was gonna get hit by a car!' and I say, 'Oh, thank you!' I've always been a fighter. If anyone rings the bell and I don't know them, I have a burglar alarm."

The shifting personal narratives about the center also changed to include some talk about the "changing crowd" and activities. This center, once referred to by Lily as "more modernized and a really a good place for people to come" was now discussed more in terms of its losses. Angela, seventy-nine, married, part-time worker, member, with a self-proclaimed mission to help everyone at the center, expressed great concern about the center's future and the needs of other centergoers: "The crowd is not like the old crowd. . . . They come for the bingo . . . [but are not really interested in any other parts of the center life]." Other local centers were mentioned for their food options or programmatic options, especially the dancing. Earlier themes of the loss of "deejays for the dances," "live bands," bus trips, and the "old crowd" with favorite activities "fizzling out" were revisited as "things ain't the way they used to be for us old-timers." The idea that you needed to "have a table" or be "part of a clique" also persisted. John explained to Maria and me, "You can't approach people; you only hope that you get the younger people in." Lily and Maria, each separately, spoke about the destructive nature of attendees' excessive talk about each other on membership. For Lily, there was simply "too much gossip—that people, like, know things [you would not want repeated]." Maria felt that this chitchat "turned off potential members." She recounted the time when she brought someone to the center and asked, "So how do you like it?" To which her guest said, "All those women do is talk."

The importance of numbers and counting reentered the discussion in a big way. Karen prided herself on getting the membership count up by a simple strategy. She would approach any new face at the center and ask, "Would you like to be a member? You're not committed to being a member of our center. But . . ." She would explain that "membership has its privileges, but there's no commitment." To me, it seemed that members were more acutely aware of keeping track of statistics, or, at least talking about "numbers." Let me relay the following conversation between Angela, who operated the sign-in desk, and Victoria, a board member. Victoria asked Angela, "We're not doing a second sheet today?" To which Angela responded, "No, we finished it," indicating that the first sheet was full of names of those signed in attendance for that particular day. Victoria closed the conversation: "People want more. We like that second sheet!" as Angela responded, "You're right!" Victoria felt that "sometimes, we get some new ones [attendees], some strangers . . . but most of the people are pretty much the same."

Number-tracking also extended to monitoring issues of the center's funding. Funding first came up in a conversation with Anita, a nonattendee and recent widow. She began to express her view about the centers in the neighborhood. So I asked her: "Anita, if you could make centers better, let's say you were to give advice to people . . ." Our words overlapped, and she responded, whispering softly as she began:

> Don't ask me that because I don't really participate in [activities, now] so I can't give you any help with that. . . . I remember when they used to deliver the food at one time to the shut-ins. And now that's sort of cut down. They are losing some funding or they may lose some funding for it. But I'm glad the center on [another street] is open now for another year. That's a relief. 'Cause my neighbor across the street, she was very upset; she always went there, and then she started to go to the other [center]. But now she'll probably go back to the one here. But the woman, she was a driver, and I guess she got an upgrade now in a different position. Well, who's picking up the people now? It's Access-a-Ride. And these are people that cannot walk for themselves, or have heart trouble, or with their legs . . . that's the ones, the people that they pick up. Now [Access-a-Ride] is closing. They're closing a lot of things.

Piecing Together the Closure

Finding Center Members and Off-the-Record Accounts

I went back in the winter of 2012 to follow up and locate the centergoers from the shuttered center after the closure was complete. I again met with and spoke with Karen. She said she left the center six months before it closed, as "things went downhill, really fast—there were really bad caterers after the chef left." She said a catering company even went out of business. Karen felt the "the director stayed up in the office [away from the attendees] more and more." She went to another center about four miles away—"but if I was sick or needed something, it was too far to go, so I came back here [to another center in the same neighborhood as that of the closed center]." When I interviewed some of those from the closed center at this other center, there was a full house with a happy and festive mood. I felt very welcomed there and happy to see some of those I interviewed in the past. It was easier for me to get into this center than any others, as well. But, sadly, many of the regulars whom I had interviewed at the now closed center were not at this one. The thrift table group of women, who also happened to be some of the board members at the closed center, was mostly missing. I was told that Victoria, a past board president and organizer of activities at the old center, went upstate to live with her daughter. One of the "German ladies," as they are called, might be able to give me a lead on her address. Jack, the ex-marine and ex–civil service worker who had paid for "lunch for the ladies," I was told, had got into some disagreements at the new center and had since died, according to some.

One of the most shocking changes was the health status of one of the women I had interviewed early on at the old center. When I first met Lily, she was running some groups and serving the coffee. At this center, I was approached by an elderly woman with striking white hair without her false teeth and using a modified seated walker. She seemed to know me and handed me a picture of her grandchildren while giving me an update and details of their lives. For a few minutes, although she seemed to know me, I could not place this woman. After our conversation, one of the new centergoers, said to me, "You know her; that's Lily." I could not believe the change. Lily had a home health aide with her during all her center visits now.

Some other members of this new center wanted to talk to me off the record. My memos about the themes of these talks are filled with tales of political moves and reciprocity. Pat, sixty-nine, and Anne, in her late seventies, relayed a tale of how the director was placed in the center by someone who heads local boards and has his own local business. Pat, a member of the teamsters' union, was on the center board and prided himself on being asked to be a promoter of the shuttered center. According to him, one of the past directors of the closed center wanted to "get me to go up [to city hall] and advocate," but he was "worn out," and his wife was not in good health. Anne and Pat felt the closure had been a "done deal." It was "all in the bag" and "it is a shame how those who have done so much for the country get very little . . . nothing in their latter years." They talked about how all the politicians had stopped by, some being "good" and on the side of the center. But according to Pat, "things began to fall apart. . . . All the activities that the people liked (like bingo) were being changed—even the dances. The dances got cut, and there was no money for a deejay. This current center we are at now is less about dancing, but at [another center in the area], you should see it. There, all the people dance—you can only move like this"—Pat gestured a few inches—"on the dance floor." They both began to leave the center before it officially closed—because of the loss of events—and think the closure resulted from mismanagement and nonpayment of rent. They also felt the director was "put there" but not really "suited to the job." Here, at the new center, they agreed, "the director cares, and things are run right."

Community Activists Tell the Tale

Local activists also made contact to tell me the "real story." Scout, a baby boomer active on many community boards and in organizations, described the history of the shuttered center building from the 1970s. Scout's account pointed to a series of political dealings and desired sales and use of the center by various groups. According to Scout, in the 1970s, a corporation "bought the building from the Masons with one cook as the staff and a lot of stealing from the building." Ever since that time, "the city never paid the rent on time. We have these five bills. We have enough to pay this one and not this one, you know? It just was a crazy time. There was bad food, and the chef got sick." Daisy, another civically engaged person, interjected, "Even under [a past director], the seniors had picked the menu. So that's why we had things like what I was telling you. Like the two frankfurters with macaroni with baked beans. And you'd have a starch—a pudding or something for dessert. It was just horrible in those days."

Scout's account continues with the 1980s, bringing a local politician into the mix. This politician "did a couple of things, important things. He put in the elevator. The elevator was huge. And, at a critical moment [the Masonic temple was removed]." The center remained in the building and paid rent. A director was brought in, as Scout explains, "doing an excellent job. [That director] was rated as one of the best centers in the city and kept on expanding it." But after the death of this director, a local realtor "got interested in the property and had a plan at some point to turn it into eighteen one-room apartments for seniors who would have lunch at the center. I think he actually had that drawn out. But it didn't work for some reason; something didn't work."

In Scout's account, the center's losing the contract with DFTA was the end result of a series of political power plays for funding and property:

> Now, in the context of politics, what happened is that the area was redistricted. One of the most corrupt politicians in the state of New York wanted this [building]. One of his [other community-based] programs has gotten the lion's share of the money.[1] And [this official] wanted this waterline just across the street. [A local realtor] probably wanted the commission for selling the building while the building is still under the influence of a senator. [At the same time], the city of New York wants to close senior centers, right? So when this one [final director] comes in, he messes things up in such a way that now there's some kind of feud between the board of directors of the senior center—and [the realtor] and the board of directors of [the holding company].
>
> We had the redistricting going on, so now [the realtor] has interest. He also was involved in putting the solar panels on top. He knew how to manipulate those funds, federal, state funds, to get those solar panels in. So he did that. Then they [the closed center's board and management company] had this theoretical fight.
>
> And the other piece of the action is a councilman for this area; a Republican and mentee of the senator, and the senator still have an interest in lots of buildings around here, including this one. So now they concoct this war between the two boards. The city cancels the contract. The next thing that happens is that suddenly who appears but [this councilman's] brother? His brother offers to buy the building. So [the realtor and the board] make sure that the senior center's charter will not be renewed. They sell the building to this councilman's brother. Now what does the brother have to do? He's got to sell the building again. So now they're looking for somebody to buy the building.

I asked why, in Scout's opinion, the building was sold, and then rented to another nonprofit. Scout explained: "That's a trick because . . . once this was a legitimate senior citizens' center and got political money for the elevator and the solar panels, it had to be sold to a nonprofit." Then I asked how an individual came to own the building—since the person is not a nonprofit. To which Scout replied, "Because [an individual] is just being the broker. He was the flipper. He could own it for a little while. I think most of [the new tenants'] money comes from city contracts. The biggest city contract is the after-school center." Scout also suggested that this new tenant was in dire need of a building, since the individual's prior landlord was raising their rent.

My final question hinged on what Scout thought was "going to happen to senior centers in this community." He replied, "Whatever the mayor wants is going to happen. You've got two other centers here. One is very politically connected because it's also owned or mentored by [the former senator]. And that's the [another local center]. What I think is gonna happen is whatever the mayor wants—which would not be more senior citizens' centers. Now, what would be good for the neighborhood would be—there really is, this center provided an excellent service." Then, Daisy joined the conversation, and she and Scout exchanged their thoughts about the closure of the center and the remaining center options in the neighborhood:

> DAISY: It [the closed center] was in competition with [the second center in the community]. And [that second center's] kitchen is much nicer, it really is. But it's also a very small facility.
>
> SCOUT: I think this [the closed center] is a good location because it would serve *this* part of the neighborhood. As opposed to either of the other centers that serve other things. So that's number one. Number two is—I think I've seen at least one person that I think died because this closed. [Scout names someone he has not seen in a while.] We haven't seen her around. She's had one illness after another, and she keeps coming back like the Eveready bunny.

Now, let's add media accounts and other local community events to our narrative time line focused solely around the center used as an extended case study in this book.

Enter the Press: Senior Center Media Coverage

Beginning in the summer of 2002, this center received two particular distinctions. It was featured as a 2002 Best of Queens senior center by a local newspaper and received a Star Award for its Meals on Wheels program. And in 2006, two years before I formally began my study, it was highlighted as a spotlight program in a DFTA newsletter for the work of its director and her novel, privately funded programs. The newsletter called the center a "vitality center" and ended the write-up with "Let there be no doubt: there's a new kind of senior center being developed all over the City by centers like [this center]." In 2006, the center received a Hunger Award for having served "more than 10,000 dinners to the community and provided supplemental groceries for 11,500 community residents" in the past year, as well as having a food pantry and common dinner table events for all.

The Media Covers the Center's Good Times

In January 2006, the mayor visited this center and delivered the thirty-four millionth meal to a member in her eighties. The Speaker of the City Council and New York City's Meals on Wheels founder were also on hand preparing holiday meals. In March that year, the center was listed as a place to drop off nonperishable food as part of a local food drive. In April, the local paper reported on the expansion of two centers in the area. Another center was expanding to create office space, intergenerational areas, and outdoor space. The media mentioned that the center profiled in this book was seeking to add on an additional floor and create eighteen senior apartments. Council members and a local realtor were in support of this project. There is mention of the potential for two million dollars in public funding for the first center and five hundred thousand dollars for the second.

Then, in May, a member from the center and some staff were featured in a short newspaper article about problems with the bus service system for elders. The member mentioned lateness, while staff suggested that drivers be held accountable in addition to seniors. In June, a local paper carried the obituary of a past center director. A news article in the same month reported that a neighborhood board meeting held a moment of silence to "honor two local activists who died earlier this month"—with the past center director being one of the honorees. In September, a local realtor and president of a property association had solar panels installed on his own roof. He mentioned that the center should have these same panels as a cost-saving measure. Then, in October, a local paper ran a story that the renovation planned for the center, as part of the fiscal year 2009 capital budget, had been "dropped."

The year 2008 was quiet in the local media. In July, a local paper covered an awards ceremony at the center as part of its thirty-fifth anniversary celebration honoring women—both as members and staff.[2] Politicians (state senators and City Council and Assembly people) were in attendance. In December, a photo of centergoers holding a holiday gala appeared on the front page of an anniversary issue of a local paper. The year 2009 brought a bit more coverage. In January, the local ambulance corps installed new members at the center. In February, an elder's obituary mentioned the center. In June, the center's director was featured in news coverage about the mayor's being celebrated for his role in increasing the number of historical landmark areas in the community at a local property owner's association meeting. A claim was filed to add more homes to the community's historic landmark portion. The article quoted Bloomberg: "For those of you who want landmarking, I think you're going to get what you want." As the crowd applauded, he went on, "[This neighborhood's] history needs to be preserved and celebrated. These landmark decisions, we think, will go a long way toward doing that." Council people attended, and two organizations gave the mayor gifts, as did the center director. The realtor also gave a presentation about contractors and home renovation. The summer also marked the thirty-sixth year of the center, and a photo appeared in a local paper about an anniversary dinner dance at the center. The realtor gave an award to a politician at the ceremony, and other elected officials were in attendance. In July, the press mentioned a dinner dance with an invitation extended to the community. A civic pride award was scheduled to be given to the district's representative, and members of the center's board of directors and the center's executive officers would also be installed for duty. The inductees included the realtor formerly related to solar panel issues and the homeowners association.

In August, a local community newspaper article featured this particular center and its centergoers and the appointment of a new executive director four months earlier. There was much adulation for a City Council member who obtained $659,750 in funding for center repairs and programming. In related news, the same council member dropped in and told members she had found "$1.7 million in the city budget" for youth- and veteran-related non-profits in the area. By December, an article in a local paper let residents know that the center would be open to serve a Christmas meal for elders and their families and praised the chef's cooking for being featured in New York's print and television media.

Reports of "Shuttering," "Management Problems," and Political Help

The year 2010 began with more mundane occurrences, expected upcoming events at the center: art and a fund-raising fashion show. But in May the tide turned, and the possibility of center closures hit Queens. Things became real as the *Queens Chronicle* listed nine—of ten—potential centers to close in Queens. Though the list was not sourced, the center in this study had not appeared on any list, including this one, to date. In mid-June, the final countdown to the closure of the center begins. On June 17, three articles ran in the local community newspaper. The first paper reported on seniors, Assembly members, CSCS, and local civic associations at a rally challenging the mayor to keep local centers from being closed, since they provided vital services for elder residents. The other two referred to lawmakers' fearing a government shutdown if the legislative budget was not passed in time. On June 24, a local community newspaper ran the apocryphal headline "Senior Center's Days Numbered" and described the differing and conflicting stories of events told by the center staff, DFTA, and the center board and management company. The paper stated that rent increases and problems with the center's holding company had led to the lack of a contract from DFTA. A spokesperson for DFTA said the center was among a host of others senior centers across the city scheduled to close as a result of "significant reduction in aid and incentives to municipalities' funding from the state. They remain on the list; the state's budget left us no other option." These comments are puzzling because the center was not on the original list of fifty centers being closed.

The center contacted two council members, a state representative, a state senator, and an Assemblyperson for assistance. The center's director felt that all DFTA requirements were met, and the contract should have been renewed.

In a local news article, the director tells the reporter: "It was obvious that these guys had written us off totally. . . . We no longer exist. . . . We're basically a carcass, and they're pulling off any piece they can. . . . They pigeonholed us into this problem, even though claims of mismanagement at the center were untrue. . . . We're not mismanaged. . . . We had problems with the landlord." He believed officials would "do the right thing." A representative for a council member noted that the center is "the most diverse senior center in the area . . . special in its own way. We don't think that it's justified that this center should be closed. We are united on one front to save this center." Center attendees stated their support for the center and confidence in the management staff. But the July 1 date loomed, soon to mark the beginning of the new fiscal year and the closures.

An editorial maligned the decision to "defund" the local center. Using census data, the author argued that "13.7 percent of the area's population is 65 years of age and older. By contrast, just 6.5 percent of [this neighborhood's Community] Board residents are five years old and under. Yet there are 23 day care centers—and just five senior centers. . . . And this week, residents learned that the Department for the Aging (DFTA) wants to defund one of the handfuls of senior centers serving this area [named]. They state the center 'serves 3,240 meals each month and is the second-largest senior center in the area. . . . It has continued to grow ever since, and from its current [named street] location, it has become a fixture in the community, offering a wide variety of senior services including Meals on Wheels to the homebound.'"

But a dispute between the center's management and the holding company that owned the building gave DFTA (under orders to close senior centers to reduce its budget) enough reason to rescind its contract with this center. This move resulted in the facility's demise. Even though the senior center and landlord had settled their spat, the DFTA insisted that the center remain on the chopping block. The editorial writer suggested, "The loss of [this center] would leave many local seniors with nowhere to spend their day and enjoy warm meals and fun activities in the company of friends and neighbors alike. Is this what the city has come to? Why must seniors be forced to compete against kids for the use of their tax dollars?"

Toward the end of June, an article appeared about the center's unveiling an energy-saving system purchased through a $140,000 grant from the New York State Energy Research and Development Authority. On June 30, in a local community paper the director noted, "It [the system] was actually a lot of trouble to get this thing installed . . . but I'm glad that we have it for the simple reason that I know it's dependable . . . and appreciate the fact that the center is able to get at least a little more help to be independent financially."

Really Closed? Conflicting Reports about the Center's Fate

Then on June 30, 2010, DFTA terminated its contract with the center and ended its funding. This senior center joined the hit list. Oddly, on that same day, there was a story in the local paper about how the center was "the first solar-powered senior center in city." The article described the June 25 ribbon-cutting ceremony, which had included "the center's president and local: realtor, the vice president of the holding corporation, Councilwoman, the president of solar panel company and the center's Director." This funding, from the New York State Energy Research and Development Authority and a state senator, had been awarded three years prior. A photo of the ribbon cutting appears in the paper in July.

On July 2, 2010, a listing added on the CSCS website for this center cites the center's history and services:

> In 1973 the [center], a non-profit corporation, was established in Queens Community Board [number] to meet the needs of local seniors and keep them a vital part of the community. The mission of the center is to serve the needs of older citizens and their families enduring the physical and social hardships of the elderly in Queen Community Board [number]. The center seeks to recognize the productive capabilities of all older adults and to deliver high-quality and cost-effective programs and services. These services include: congregate meals, case assistance, information and referral, recreation/educational activities, nutrition counseling, telephone reassurance, health promotion and screening and friendly visiting programs.

Then, the tide seemed to turn again—in favor of the elders. A local Queens paper, under the headline "Seniors Win Big," gave an account of how a local councilperson may have "saved" this center by finding extra funding to keep it open. The director commended the councilperson for "dedication to the cause of the poor, the helpless, and the forgotten." A second councilperson joined the effort and stated, "The budget is not about numbers, it cannot be balanced on the back of seniors. . . . The city has to do right by seniors. This is not the end of a victory, it's only the beginning. . . . It's a battle, we have won this one, but there still are more. I fought for this center, and I will continue to fight until it closes." There were reports that the center might have to close for a few days until the funds came in and would reopen for a scheduled almost-forty-year anniversary celebration later in the month. A picture of councilpersons with seniors and a sign heralding them as "saving the center" and as "our Heroes!" was hung outside the center.

In another story, the local community paper ran the headline "Senior Center Saved from Shutdown" and reported that the center had funding for one more fiscal year. The center board praised the efforts of the local council members in keeping the doors opened. A public relations officer for the center said that they would get a contract extension "as soon as we are stabilized." There was a "constant battle" over why the center did not reopen. The holding company was accused of not renewing the lease despite the promise of City Council funding. The funding from a local politician would keep the center open at least until summer. Politicians felt that "permanent solutions" must be sought. The president of the center's board praised the City Council member's efforts: "The door would be locked today without her tenaciously doing what she had to do to keep this center open." The council member's spokesperson said, "Once the funding had been secured, the agency agreed to extend the provisions of the contract through the 2011 fiscal year, which concludes on June 30, 2011." The holding company was blamed for a rent increase one and a half years ago, although later rescinded, and cited as the cause of the dilemma. Some raised concerns about the overlapping membership of the holding company and center's boards.

The "Saved from Shutdown" article provided some history. It seems that on June 3, the president of the center's board informed the holding company by letter that the "sole reason for DFTA's decision was the impasse between the landlord and the senior center." The center solicited the assistance of elected officials. The article reported that DFTA was made aware of the resolution but "declined to overturn its decision to kill their contract with [the center]." The center's public relations officer reportedly stated that the administration would work with DFTA on a long-term extension of their previous contract "as soon as we are stabilized."

Mid-July, a letter to the editor of the *Queens Ledger* online received 2,213 views. Its writer evoked the meaning the center had for her uncle:

> I would like to thank everyone who helped save [the center]. This center is an asset to the area. According to the reports, Council Woman [name] helped secure funds to keep the center open. Thank you very much. Thank you also to Assemblywoman [name] and Assemblyman [name] for writing a letter to Lilliam Barrios-Paoli, the Commissioner of the Department for the Aging, urging her to reconsider pulling funding to them. This center is very close to my heart. My Uncle Eddie, who passed away in 2005, spent many years going to this center. When he could drive he delivered Meals on Wheels for them. When he couldn't drive anymore he helped prepare the meals for them in the center's kitchen. He also served on the Advisory Board for the center. He made many friends there and had much enjoyment there in his last years. Thank you for saving the center that gave him so much joy.

The *Queens Courier* ran a front-page story, "Senior Trips: Seniors Suffer and—Free Rides for the Displaced," highlighting the difficulty elders had in getting promised rides to new centers. A councilman from another district talked about how he saved one center; another councilman announced he is going to fight for his two centers in peril. The article cited the shuttling of elders between the centers as "horrible." In terms of the center, a local paper reported that the center held its thirty-seventh Anniversary Dance and Awards Presentation. The council member who had "saved the center" received a Civic Pride Award. A representative would bring an extra $230,000 from Congress "to help keep the center open while it develops future funding plans." After many calls and discussions with interviewees and elders in the neighborhood, I sent a letter of support to the associate director. I called repeatedly, but there was no contact from the center until August 11.

On July 30, the center board officially closed the center. The dissection of the trail of events that led to this event begins in the media. The local community paper ran the headline "Seniors Screwed: Red Tape Forces Temporary Closure of the Center" for its cover story. The story cited DFTA as not providing an advance of funds. Quotes from councilpersons attested that that the monies promised were "yet to be disbursed pending completion of various governmental bureaucratic processes." According to another councilperson, "They [center staff] knew there would be a lag" and "they should have communicated that to seniors." At that point, the staff and director believed that the center would reopen. The director told the reporter they would know their fate after Labor Day; the center would "reopen in better shape. . . . That's the silver lining"; "we're dealing with politics on the backs of 80-year-old people." The reporter called the events a "nightmare com[ing] true for seniors" and quoted a centergoer: "When the money comes in, we're going to have lobster for lunch. Hopefully, we'll get what we deserve, what we worked our whole lives for."

Confusion about the actual status of the center abounded. Two other local community papers ran articles about the closure being only temporary and the "jubilation" about being saved from closure as "short-lived" because the promised federal and city funds from elected officials would probably not come through (or at least for many months) and that only other sources of revenue could really "save" the center. Yet, in direct opposition to these statements, another article expressed the director's belief that the center would reopen in October 2010 when some state funding came through. Maybe this was denial, since reporters cited a DFTA spokesperson as saying, "There is no more DFTA funding" and no contract for the center with DFTA. A senator said, "The center is going to have to become a different kind of senior center that does not rely on city aid." The author of the second article also restated the funding issues and spoke to directors of other centers in the borough that were willing to take in seniors when the center closed. One director of a neighborhood center that would embrace the relocated elders stated, "I'm on good terms with [the director of the closed center]; it's always a pleasure to take in seniors."

An online story called the center closure "temporary," noting it would need to "survive in years to come" without DFTA money. The article received 976 views. The center, "cut from DFTA" in June, "remained open through July, and even received a boost from elected officials who said a combination of federal and City Council funds would prevent it from closing." The article reported that monies from the City Council and other governmental sources would arrive in November—but "forced to wait, cut off from city aid and faced with the prospect of going deeper into debt by staying open, the center's board decided to suspend operations as of July 30." The director was quoted as saying, "The center will receive a state grant of roughly $123,000 in October, and a final payment from the city sometime this month. The center will reopen once the state grant comes through. . . . It would be irresponsible for us to reopen [before then] if we don't have enough money to run the place." The associate director and center members told me that they had raised enough money through donations, bingo, and other charity events to pay to keep the center open for at least fourteen days.

Even though this self-raised money worked to keep the center opened for two weeks, and hopes were raised about the potential contract, concerns remained. In this last article mentioned, the director stated, "I don't think DFTA is a reliable partner. Not because DFTA is unreliable but because the mayor has been decimating funds for senior centers for years." In April 2011, seven months later, a comment is posted about the closure article: "Why is this going on when this particular center has been a real 'God send' to those in the area? With seniors who might have nothing to do but sit at home and watch TV, lie in bed, etc., centers like this are a real blessing, but once again why should that matter to the Mayor or others in office, who I'm quite sure have somewhere for their elderly parents (or grandparents) to go? There has to be a viable solution to keeping this center open, and I pray to God it happens 'very soon' because to see this center close down for good would be a horrific blow to those who need it the most."

On August 11, the associate director of the center sent me the e-mail that opens the introduction of this book. It bears repeating: "My dear, it is horrible, even though our center was promised so much money, none of it came in. We had to suspend our programs and do not know if we will be able to open up again. Our seniors took it so hard, and we are so sad." The next day, the *Queens Ledger* ran an anonymous commentary about the state of the center and discussed more unanswered questions. The author asserted, "Several things just don't make sense. When DFTA released its list of centers to be closed, it stated that the centers on the list possessed the following criteria: (a) served less than 30 meals a day, (b) were part-time or satellite centers, and/or (c) had maintenance or management problems. [The] Senior Center certainly doesn't fit the first two options, so why is it no longer open? The seniors now without a place to go are the ones who deserve some answers, so people, stop all the finger-pointing and think about the people you serve for once."

False Hopes of Reopening as the Building Is Sold

In September, a local paper reported on another local center whose attendance was up since the closure of the other center. The center accepted the seniors who had previously attended the one that closed. This center's director, of thirteen years, spoke of "doing more with less" in terms of DFTA funding and the need to be creative in fund-raising. Interestingly, in September, a related nonprofit organization that borders this community in Brooklyn came under scrutiny at one of its centers by the New York City Department of Investigation. The city wanted some budgeting issues rectified. There were accusations that elders who were board members were paid to sign documents, and there were activities billed that did not occur as presented. A city-generated "Corrective Action Plan" was accepted by this elder-centered organization. And a local community paper reported that many buildings were being "controversially" converted into "co-op[s] for senior citizens" and that even area religious institutions were considering this option because of the high cost of living and decreasing school enrollments. There was also an undated list generated by a senator requesting federal funding for fiscal year 2011 for Transportation, Housing and Urban Development, and related agencies. The request was for one million dollars to expand the focal senior center of this book to another site, the West Community Center, at another address in the community: "This project will allow the community center to provide the necessary services to meet the growing needs of low-income seniors. This project will also meet the needs of a multi-ethnic immigrant community by providing job training, language education and programming and assistance on nutrition." Yet this West Community Center expansion was not mentioned elsewhere.

The end of 2010 left the center, once dead, now with slight hope. An article appeared in the middle of a local community paper with a headline featuring the fact that the center remained "empty," its "future in limbo." Council members lamented that "it's just a slow, slow process" getting the funding, and the director of the closed center stated that it "will have a new life once monies come through." The reporter noted that members of the closed center "have already moved on to two other area centers."

In early 2011, the center's building, according to a local paper, had been put on the market "for $1.8 million" by a Long Island realtor. The broker describes the 7,569 sq. ft. property as "priced to sell fast" and ideal for a "church or other large organization." The center board's president claimed, "We're going to do several things [to get the center back in the building] and whatever happens, happens." The article went on, "The Board President indicated that the senior center has good contacts with a potential, unidentified buyer who would allow the facility to reopen. We don't know which one is going to work, but we're going to pursue all different directions." A commenter, Jeanne M., responded to the story online, using all capital letters (modified here): "I do not understand for the life of me why this 'institution' which has been around since before I moved to [a neighboring community] (over 20 years now), is going through a legal battle when it's been the life of this community and has helped so very many. I pray to God they're able to open back up soon, even if it means they must do so without the help of the government."

In a related story in a local paper about the "state of things" in the community, an Assemblyperson "touched on the recent plight of [the center] . . . forced to shut its doors in hopes of reopening once the site received extra government funds." That money, he confirmed, "never came in." In June, the director of a local center that embraced the centergoers displaced from the shuttered center is quoted in an article asking that a local casework program not be cut or moved out of the community district; the commute is extremely difficult for older persons to make to obtain benefits. The director bemoaned that "it's just been cutting and cutting and cutting. For the DFTA, their motto is 'do more with less.' You can't do more with less when you keep cutting us. [DFTA is] slowly taking away pieces of the program that we have until we fade away [in favor of] mega senior centers."

October brought false promises. Hopes were raised as a local news article reported that a "third party" would buy the center building. The center board's president believed that this unknown/named/not-finalized new owner would "permit the site to be used by the center—which suspended its operations in July 2010—as well as a youth organization for its various functions." But, as expected, in November, the final shoe dropped. The center would not be given space by the new owners of the building. Instead, the building would house a youth organization, a prekindergarten program, offices, and other initiatives. According to the article: "The [youth organization] has also agreed to house a senior center in the basement . . . as part of an 'intergenerational program,' and [the youth board president] noted that the Senior Center . . . has the opportunity to reopen. I [the youth board president] have all intentions of having [the center] come back in as a viable entity if they can get their funding from DFTA."

But the senior center board's president told the reporter that the center would not reopen at its original site and was in the process of dissolving completely. "They may constitute a new senior center there, but we're not going to be a part of it. . . . [The new tenants] didn't give us the means to do it. . . . You would think that at least in part some of those proceeds [from the sale agreement] would have gone to [the center] so we could start up. But we didn't get a penny."

The building, according to the article, was held by a holding company, and any profits had to go to a nonprofit, but in this case it is the new tenant and not the center. As the new tenants paid rent, newspapers reported, the center could come back within an eighteen-month period. Sources did not think this was the case. The new tenant's president would house the old center or another. He stated, "I want [the old center] to come back. . . . They have a certain amount of money in their budget for this year. I want to see them utilize that with us."

According to the center board's president, there was an "unwritten agreement" with the current owners that was not honored, and the space was reallocated. "We're a footnote. . . . I didn't want to go through the same battle that I did with the holding company. We just have to wait until the end of the year to file our final tax return. [The community] is okay with two senior centers. We can approach it with two."

In opposition, the new tenant organization's president said, "We're preparing for our pre-kindergarten to come in on the first floor and to have the young adult internship and director staff on the second floor. We're going to reopen the senior center in the basement one way or the other." The article ended with a question about whether or not the new tenants would open another site in the area.

At the end of November, the *Daily News* reported that Kathleen Turner and Mayor Bloomberg served a holiday meal at another local center. Bloomberg told New Yorkers not to forget how lucky they were instead of looking at "the handful of things that don't work." In December 2011, the year closed with a posting on the website of the Independent Budget Office (IBO). The *IBO Web Blog* piece was titled "Senior Centers Come, Senior Centers Go" (Salas and Turetsky 2011). The piece described the way the City Council allocated monies for closed centers: "The Council has again provided $1.6 million in the current fiscal year for the 17 centers, including $130,000 for [this center]. But the building [that the center] had operated in has been sold with no immediate plan for the senior center to be allowed to reopen there. The president of the senior center's board told the [local paper] last month that [the center] is 'in the process of dissolving completely.' IBO assumes the [center's] funds will again be reallocated to other organizations by the Council." Now, sadly, there is a new photo taken at the center that appears in the local paper—but it's Santa paying a visit to the new tenant's groundbreaking ceremony.

A Case of Discretionary Funding?

Since much of the blame cast about by the various players in the shuttering process was placed on the late arrival of the City Council's discretionary funds (when it was not placed on DFTA), I wanted to explore the council's

2012 funding trail more thoroughly. To understand the process, I spoke with Paola Miceli, director of Health, Human Services and Senior Services for the Queens Borough President's Office on December 19, 2012. Our meeting occurred after the center had closed. As one would expect, just as with the trend of state and federal monies diminishing for centers, the amount of discretionary funding available to the City Council to give centers is also decreasing. Miceli explained that the discretionary money pool had been lessened "from 2.9 to 1.6 million" over the eleven years that Borough President Helen Marshall had been in office. Miceli described the many larger sources of funding for centers (such as DFTA's receipt of federal funding from OAA's Title XX and "United States Department of Agriculture money for the food"). She explained that "the Queens borough president provides a tremendous amount of funding to senior centers. It's historical; it goes back [for each of the three borough presidents she has worked for]." But she continued to explain the City Council's discretionary funding process in relation to the center:

> There's discretionary money, which means it's money that comes from elected officials to fund certain projects, certain services. But that's separate and apart from what's considered baseline funding for aging services. So what happened with [the center at the heart of this book] was that they no longer had the contract with DFTA. Their government money was not flowing, and when the City Council added the money to save them, they couldn't add it into a contract to get them going because there's a lag. When you have federal money and state money that flows through DFTA, the fiscal year is July 1 to June 30. So July 1, that money is in the contract, and they're ready to go. . . . The money may not be flowing, but they get cash advances on it, so they're able to fund the basic services for the center. Discretionary money goes through a different approval process. It takes forever. . . . Although it's [discretionary funding] not considered part of that baseline, these centers would never survive without it. So, for example, I give the approved list to DFTA, the Mayor's Office, the Comptroller's Office by July 1 or early July of every year. And the money is only starting to flow now [in December].
>
> So that's how long it takes for it to go through all the necessary [channels]. We don't make any changes because, again, as I said before, if I were, or if the borough president were, to start fooling around with it "we're going to take it away from you and give it to you," we're looking at the destabilizing of community centers. We would never do that. So it's the same list, over and over and over, and it still takes this long to go through the process because it's a discretionary process. So that's what hurt [your particular center]. They were given the extra money that they needed. But they couldn't get it fast enough. . . . It was the time. It was just the bureaucratic process and the time that it would take. So they never reopened even though the money was there. Which is a shame, and that's happened in other instances before.

So, the City Council had provided discretionary monies for this center for quite some time, and often it took time for the funding to arrive. The end of 2012 brought an end to talk of the center in the local media as well.

In 2013, the local paper ran photos of the center's building but not in its function as a center. The photos show all the local politicians and elected officials involved with some additions as the center is now the site for a lunch sponsored by the new tenant—a youth organization. As of a February 17, 2013, website listing, the senior center's holding company, which had once owned and sold the senior center building, is currently not registered with the IRS because this organization failed to file a nonprofit tax form, a 990, for three consecutive years.

While we leave the center as closed in this chapter, in chapter 5, I will reexamine details about the closure process and the key players involved through a sociological lens. Specifically, how did social capital move in each of the relationships and between the groups throughout the events of chapters 3 and 4? When were social ties advantageous? And when were the generated social capital and corresponding ties ultimately negative?

5

The Organizational
Embeddedness of Capital

• •

Being Saved and Being Sunk

> The personal experience of individuals is
> closely bound up with larger-scale aspects
> of social structure, well beyond the pur-
> view or control of particular individuals.
> —Mark Granovetter, "The Strength of
> Weak Ties"

Social Capital and Ties at Multiple Levels

Much has been written and disputed about the way individuals in "disadvantaged groups" can or cannot generate social capital. We generally discuss how
social capital is generated and maintained by an individual through his or her
personal social networks. We tend to think of this capital at the individual
level—that is, social networks that are made up of ties with other individuals, typically friends and neighbors. Sociologically, *social capital* refers to the
sum of resources linked to a network of friendships or repeated social contacts
(Bourdieu 1986). However, we must expand the scope of social capital and
ties to go beyond the level of the individual. Using James Coleman's (1990)
findings that educational differences are influenced by school type, we see that
social capital goes beyond the individual level and incorporates relationships

with institutions. Mark Granovetter, in "The Strength of Weak Ties" (1973), finds that "numerous well-documented cases show that some working-class communities have mobilized quite successfully against comparable or lesser threats" (1373). His work goes a step further by providing a way to see social ties as a bridge between individuals (microlevel) and societal (macrolevel) interactions; he ties individuals to communities. Granovetter's work deeply explores why "some communities organize for common goals easily and effectively whereas others seem unable to mobilize resources, even against dire threats" (1373). Granovetter suggests the need for "a sharper analytical tool, [an] examination of the network of ties comprising a community to see whether aspects of its structure might facilitate or block organization" of capital/ties (1373). At the time, the role of a community in relation to the generation of social ties created great debate that led to two views about the respective weight of individual social networks versus more macro forces in effecting or not effecting neighborhood change. While Granovetter felt that ties were key, others, such as Herbert Gans, believed larger social structure prohibited change.

In the 1980s, a gerontologist, Jaber Gubrium, suggested that families are "organizationally embedded" in agencies, meaning the way an organization "sees" or "talks" about a family, or puts the family in a certain context, affects the family group itself. This concept of embedded families in organizations was picked up in Mario Luis Small's book *Unanticipated Gains: Origins of Network Inequality in Everyday Life* (2009). Small looks at how social ties are generated at daycare centers in terms of whether or not the mothers can use their social ties at the center to make connections at other organizations/agencies. His approach takes Coleman's and Granovetter's definitions of social capital and offers us more expansive sociological directions. His neighborhood hypothesis suggests that "people in poor neighborhoods do not always do worse" in terms of building capital, but the neighborhood's level of advantage or disadvantage is very closely tied to the group's ability to use the capital generated (195–196). Small combines individual social capital with groups' links to organizations. Small's theory can serve as a bridge or way to examine how the accumulation of inequality across the life course affects the ability to build social capital at the individual and institutional levels.[1] In his multimethod examination of centers in a variety of social class settings, Small examines social capital building among perceived "underprivileged groups" to learn which organizational structures allow specific class groups to build better capital.[2] He focuses on the way capital is also embedded in relationships between particular institutional structures, rather than examining only social exchanges among individuals. For example, a centergoer's capital is not limited to personal relationships with others at the center; there are ties to other centers in the area and other organizations, such as the DFTA.

Here, in the case of the organizational embeddedness perspective, we can more closely separate out attempts by the individual to generate capital or challenge adversity while also taking into account the unique role of organizations in either supporting or challenging an individual's efforts. The multilevel process provides greater flexibility in assessing roles—so that we do not automatically associate lower social class with less individual agency and capital. The focus on a larger perspective lets us recognize the way institutional constraints can affect individual efforts at lessening inequality, achieving resilience, and generating "good" social capital. By deeply focusing on one case with many principle actors, we can disentangle the multiple and complex levels at which both equality and inequality are simultaneously operating.

Not all capital generated by a person's interaction with an organization is positive. As Small states, "Not all centers broker social and organizational ties in equal measure . . . so that social capital is directly tied to institutional practices of an organization that a person routinely participates in" (2009, 177). Small suggests we change the way we look at an organization's function or purpose. A senior center does more than feed and provide services for seniors. Small sees the need for the multiple exchange of "extra" information to call attention to larger network dynamics that are often ignored in the study of social inequality (186).

Organizationally embedded ties can become a form of "negative social capital." Small stresses the conflict or coercion placed upon the individual by an organization: "Organizationally embedded networks can be captured under the rubric of institutional coercion, by which people are forced, for the good of the organization and its members, to forgo at least some rudimentary rights such as the right to refuse to represent the organization or the right to privacy about contact information" (188). Specifically, Small describes three ways in which being embedded in an organization can negatively affect a member. First, the requirements of the organization can reduce the amount of free time and leisure for members. Second, the demands of membership may be coercive or force members into behaviors. And third, organizational membership places members into relationships with other third-party institutions or organizations that may be unfamiliar to the member.

Before I apply the organizational embeddedness perspective to the study at hand, let me provide a quick critique of Small's concept. Its strengths are that this perspective makes social capital institutional. For my study, this level of scale allows the incorporation of exchanges between organizations such as the center, its boards, building owners, DFTA, and real estate companies. Small sees society as a network of linked organizations (or public issues rather than merely personal troubles).[3] His "unanticipated gains" are the benefits an individual experiences while being a part of the organization. But critics have found several gaps in this organizational embedded perspective. Some say that a guide to the ways organizations can practically broker social capital in everyday life is missing (Crouse-Dick 2010). In his review, Steven Marcum (2010) discerns in Small's work a lack of emphasis on the potential negative capital built by individuals' interaction with organizations. Marcum argues that Small, by focusing on the positives of social capital theory, misses some "unanticipated losses" for his participants (349).

Brokering Ties: Insider or Outsider, Actor or Institution Driven, Coercion, and Weak Ties

Brokerage, in its most basic terms, is the way a third party links two other parties to each other. The joining of the two parties is commonly beneficial but can also have negative consequences. Paradoxically, there is some strength to be found in "weak ties" linking individuals (Granovetter 1973). In a 2012 meta-analysis, sociologists Katherine Stovel and Lynette Shaw define *brokerage* as "the process of connecting actors in systems of social, economic, or political relations in order to facilitate access to valued resources" (141). While brokerage has been studied heavily in other fields, Stovel and Shaw make a call for brokerage study to have a "prominent place in the [current] sociological canon" because of its dual focus on micro and macro scale (140).

Ronald Burt's *Neighborhood Networks* (2010) is one such earlier brokerage work. Burt describes his concepts of outside and insider brokerage.[1] Here, I adapt Burt's usage of *inside brokerage* to refer to those who have achieved credibility and membership within a group or relationship. In my adapted analysis, being an insider can be both positive (membership has its privileges) and negative (as a form of social control or limitation). Being an insider is positive, as insiders have "tacit knowledge" or are in "the tribe," as Burt explains. Insiders have a great deal of knowledge about the organization and other members. Insiders also have some limiting traits. They may lack knowledge of the outside world beyond their view of their particular setting or are "overprotected." Their experiences can be restricted to their social world as they are wary of outsiders, labeled as "other." Burt sees outsiders as locked out, barred, or excluded from a group or relationship; they are viewed with skepticism and do not readily get trust or respect. In my analysis, outsiders, who do not feel a part of the group, can also have what I will call "outsider advantage." This is the ability to leave an organization to find more favorable circumstances for themselves.[5]

Small takes brokerage up a notch by examining the brokerage of organizational ties (or those relationships between institutions). This organizational element is essential because, according to Small, "the brokerage of organizational ties arises from the highly bureaucratic nature of contemporary society, where exchanging goods and resources constitute much of what businesses, government agencies, and nonprofit organizations do" (2009, 185). The relationship between these institutions and organizations can also generate supportive, coercive, or mixed results for an individual member of the organization.

So, for Small, brokerage is the way organizations link individuals to other individuals, organizations, or resources they contain (2009, 19). He outlines two types: actor driven and institution driven. Actor-driven brokerage occurs when an individual in an organization links another individual in that organization to resources. Institution-driven brokerage occurs when two institutions share resources. Institutional brokerage occurs through processes of referrals and collaboration. Small suggests that brokerage can occur purposively during a formal, institutional, or organization-sponsored activity. Or brokerage may occur nonpurposively, meaning ties or good outcomes may develop from just being in regular or predictable contact with the other organization.

A Framework for the Center's Social Capital and Social Ties

Organizational embeddedness operates at three levels: micro, meso, and macro. At each level, the brokerage of capital can be leveraged as an insider, outsider, or mixture of the two types. Either an actor or an institution can initiate or drive the brokerage. We can think of the relationship between organizations at each of the three levels as having some type or quality of organizational match.[6] This match is critical in assessing the way capital moves between the three levels. This framework allows for a more complex analysis of the way center members' microlevel activities at building (social, political, and economic) capital were halted. Also, the framework applies to why the center closed despite varying mesolevel, and some macrolevel, network affiliations that produced promised political and financial support.

In this model, organizations can have positive, negative, or neutral individual brokerage of social ties with other organizations across several levels of interaction. We can trace the trail of social-capital building and halting in the center-closure process at the micro, meso, and macro levels. Relationships between varying parties on each level can be classified as brokering positive, negative, or mixed/neutral capital and linkages.

Microlevel Relationships: Types of Organizational Embeddedness between Individuals and the Center

As you may recall, in the halcyon days of the center, members reaped the benefits of membership and their relationship to the center as an institution. Through almost daily contacts, regular members reported many positive aspects of membership. Center regulars felt that the activities the center offered or that they created enhanced their experiences and enriched their lives. Member-initiated activities like the health-based conversation groups, bookmobile/reading library, and specialty dances (such as a past Hawaiian-themed luau) wedded the centergoers to the center. The regular members felt that the center trips offered them opportunities they would not have otherwise enjoyed.

Members were also proud of the individual programs they created or ran within the center. Several key examples come to mind. Lily, seventy-three, was a homemaker whose children and grandchildren live with her. She held a health group about "good" numbers for health problems such as high blood pressure and diabetes. Joe, the sixty-two-year-old "baby" of the center, as he stated, wanted to enliven an "Alert and Alive" group. Victoria, seventy-four, an active member of the center board and someone who took pride in being an organizer of center trips and parties, talked openly about her accomplishments in battling to have milk with meals in cartons (not cups) for take-home and later use. Some felt a sense of agency in their roles as center volunteers and helping others (such as "letting the Mormon boys help with meals," "spending time with college students," teaching grammar school pen pals how to read and write, and providing a worksite for those on Workfare). Others felt they created the vital aspects of the center such as the summer vegetable garden and newly expanded food pantry.

A theme expressed early on in my first visit in 2008 by Victoria was that she ran a thrift table and raised a lot of money for the center, just as Karen, a seventy-three-year-old woman with macular degeneration and lupus, legally blind, talked about the way she "used her blindness" to get merchants to donate better prizes at bingo. Karen stated, "I go grubbing with my dark glasses and my cane, and we got a twenty-five-dollar gift certificate to buy snacks for the party." Lily and other regular volunteers also stressed that their volunteerism was a "huge money saver" for the center.

The center staff also recognized and commented on the ability of centergoers to generate capital, even within their modest social class status. The center, as an institution, was responsive to members' needs. The most-talked-about example was the switch from serving milk in a cup back to the preferred carton form. Center attendees preferred this because they could take away the milk for use at home on the weekend. A board member and thrift table starter related this story of her "win" to me with great pride. The center was seen as expansive and giving reciprocity to its members. Center staff provided referrals to utility reductions and van rides home at the end of the day. The center also linked members to local politicians through events like the thirty-sixth and thirty-seventh anniversaries of the center or art shows. An offshoot of the positive relationship between the center and its members was the organic effort by members to raise enough monies to keep the center open an additional fourteen days during the on-again-off-again closure process—during June to July 2010.

Bingo and menu center members benefited from dances (like Maria, who loved to dance), hot meals (for recent divorcees, like Jack), bingo (like the

Teresa, Joan, and Linda group) or a place to bring your brother (like Joe). Even those who saw themselves as nonattendees, who would rather engage in non-center-based activities, and the baby boomer activists also ate an occasional meal at the center or partook of the camaraderie of centergoers. Yet, the nonattendees and boomers saw the benefits of membership—mostly for others—and not for themselves.

Being a center member also had negative effects on individuals—a "cost" for membership. With the loss of two directors (one through a death in 2006) and key staff in later years and with a final, new director, center members felt the quality and variety of center activities (bad trips, ever-shrinking staff, and poor catered food) to be slipping. As members, they wanted to remain a part of the organization they had come to grow in and love but also felt this tie as binding. Some members were on the center's board and felt they should remain loyal to it—even after the board voided its agreement with the center's landlord, and "things went downhill fast."

Center members "held on" with a new, "less mingling" director and the loss of a social worker who could complete their benefit forms. Attendees tolerated ongoing construction and new security cameras. They felt they needed to keep "the [attendance] numbers up" and get to City Hall "to advocate," even though, in some cases (like Jack's), their own health was poor. Karen felt they must remain loyal "even though things were falling apart." Local activists felt obliged to aid them, occasionally eating the "bad food" of "poor nutritional content" at the center despite what they felt was an almost unstoppable political machine. Less frequent members kept trying to join in despite the stagnant activities. These obligations to the place kept members hopeful (despite rumors of mismanagement and DFTA's contract removal) that the closed center would reopen in October 2010.

A member of the closed center interrupted a conversation I was having with another center director of a catchment center for the relocated members. He offered his version of how the center went downhill: "I was on the board of directors. It just didn't go right. What more can I say? We'll talk." His implication of wanting to share some secret information with me about the closure of his former center in the presence of this center's director made the three of us laugh. He then made a comparison between the prior director to the current director: "But I tell you, we got a wonderful director here. The whole staff; they do their job, they do it well. They stayed open for so many years. And it's run very efficiently. No, it's not run like change this, change that, change this. No, it's run like it should be run, on a dime. Trust me. Like I said, I'm not bragging; I was on the board for a long time. They asked me three times; twice I refused. But I went on a third time because it was sliding down. But this place is excellent. She's excellent. Very happy to be here. I don't like lying and bribing and all of that. No, she's here. This place

Table 4
Levels of the Center's Organizational Embeddedness

	Positive	Negative	Neutral/mixed
Micro (individuals at center)	Member-created activities supported Original staff	Changing membership and activities Staff changes/loss	Initial interactions with the new tenant
Meso (center-specific)	Local media DFTA in earlier years Direct contact with borough president and City Council Many local/borough-based politicians	Building's landlord/holding company Center board Local real estate market and developers	DFTA/City Council reducing funds Department of Energy's solar panels Mayor's direct center visit and contact Neighboring-borough organizations
Macro (larger, policy based)	NCOA/NISC CSCS DFTA, NYAM, and Mayor's Age-Friendly NYC report Brookdale Initiatives National media NYS Office of Aging hearings City Council speaker	Some national pro-Boomer media State diversion of Title XX monies DFTA's modernization and innovative centers Mayor's Health Aging model OAA reauthorization delays	NYAM's Age-Friendly NYC collaboration used to modernize centers DFTA's continued modernization and Innovative centers OAA reauthorization

NOTE: The assigned values (positive, negative, or neutral/mixed) do not apply to the individual groups or organizations themselves. The positive, negative, or neutral/mixed assessments refer to the relationship that each item listed had to the center used as a case study in this book.

is here because it's been run right. It's simple, the proof is in the pudding. That's it."

Interestingly, center member embeddedness also produced some mixed results. Centergoers could have worked to secure a place in the new tenant's organization. The new tenant had more money and resources, so the experience could have been that of socioeconomic assent, or a collective increase in circumstances for all, as a product of "gentrification" by the new organization. But duty to the center meant holding on to see if the new organization would, indeed, leave some room in the basement for the center. So, in this case, the members' loyalty led to a negative outcome for themselves and the senior center setting. See table 4 for a complete list of centergoers' relationships at the micro, meso, and macro levels and their impact on center social capital and ties.

Mesolevel Relationships: Types of Organizational Embeddedness between the Center and Other Local Organizations

Not only do individuals have relationships to organizations, but organizations can have relationships with other organizations. Now we will focus on the relationship of the senior center, as an organization, with other local, small organizations. Smaller organizations are those that have direct impact on or relationships with the center at the level of the borough. In this case, the borough is Queens. One of the greatest allies of this center was the borough-level media. News articles gave this center distinction early on as one of the "best centers in Queens" in 2002 and covered awards and praise for its cooking and Christmas meal provisions in 2006 and again in 2009. Each thirty-year-plus anniversary received press coverage with photos in the local paper of politicians in attendance. The local paper covered the possible center expansion and later decisions about designating areas of the community as historic landmarks.

Local media also printed the unofficially released hit list, the list of potential closures (not this center) as mostly negative with headlines like "Seniors Suffer: Nine Senior Citizens Centers Shut Down" (Davis 2010). The role of the local media was most vividly in play as the decline of the center began. Community papers ran headlines like "Center Days Are Numbered" and cast blame on DFTA and the holding company. Editorials blasted those wanting to close the center and, using the age-old argument, asked why we placed the needs of kids above those of seniors "for tax dollars." Editorials pointed out how "things don't make sense"—why, if the center met two of the three criteria (numbers of meals and full-time status), would it be closed? Authors raised questions about why the center that was meeting its meal quota and that was the "second largest center in the area and continuing to grow" was being targeted. Queens residents wrote poignant letters to the editor to print media and blogs. One writer described how the center had helped her uncle. Another decried the closure process and lashed out: "Shame at how the politicians are trashing the quality of life in the city." Others spoke of how the center had "breathed new life" into a parent. The *Queens Courier* rallied for "free rides for the displaced" and told stories about the successes of politicians in other areas in fighting to keep their centers open.

In a headline that expressed the exhaustion and disgust at the closure process in the center, a paper claimed, "Seniors Screwed." The story covered the whole political debacle and the director's still believing that the center would reopen in October. In reality, of course, it would not. Two other local papers joined in the crusade and reported the rise-and-fall saga. A local paper reported the sale of the center to its new owner and mentioned the new tenant, the youth organization. And in 2013, a community newspaper announced events with the new tenant, and politicians were featured in photos accompanying the new stories.

DFTA can also be listed as an early supporter and ally of this center because they provided a contract and services for several decades. DFTA also gave this center a "vitality center" and a Hunger Award in 2006. DFTA, in fact, supported the center until its new "mismanagement criteria" for closures came into play. The Queens Borough President's Office and the New York City Council had a long history of funding and supporting this center with programs and activities. Politicians at many levels (state representatives, Assemblypersons, City Council members, etc.) directly tried to aid the center in its struggle to stay open. For example, Assemblywoman Catherine Nolan of Queens released a statement on her website about the changes: "While I am intrigued by the streamlining goals of the DFTA Healthy Aging Centers proposal, I believe we should move forward with caution."

For their show of support, the center had given many politicians civic pride awards, beginning in 2009—for projects such as City Council members' getting almost seven hundred thousand dollars for repairs and programming in 2009—and finding even more monies. City Council members were lauded as "heroes" in headlines such as "Seniors Win Big" and "Council Member Saves the Center from Shutdown." Council members were praised, while the center's holding company was seen as the "bad guy." An assemblyman for the borough reported he was touched by the sad case of this center's closure in early 2011.

There were also plenty of negative embedded relationships that the senior center had with other institutions and organizations. The entanglement of the senior center with the two organizations, by many accounts, sealed its fate. The center's board and its holding company each had a difficult and complicated relationship with the center. The board, which included center members and a local realtor as its chair, would be accused by some of mismanagement (lack of rent paying) and misdirection (or ulterior motives with the president having role conflict as a realtor in the neighborhood). Advocates said the center's board was a "dummy/fake/phony board" intentionally composed of people unaware of the bigger picture. It would be the center's board that officially closed the center on July 30, 2010. The center's board president (in October 2011) would cast blame on the new tenants for "messing up" and not letting the center back in. The holding company that owned the center during the closure process is listed on some websites as "dissolved in 2013," since there were no corporate tax returns filed for three years. A new owner was listed on New York City tax records in November 2011.

Also, the real estate market and developers acted as a roadblock for the center. As the potential sales cost of the center's physical building rose in value, at one point to $1.8 million, the center became a less viable tenant in an open real estate market. The new tenant also had allegedly promised a place for the senior center in its basement, although this turned out not to be the case.

The center also maintained a complicated and enmeshed relationship with the City Council and DFTA. As these organizations provided critically needed monies and services for the center, its reliance on their continued support at the same or increased level was tenuous and nerve-wracking. For example, though the City Council was a supporter, at points, such as in 2007, center renovations were dropped because of cuts in the capital budget. As DFTA experienced state cutbacks and its modernization and innovation programs were carried out, DFTA terminated its contract with the center on June 30, 2010. DFTA did not reinstate its contract with the center even after holding company and rent issues were supposedly resolved in July 2010.

Some organizational linkages neither helped nor harmed the center. The center partnered with the Department of Energy to install solar panels in 2010 with the help of local politicians and the holding corporation. The panels could have, ultimately, saved money but also took the time and efforts of the center. Some snafus in related organizations could have cast a negative light on the senior center by distant association. For example, in September, an elder-focused organization with a similar name in the neighboring borough of Brooklyn fell under investigation by the city for serious budgeting issues. A senator also posted what seemed to be an out-of-the-blue listing for an expansion project with a name very closely related to that of the center.

At the meso level, the mayor had mostly tangential relationships with this center. In 2006, he used it as a site for a photo opportunity for his good deed of delivering holiday meals to the homebound.[7] A center director gave the mayor a token gift as the mayor announced his support for landmark status for an area within the center's community district in 2008. In the same vein, a local realtor had a complicated relationship with the center. At first, the relationship was positive, as the realtor was inducted as president of the center's board.[8] But the board could not keep the center afloat. Although not happy about the closure process, one other senior center in the area embraced displaced members with a welcoming ceremony.

Macrolevel Relationships: Types of Organizational Embeddedness between the Center and Larger Organizations

The center had embedded relationships with organizations much larger than itself in terms of weight, power, and class. While these organizations directly influenced events at the center and the center's existence, the relationship was mostly unidirectional—the center had little direct effect upon these greater entities. Organizations and other factors at this level included center advocacy groups, the larger national media, DFTA's policies, mayoral- or city-level policies, state-based politicians and state policies, the Administration on Aging, and the OAA. These larger organizations had three types of relationships with the center: positive, negative, and mixed/neutral.

Centers had huge advocates at the city and national levels. Nationally, the nonprofit National Institute of Senior Centers (NISC, part of NCOA) organizationally rallied to protect and support centers, while CSCS's advocacy focused on the New York City area. NISC, as suggested by its name, has been a proponent of senior centers. Its support ranges from the production of senior center facts sheets to that of legislation briefs. During the hardships of center closings in fall 2011 and OAA reauthorization, NCOA and NISC's issue brief "Older Americans Act Reauthorization: Multipurpose Senior Centers for Positive Aging" argued for the necessity of neighborhood centers and Aging and Disability Resource Centers as one-stop-shop service points for elders. NCOA did not dismiss charter or innovative models. In fall 2012, the organization embraced those changes, as well, calling for centers to rebrand and change with the times and reach more isolated persons. NCOA set policy priorities for the 113th Congress (2013–2014) and created an online form for centers to record the effects of the sequester on them in March 2013. NISC provided resources for members and also accredited centers, which could improve their stability and solvency. NCOA and NISC not only advocated for senior centers but also provided a platform where elders could advocate for themselves (at the center and legislative levels) and tell their own stories about how changes in laws and funding directly affect their individual centers.

Taking up the cause of centers in New York City is CSCS. The leadership of this organization has been an outspoken supporter of senior centers. The nonprofit is best seen as an activist body fighting injustice done to centers. The titles of its reports and other texts reflect its mission: *Hunger Hurts* (2007), *More with Less Is Impossible* (2010a), "The Shoe Drops" (2010b), *21st Century Senior Centers: Changing the Conversation* (2010c). This group is not afraid of telling it like it is using facts and strong visual images. CSCS produced an infographic, "How Age-Friendly Is NYC?" (n.d.a), which tracks proposed cuts to all age-based services in New York City (with about twenty million dollars in cuts from 2008–2012 for senior centers alone). The infographic predicts an overall spending cut of ninety million dollars and tracks the losses, using images of an elder with a cane and another in a wheelchair in the last bar of the chart reflecting the most loss.

CSCS advocates on multiple levels. In my January 2013 conversation with Bobbie Sackman, the director of public policy, she told me, "We do a lot of advocacy; [we are] known for it. What's good about it is that this is how seniors have their own voice in their future. This is our grassroots base." Sackman gave an example of CSCS's role in fighting an initial RFP and closure process for all centers: "There was this proposed Title XX cut that would have closed 105 senior centers in NYC that came from the state. Instead of waiting for the third year for the cut to be proposed, get hysterical, and get the money back, we did a letter-writing campaign to the governor, to Cuomo, 16,642 letters— I'll never forget the number—letters in English, Spanish, and Chinese, and he didn't put the cut in the budget." In another instance, Sackman spoke about "even [going] up to the state legislature because federal funds come through the state Office for Aging down to the city. We wanted anybody in that conversation we could get to try to help us. A bunch of political things came at the same time, but . . . it's a clear case that had we not been doing advocacy, we wouldn't have been there at the moment."

CSCS has a senior Activator program and commitment to develop it further. Sackman explained that for older New Yorkers, "we want them to know what the city budget process is, and people are interested. When we first started the Activator program, which is in its beginning stages, we got a teeny tiny grant of about five thousand dollars [from a family foundation]. . . . When we first brought together that first group of activators, a lot of them turned out to be people active in their church, active local civic groups, or active in their senior centers, but you need to give them an organization and a mechanism to fight City Hall. You can't just say, 'Go fight City Hall.' So we're trying to give them training and a mechanism and support to fight City Hall." Igal Jellinek, the executive director, added that the program received funding from the City Council, to which Sackman replied, "I think that they're interested to see seniors speak for themselves."

Sackman explained the history of elder-driven advocacy campaigns: "We got off to a beginning start back in spring of 2012 when we trained twelve or fifteen older adults from senior centers across the city how to do advocacy and understand the city and state budget process. And they joined us, and one spoke at a public hearing. They spoke at press conferences we do at City Hall. We do our City Hall Advocacy Day; we've done that for seventeen years now. We set up delegations; seniors meet with their council members. They would be part of those delegations." Jellinek wants to create a leadership institute that "deals with staff training" while most are focused at the center-accreditation level. He wants to further empower the volunteer organizers in senior centers to use the "human assets" available and "something we're gonna fight for . . . where you can mobilize volunteers in a much bigger way. . . . The Older Americans Act says [older persons] should do advocacy."

CSCS leadership also discussed some advocacy struggles. Sackman talked about "advocating for social workers in senior centers for probably fifteen years. We had actually won about three and a half million dollars or something through City Council in June of 2001. And so DFTA was figuring out how to spend this money, and what the plan was. And then 9/11 happened, and the money disappeared overnight—gone." In 2013, she reflected, "Now we're terrified of what's going to happen on the federal level with Title XX. We don't win everything. We've lost millions of dollars in the last five years from DFTA, almost a third of their city budget. So I'm not pretending; we've lost a lot. But we've also been able, I think, to not only stem the cuts; we helped put the senior centers and other senior services on the map because we've made it so visible. The way you do that is with senior centers. I mean, you can't organize homeless people to come out; you can't organize homebound people to come out. You organize senior centers."

The New York Academy of Medicine's Age-Friendly NYC initiative (with the mayor and City Council) and the Brookdale Demonstration Initiative in Healthy Aging both supported centers and validated their role in the daily lives of elders. Each initiative produced models or toolkits to make communities age friendly or supportive of elder health programs. For the center, DFTA, and the mayor, NYAM had some up times with the center-supportive, age-friendly initiative.

I was surprised to find that trends in local media were echoed in the national media, which were almost unanimously in support of senior centers. The greatest risk a newspaper took was a 2010 *New York Times City Room* blog post that released the full list of the fifty shuttered centers on its website. The list was reported as leaked from a City Council meeting. This hit list of sorts, directly naming centers, gave those named the power to take early action on their behalf. It helped the center in this book to an extent, as it was not on the hit list. The "deadly cuts" began to gain speed online.

The *New York Nonprofit Press* (which claims in its About Us link that it is "the only newspaper devoted exclusively to the information needs of the greater metropolitan nonprofit human services community") provided centers with more details online about why and under what category each was closing. Later articles detailed looming financial cuts and promoted the efforts of senior center advocacy groups, collected together as the Don't Cut the Core Coalition. The *NY1* blog story "105 Senior Centers Slated to Close" (2011b) elicited a flood of readers' comments all favoring the center-grown advocacy movement. Then, protests by elders and politicians against the center cuts and closures drew print and online media support. *NY1, CBS New York*, and the New York Beat website covered the anticlosure City Hall rallies. In fact, in addition to a CBS New York (2011) article covering the rally at City Hall to protest center budget cuts, a second article told a heroic tale of the efforts of another Queens center to stay open. The *Huffington Post*'s political blog ran a story, "Bloomberg Shuttering Lifesaving Senior Centers" (Torres 2010). Only one media outlet mentioned the center in this study by name. A NYC Independent Budget Office blog (*IBO Web Blog*) posted an article about the passing of centers that drew attention to the plight of this particular center (delayed funding and DFTA contacts) by name.[9] The article blamed the delay in funding ("funds took awhile to reach the centers") as the main source of this center's closure and suggested that the "funding for [this center] was subsequently redirected by the Council to 12 different agencies serving seniors."

The center had more positive, rooted relationships with major institutions. In a supportive context, in 2008, the director of the New York State Office of the Aging, Michael Burgess, made efforts to ensure that "senior centers retain[ed] access to essential supports during the aging services modernization initiative in NYC." In late 2010, the New York State Assembly's Standing Committees on Aging and Children and Families held another hearing, "Senior Centers: Funding, Challenges, and Value to the Community," to evaluate the center funding cuts and other related challenges across communities.

Many City Council elected officials also rallied arm in arm with elders in the Save Our Centers campaign—literally on the steps of City Hall. Politicians such as City Council Speaker (and potential mayoral candidate) Christine Quinn remained a staunch supporter of keeping all centers open and used her role to protect them. She openly challenged the mayor's closure plan and wanted to place it, as you may recall, "in the garbage can." During the closure process in 2011, the council was a strong ally. It helped to keep centers opened and was proud of its success in keeping seventeen centers (on the closure list) running. The council raised pointed questions, such as, Why, if so many centers were in a bad state of management, were they allowed to stay open without guidance from DFTA about how to resolve these issues? The council stated its position that all centers should remain open and "fixed."

Then, DFTA along with the mayor undertook the modernization plan for centers—proposed to improve neighborhood centers and create innovative ones. When Lilliam Barrios-Paoli took over as DFTA commissioner from Edwin Méndez-Santiago, she extended the contracts for all existing centers for one year while the center-model transitions were planned and studied. DFTA brought trained artists in residence to centers as well as fresh food via farmers market visits. DFTA provided resources for existing centers and research on ways that "successful" centers operated. Also, DFTA called for a NORC proposal in 2012, which could include neighborhood centers in the model.

While organizations' affiliation helped the center, ultimately some affiliations were detrimental to the center's existence. Although the press overwhelmingly supported existing centers, some stories covered rebranding, such as "Its Appeal Slipping, the Senior Center Steps Livelier" (Gross 2008), from the *New York Times*. Such stories presented existing centers as artifacts in need of a complete overhaul.

Federal and state organizations and policies also left existing centers in this limbo state. In 2012, the Administration on Aging asked people to write in about how they saw priorities of the OAA reauthorization. Funding for centers was not on the top ten list; only congregate meals made that cut. The decision on the part of state lawmakers to divert Title XX monies (such as those in the fiscal 2010–2011 state executive budget) to alleviate state funding for adult protective and domestic violence costs was the impetus for the center closures. The state's decision to use federal funding for noncenter programs sealed the fate of many centers. DFTA picked up the relationships to centers inherited by the state's policies. DFTA also had some policies before the states' Title XX monies decision that would come to be detrimental to centers.

DFTA policy changes also had a negative impact upon centers. An early 2007 mandate converted centers' case management services through an RFP process—which left many centers and directors at a loss to compete for service contracts. The modernization-plan concept, begun by Commissioner Méndez-Santiago, was to be a community-specific way to match services to specific needs of communities. But this focus changed over the terms of Commissioners Méndez-Santiago and Barrios-Paoli to support the mayor's focus on healthy aging and a more "active" aging lifestyle. These "15–30 [new] comprehensive wellness centers" would have an RFP process and (intended or not) shut down neighborhood centers. This was part of the downward spiral for some centers, as the fifty-plus center closures were determined based on "fewest meals, fewest hours," and a new criterion: "most management/maintenance problems." New procurement procedures were released, and the eight, then ten, innovative centers sprang up after the neighborhood centers closed. The new neighborhood centers' requirements also fell into place. These centers needed to have "a consistent set of services, including a minimum of 60 meals per day, an average daily attendance of 75 persons, and a required health and wellness component." In November 2012, 234 (of 249) neighborhood centers were prequalified to provide senior center services on the DFTA website.

It would be impossible to look at the way DFTA changes affected centers without including policy changes handed down by the mayor and the Mayor's Office. Early reports in 2008 cited conflict between Mayor Bloomberg and Deputy Mayor Linda Gibbs about when and whether this modernization plan should roll forward. This go-forward-or-not decision, along with the center-consolidation idea, was tossed around for a while as DFTA commissioners changed. The mayor was in office for the transition of DFTA's commissioners. According to the *New York Times,* this transition occurred after a lawsuit against a prior commissioner cost DFTA $225,000 to settle.[10] DFTA was the agency responsible for creating the closure list and selecting centers on it, with, of course, the mayor's approval.

Some senior center directors in the field see these health and wellness models as "bad" for current members. A local director explained to me why the changes are seen as negative: "Mr. Bloomberg hates them playing cards, and he hates them doing board games, and he hates them playing bingo. He despises bingo. I don't like bingo myself. Okay? But it's in there for them. It's not in there for me. If it was for me, I'd have music and there'd be dancing every day. Do what I like to do. But that's not what they want to do."

In early 2011, a preliminary Mayor's Management Report for DFTA reported on the twenty-five million dollars redirected by the state from the operational costs of senior centers. This redirection would "severely cripple the City's senior center network, forcing DFTA to close 105 centers, or approximately 40 percent of the current system. . . . DFTA estimates that 7,800 seniors will be affected by the citywide closures, many of whom will be left without services entirely." This estimate was reduced to about fifty centers actually closing.

I would also classify a third type of embedded relationship between the center and larger organizations as neutral or mixed in nature—for example, the relationship of the center to its place in the OAA reauthorization effort. Senator Bernie Sanders of Vermont has power over how the legislation reads and supports senior centers. He lists the "modernized senior centers and community planning for an aging population" as one of the nine key areas of interest on his website. While this can be a good thing for centers, the full plan is not clear and could involve additional closures. The innovative-center models of DFTA can be placed in the neutral category. I see these as a "wait to be seen" concept in terms of their relationship to and coexistence with neighborhood centers, since the concept of modernization or chartering, as created, has been implemented differently. Also implemented differently from how they were conceived are the Age-Friendly NYC guidelines in the way they relate to senior centers.

The Role of Organizational Embeddedness in Generating Negative Social Capital

Even with the generation of some positive social capital by the center's members, the shuttering occurred because of a lack of organizational embeddedness of the center within local institutions. Independent structural changes (such as financial cuts or board and city political directives) could not be altered by efforts made at the individual level. The organizational nature, in which the capital was generated, prevented the capital from seeing its full use. Centergoers were able to create some "good" social capital via advocacy and fund-raising at both local and county levels—even getting local political figures to intervene as advocates in obtaining grant funding for the center. But the center itself (as the primary organization) was not able to use, sustain, or promote the building of such capital.

The center remained embroiled in a political and power-based tug of war with several entities vying for control: the center board, the center's holding company and landlord, center staff, local elected officials, politicians, non-profit coalitions, and DFTA. All were major stakeholders working out their roles and relationships, in terms of the center, with a lesser regard to the promotion of centergoers' positive capital building. These actions, when taken by organizations, are what Small refers to as "institutional coercion." The senior center did not "broker" or serve to generate capital but rather dispersed it. The center could generate capital from its embedded relationships across the micro, meso, and macro levels. The greatest stops/blocks/barriers were at the levels of relationships between the center and the center's board, the center and realtors, the center and DFTA, and the center and the mayor. Lesser halts were made by the embedded relationships between the center and the state and by the center and the City Council. In addition, some micro halts of the center occurred because of its director changes.

When Insider Brokerage Fails, Do Weak Ties Remain?

We will close the chapter going back to the brokerage principles we began with—noting that all ties are not created equal. The greatest deficit in the ties formed by the center members was that they were insular or insider based (à la Burt's theory). The disconnect between the senior center and its members over time can be heard in the intra-individual changes in narratives about the function of the center in one's daily life and accounts dismissing a lesser quality of goods and services offered. These ties bound the center members to the center and lacked any sustainable insider advantage. The center tried to employ Small's actor-drive ties to political larger and funding sources, but the lack of collaborative resource sharing, or institutional brokerage, prevented the larger-level interventions and interactions needed to keep the center afloat.

Although I do not formally quantify ties, my framework (seen in table 4) provides a visual model and guidelines for the flow and blockage of social ties between key players in the closure process. As Granovetter suggests, the "strength of weak ties" must be evaluated in looking at how individuals join together for neighborhood change. Herbert Gans (1974) found structural issues (such as the lack of political organizing history, residents' reluctance) to be political. He suggested that if institutional support for a change is lacking, the process of change stops. For the center, networks were insular and limited to the within-the-neighborhood level. Most harmful was the fact that centergoers' perceptions about the reality of the center changes and closure threat happened too late in the process. Residents' limited political interest and their social networks being restricted to the neighborhood-only level were indications of the havoc the lack of weak ties can bring. In the next chapter, the case of the center will be put in the context of physical place and space it occupies within the community. The neighborhood becomes an actor now as it relates to spatial dynamics and the gentrification processes at work.

6

Poor Centers

● ●

The Politics of Age and Class
in the Neighborhood Context

> When the theaters of social life are
> the home and the block, passions run
> deep over who owns every crack in the
> sidewalk.
> —Sharon Zukin, "Changing Landscapes
> of Power"

Not only do networks matter, but location and specific neighborhood characteristics influence which centers remain open and which close. Several theories about the role of neighborhood and place, spatial dynamics, gentrification
and displacement, elder empowerment, and social movements suggest that we
must address the social conditions of the neighborhood and people where the
now closed center was housed. Some theorists even argue that the combination, or intersection, of these characteristics (age, race, ethnicity, immigration
groups, socioeconomic status, and location) can make aging in place more of
a "stuck in place" model (Torres-Gil and Lam 2010). Physical space and the
built environment become places of attachment for elders.

My (Poor) Center, My Home,
and My Community: Stuck in Place

While many argue that all older persons want to age in place in their own communities, Fernando Torres-Gil and Brian Hofland (2012) point out that a combination of being a member of the "oldest old, racial/ethnic groups, immigrants, people with disabilities, poor, homeless, and women" can keep older persons who are residents of a community "vulnerable" and "stuck in place" (223). Aging in place is, therefore, detrimental to these groups of elders. Being "stuck in place" reflects limited choice and often absence of these elders' concerns in social policy. Researchers have also discussed the way many age-friendly initiatives suggested as "good" for urban elders—such as AARP's AdvantAge and the National Association of Area Agencies of Aging's Partners for Livable Communities—may not be as beneficial as they first appear. They found little empirical data about aging in place universally; rather, aging in place is based more on class and social network. The one-fit, aging-in-place model was criticized for not acknowledging the necessary financial and social resources needed to do so (Lehning et al. 2013). Faced with fewer economic resources or poor social support, one may indeed remain stuck in place. In fact, older persons in working-class communities with waves of new elder immigrants—even if not completely stuck in place—may be more bound to local institutions for goods and services than more affluent elders, who have more choices in places to go to.

So are centergoers stuck in place in their local community? Some of the changing demographics of the center's community district meet the criteria suggested by Torres-Gil and Lam's (2010) model. In terms of age, the neighborhood that housed the closed center saw some key changes between 2000 and 2010, according to the latest U.S. Census (2010). While those sixty-two years of age and older are about the same, younger age groups (those 50–54, 55–59, and 60–64 years of age) are each rapidly increasing. More of these older persons are now living in family households of the U.S. Census–defined category "other relatives, non-spouse" instead of renting their own places. And those seventy-five and over and eighty-five and over are more likely to live with others than head their own households.

In terms of changes in racial and ethnic groups, this neighborhood is known for its greater diversity of groups compared with those in than many other parts of the borough of Queens. Since the 1980s, and as shown by Geraldine Grant (1981a), studying the "ethnic relations" of this neighborhood, it has contained many new, coexisting, working-class immigrant groups. Further, their countries of origin are changing over time. From the 2000 to 2010 censuses, this community has seen an increase in African American, Asian (Cambodian, Filipino, Malaysian), South Asian (Pakistani, Bangladeshi, Sri Lankan), and

Hispanic (Mexican, South American, Central American, Dominican) groups. In terms of socioeconomic status, CSCS (n.d.b) reported on NCOA's analysis of American Community Survey Data looking at the citywide rankings of those sixty years of age or older and eligible for food stamps in 2011 but underenrolled in that program. An alarming 83 percent of those sixty and over in the closed center's community were underenrolled in the food stamps program. Actually, older persons in this community district were listed in the top five of those underenrolled communities for this public benefit.

A director of a local area center that took in many of the displaced members from the closed center talked about her observations of changes in this community in terms of the shifts in racial, ethnic, and cultural groups she saw with the new members of her center: "We're not one homogeneous group here. We're having a big influx in this neighborhood of Polish and Egyptian seniors. Neighborhoods change. 'Cause a lot of [new immigrant groups] are coming in for the food pantry program. There are a few Egyptian seniors that do come here to the center we've befriended. One gentleman comes here, usually in the morning; he picks up a meal for himself and his wife." The director explained a situation where translation from English to Romanian involved two other center members and three languages: "One time I needed a translator, and I had someone [who] had the English to the Hungarian, and then the Hungarian was translated to the Romanian."

Physical Space and Environmental Barriers in Neighborhoods for Urban Elders

For older persons living in urban settings, we need to look at their use of public space, a topic often omitted when analyzing the relationship of poor elder residents to their neighborhoods (Smith 2009). Researchers Judith Phillips, Nigel Walford, and Ann Hockey suggest there is a physical "insiderness" that makes one very familiar with one's local space. It is a social tie that links the group by having this feeling of "insiderness" within a particular neighborhood built over a lifetime. According to these researchers, people in "deprived neighborhoods" and those "who have few physical, economic and social opportunities other than place around which to focus a sense of belonging" would be more place bound (2012, 79). Those with more wealth "have agency to detach themselves and move to other environments and become attached elsewhere" (79). Yet we cannot simply assume that all elders would simply be attached to their neighborhood in the same way. Early work by Mark La Gory, Russell Ward, and Susan Sherman found living in a neighborhood can be perceived differently by residents. They found that "persons sharing the same spaces do not necessarily occupy the same environmental worlds. The environment is both 'outside' and 'inside'"—so that interpretive value of place must not be lost (1985, 716).

Displacement and Root Shock

What happens when people are removed from a familiar setting within their neighborhoods? According to Mindy Fullilove's concept of "root shock," this loss is akin to a plant being pulled from its roots.[1] Materials posted on the Rootshock.org website (2012) defined *root shock* as something that happens as a result of displacement or "traumatic stress reaction to the loss of some or all of one's emotional ecosystem. . . . [It] can follow natural disaster, development-induced displacement, war, and changes that play out slowly such as those that accompany gentrification." Fullilove herself wrote, "Viewed through the experiences in one place and of one person, we can begin to delineate the kinds of problems caused by the massive structural intervention of urban renewal of American cities. We can identify some of the costs for the community and some of the pain experienced by individuals" (2001, 71).

Even after the center closed, some members were bonded to the physical setting. The success and failure involved in moving to a new center in the area are evident in the words of a director of a nearby center who embraced displaced center members: "[To make the transition easier] we had a welcoming ceremony. We gave them a T-shirt from our center to let them know that they were a member [here] now. We're just trying our best to welcome them. We told them, 'Look, we want you to come here. We don't want you to feel we don't want you here.' And at first, I would say the majority of them did come here. And, then, as aging [and things happen], you know. [They] say they can't walk here or [they say] whatever difficulty it was to get here and it's not that far." With some members from the closed center, it was more than just reestablishing a group of past friends—since some had migrated and established their identities at other area centers. The loss of space was a barrier in their daily lives. The distance from the closed center to the two other closest area centers was about six to ten blocks, with city buses or center van transportation readily available. So for this group, their attachment to the prior familiar setting remained, and they did not make the trip.

Two and a half years after the closing of the center discussed in this book, I visited another local center. There, I met Anne, a former member of the board of directors of the closed center. We sat and talked for a while. She spoke about her longing for the old center space. She explained that despite her account of the closure process ("There was a dispute over back rent, a DFTA investigation; they broke the contract, and the center closed"), the current tenants "kept the basement like it was in the past. I see it for the AARP board meetings." Anne was convinced that the center could very easily be reinstated, and the old crowd could return to the basement to things as usual. I hearken back to the words in the e-mail from the associate director of the senior center in August 2010 that began the introduction to this book. She spoke about how the turbulent center closure process had some long-term detrimental effects upon members. For many elders, even those integrated into other centers now, those effects are still felt.

Gentrification and Socioeconomic Assent

The gentrification of the center's physical setting and its neighborhood are essential components of this book. When discussing gentrification, I use two interpretations of this concept. The first is the formal definition as displacement of the working class by those of a higher social class, as Ruth Glass originally defined it in her 1965 work, *London's Housing Needs*. But, second, this definition of gentrification goes beyond the common application of neighborhoods as the units of gentrification. I apply the concept of gentrification, not at the neighborhood level, but to the case of the elders' center building itself. Political entities and organizations are included as agents of gentrification because, according to Sam Miller, a housing advocate in New York City, "the 'audience' for gentrification is always the poor, people of color, immigrants, working-class seniors, and combinations of the above. The realities of gentrification are usually 'invisible' to those who shape the public's understanding of the issues" (quoted in Slater 2008, 6).

Some see gentrification as a lose-lose situation for older persons. For example, Ana Petrovic describes pre-gentrification elder neglect. She sees the process beginning with older persons living alone, without social ties, being abandoned by businesses and police and living in dilapidated housing among unsafe streets. The presence of older neighborhood residents is masked in several ways, she maintains, for example, through predatory real estate practices. These practices put elders in "grave risk from predators who desire to capitalize on the economic rewards of a future revitalized neighborhood. Despite the elderly's distrust of outsiders, many fall victim to predatory practices" (2007, 13). Lenders and developers will seek elderly residents out, manipulate them and pressure them into selling their homes, and then take their property at unjustifiably low prices. Some developers do not even try to persuade elderly residents. Instead they file code violations that incur expensive repair costs. Petrovic calls gentrification for elders the experience of being "stuck in another's paradise" (15).

Some feel gentrification can have mixed results for elders based on social class. Phyllis Nyden, Emily Edlynn, and Julie Davis (2006) studied elders in a Chicago neighborhood during gentrification and found that the process brings financial strain from developers pressuring elder homeowners to sell. But they also found that the gentrification process varies by social class, so the experience of working-class elders differs from those of older persons in other social classes. It could be that older persons in the higher social classes ultimately benefit from their neighborhood being scaled up.

Clearly, we cannot paint gentrification with a broad brush. While the bulk of literature on gentrification sees the process as having negative or mixed effects on elder community residents, some say it can bring increased benefits to all. Stephen Crystal and Pearl Beck (1992) and, earlier, J. Kevin Eckert (1980) found that single room occupancy residences (SROs) functioned to fill a need for elders living alone in gentrifying communities. Ann Owens (2012) sought to broaden the gentrification model, introducing a typology of socioeconomic status (SES) ascent, or the idea that gentrification improves conditions for everyone in the neighborhood in a sort of ripple effect. According to Owens, poor and immigrant neighborhoods can be places on the ascent track.

Looking at the center, in the same location for over thirty years and a rent payer, albeit sometimes late, but faithful, its plight might be similar to that of an elder homeowner in a gentrifying neighborhood. With the sale of the building and new younger tenants, it was hoped that SES ascent would occur at the center level for its setting and members. Members had hoped, and some felt promised, that they would benefit from the real estate transactions and have a new and improved—even intergenerational—center. As the advocate Sam Miller suggested, noted earlier, the vulnerabilities of this group were exploited, at some level, such as by the center board or the new tenant organization. Each entity would seem to create synergy between the new tenant and the old. But in the building's construction and gentrification process, the elder group's interest was largely lost, "invisible" in the fray, as the negotiations between the building ownership and center board broke down. From the solar panels to the frequent internal construction, the building was upgraded and redesigned for a younger, higher-paying tenant.

Applying to the center site what Petrovic postulates as negatives of neighborhood gentrification, conditions were increasingly poor at the center. Social workers doing case management left, food quality decreased, activities declined, and funding was pulled as management practices shifted. Some predatory real estate practices, as defined by Petrovic, were involved with the center site, as well.[2] Holding companies bought and sold the building. Landlords did not wait for late rent from the center, although since the center's funding was from city sources, delays had been common in the past and had not been a problem before.

Being Authentic

Each neighborhood has a unique sense of character of being "real" and established or rooted. This neighborhood personality or flavor is what sociologist Sharon Zukin calls "authenticity." Authenticity includes a cultural claim to time, space, and place. Gentrification can create a new neighborhood identity or, most often, destroy an existing one. Zukin points out several key agents in the gentrification process. The business class can create a new "landscape" through purchasing power with little regard for associated cultural changes. Then, "politicians want to please local real-estate developers by subsidizing the cost of acquiring inner-city land and providing incentives to start new construction. Caught up in the universal desire for growth, for visible signs of progress that would attract new investment, and for money to finance the police and fire fighters, public schools, streets and all the other things that local governments provide, mayors and city council members [seal] the old neighborhood's doom" (2009, 548). Elected officials are in a particularly sticky situation: "Dependent on both private developers to invest and build, and voters to keep them in office, officials walk a fine line between promising support for housing rights that will help to preserve communities and redevelopment projects that will eliminate or change them. . . . The new priority is 'making markets' . . . rather than helping poor people and small businesses to stay in place, or permitting local communities to veto developers' plans" (549).

Adding to the role of realtors in the process of gentrification is the way groups fight for control of "owning" place. Politicians and business interests place the authentic or bona fide character of a place, such as the center and its place in local neighborhood, at risk (see Zukin 2009). Politicians had to straddle many groups in dealing with senior center issues. Some elected officials at the City Council levels had sought monies to appease the older persons and center director and boards—since these groups were voting constituencies. Yet political actions on behalf of "poor, older people" were weighed against the interests of realtors and the market value of the center itself. Politicians had to deal with complicated relationships with their peers and what their support of the center meant for their own political parties. Political commentary and action by elected officials also influenced their relationship with the mayor and the state—each of which could affect the career and political future of officials. Five of the politicians involved in the center were on the New York City Power 100 list in *City and State* magazine's first list of rankings. These included Assembly people, members of the City Council, and individuals in the Mayor's Office.

Enter the Hipsters: Making "Old" Neighborhoods Cool

Somewhere in the hinterland in the process of neighborhood change are the modern-day hipsters. Although difficult to define, they can be described as counterculture younger persons who mock elements of the larger culture through dress and art. They recognize the irony of being more affluent, often White, consumers in a society while challenging these same materialistic societal norms. They are strongly linked to the arts and independent music (see Gianoulis 2013; Greif 2010).

These hipsters are part of the contested gentrification scene in New York City. Zukin describes the dual nature of the hipster influence in her work. First, this group can redefine neighborhood identity: "In NYC, both the recent gentrification of Harlem and the slightly earlier emergence of Williamsburg, an industrial neighborhood on the Brooklyn waterfront, as an artists' and hipsters' district reflect the importance of new retail entrepreneurs who reshape local character" (2011, 163). On the other hand, these same "loft dwellers and historic townhouse owners, hipsters and gentrifiers lay claim to the bricks and mortar of the historic city, while the media either romanticize or form a collective amnesia about who, and what, has been displaced" (2010, 549). The tension between hipsters' night-life (read bars, clubs, art galleries) and neighborhood residents and businesses has led to code and law changes within Manhattan. Increased code enforcement has sent hipsters looking for less regulated parts of the city (read boroughs like Queens) to live and hold events (Hae 2011).

Early 2012 saw a flurry of articles about hipsters and artists' collectives "invading" this local community. The hipsters sought the low rent, ready transportation, and deregulation of cheap arts spaces in this community. They sought to free the local community "from the shackles of lameness" (Khan 2012, 1). An arts crawl to promote a relationship between the new residents of the center's neighborhood and the existing ones went a bit sour. In an article in the local paper, one resident expressed his dismay about the way hipsters were taking credit for creating a neighborhood almost in a vacuum without acknowledging its current residents: "You keep talking about [this neighborhood] as a place people are coming to but, I mean, people are already here." A Brooklyn art collective was scoping out potential mixed-used rentals in the Queens half of this neighborhood, since the Brooklyn half did not "work" for them anymore. Ultimately, the group returned to the "more hip" Brooklyn. A blog about safety and crime rates in the neighborhood brought more of the ugly gentrification debates back to life. A local neighborhood resident wrote in an online discussion group about this neighborhood in Queens: "If you live in [this neighborhood] you are not part of the gentrification LOL. . . . [This neighborhood] is not ghetto. . . . Maybe to people living in Ohio or Iowa it may be classified as such because of all the Hispanic and working-class European folk, but [this neighborhood] is not a ghetto at all and has a significant working-class white population." Another blogger and original resident expressed dismay at being ostracized in the Brooklyn half of the neighborhood by White hipsters. In addressing the way the hipsters saw themselves as the minority and the original residents as a safety threat, the blogger replied, "Now the tables have turned." A local community leader had expressed concerns early on, when portions of the neighborhood were made a historical district, that there would be an influx of city residents, or what they sarcastically call the "quiche crowd."

The Role and Effect of Neighborhood Context

An early work based on the cumulative inequalities of race, class, and neighborhood in a Queens neighborhood, Steven Gregory's (1998) *Black Corona: Race and the Politics of Place in an Urban Community*, challenges the idea of labeling a group as powerless based on social position alone. In part, Gregory followed the struggle of a community of working-class African Americans to keep services in a local housing development and to prevent a monorail from being built over the Corona community. He found that the struggle of individuals and groups was closely tied to the power dynamics of actors in local organizations and not just the agency of individuals. With a call to examine individual issues in a larger structural context, he concludes his text:

> The struggles of the activists in Black Corona contribute to our understanding of the social processes through which collective identities and shared political commitments are historically constructed, practiced, and disabled across multiple crosscutting hierarchies of power. In their struggles for political power, neighborhood services, and environmental justice, Black activists strove to construct common definitions of need, empowering social identities, and alternative political spaces in which to negotiate interests and allegiance across racial, ethnic, and gender lines. In contrast, their adversaries—sometimes the state, sometimes the capital, and often a complex amalgam of the two—worked to undermine this empowering political identity by employing practices of divide and conquer which constituted and braced disabling and power-evasive constructions of racial, class, and spatial identity. (251–252)

Just as Gregory points out in *Black Corona*, if we fail to taken into account the role of larger organizations and institutions in "undermining," we may be misled about the levels of agency and capital generated by "disadvantaged" groups.

In the case of the center, if we do not account for structural barriers, the role of centergoers in attempting to create change and keep "their" center open will be overlooked. For example, when I last spoke with the associate director, in June 2010, in the midst of the center-closing process, she was working on a thank you page for the center's newsletter that would probably not be published. She told me it was extremely important to write the acknowledgment anyway and "somehow thank the seniors" because "the seniors raised enough funds to keep the center opened an additional fourteen days after it would have closed" [during the rent disputes between the center board and landlord]. The advocacy of the center members and staff, through letters and direct-support requests made to elected officials, generated potential funding promises of over three hundred thousand dollars.

Without an understanding of the continued efforts of individual members to raise funds to keep the center open and rally support from many local and higher-level politicians, the centergoers, as actors, would seem to have been largely absent from the fight or would be merely cast aside in a light of compassionate ageism. The role of centergoers as key players needs to be understood in the neighborhood setting. The setting includes the role of the management company raising rent and even talk of real estate developers wanting to end the DFTA contract so the building could be sold to create "senior apartments"—a controversial move by realtors in the local community. The allocation and support, then subsequent removal of grant funding and DFTA funding, must also be recognized alongside larger forces weighing heavily against the efforts of the older adults. These institutional changes trumped individuals' agency and changed the way centergoers saw the center's future.

We need to account for elders' voices about their roles in the local fights and disputes, such as the battles to keep the center open. As Gregory suggests, the weight of these "advocates" must be measured against the power of "adversaries" (ranging from local entities to federal agencies). All these struggles occur in the local neighborhood context. The center sat in a largely working-class neighborhood of many immigrant groups with older persons increasingly living with relatives and qualifying for public aid. Some interviewed, like Scout, suggested that those favoring selling the center building played on the naïveté of some senior center members on the board who were chosen because they were not truly aware of their roles on it. Without the dual focus of agency on advocate and adversary, elders in poor neighborhoods are labeled as passive with institutions (such as the center) as "caretakers" doing all the work.[1] Elder residents, as center members, see a social order in their space, while outsiders may see the neighborhood and advocacy efforts as disorganized. Elders fought in the struggle as activists and gained some political support and power, but the weight of their adversaries won out in the end.

How Empowerment and Social Movements Challenge Displacement

Much of the work on empowerment and social movements involving older persons tends to focus on the older person as a passive actor receiving the benefit of empowerment through the work of others. There is some call to action and mobilization on the part of baby boomers and senior center directors to influence public policies (Haber 2009; Pardasani and Goldkind 2012). But, to more deeply understand the role of social movements and the impact of organizations in seeking empowerment, we need to look at Neil Fligstein and Doug McAdam's (2011) general theory of strategic action fields. In their theory, in strategic action fields or multiple mesolevel social networks, actors at varying power levels vie for power. There are incumbents who have the current political moxie. There are the challengers, those who lack the privilege of the incumbents. And there are governance units that enforce compliance with existing rules and norms. Further, there is an element of social skill in securing cooperation and mobilizing after reading a situation, as a strategic action. All these events take place in the broader field environment in a complex set of ties. Fligstein and McAdam argue that "actors are using [institutions] to create social positions, advance claims on what is at stake, and leverage their resources to achieve desired outcomes" (49). Exogenous, or outside, shocks, field ruptures, and contention are created by different actors' actions. Episodes of contention occur because of the uncertainty of power within relationships. Finally, settlement occurs with the emergence of new norms in the field. What this theory brings to the table that others lack is the role organizations have in propelling or stopping social movements and power at the interpersonal level.

Why do we care about how social movements work or how they lead to empowerment? Well, at the most basic level, social movements represent "a sustained challenge to power holders in the name of a population living under the jurisdiction of those power holders by means of repeated public displays of that population's worthiness, unity, numbers, and commitment" (Giugni et al. 1999, 257). David Meyer's "How Social Movements Matter" provides several concrete ways that social movements do matter. They influence public policy and strengthen the minority positions within a setting. A strong social movement gets politicians to reconsider their policy positions and can, in some cases, make new organizational elements address issues. Social movements "get diverse voices heard" (2003, 33) or give birth to new nonprofit organizations picking up their cause. Social movements can also "ignite passion" in participants and create a level of activism that surpasses the movement itself. Yet social movements do not exist in a vacuum, nor are all actors equal.

Moving beyond stereotypes of disempowered elders, we have the reality of elder center members with limited generated power. Their social movements as "challengers," those without power or class privilege, lacked the momentum to create leaders or take the passions that arose to another level. No greater movements or organizations were created from the center members' protesting the closure or garnering support from political leaders. Small grassroots efforts did not build into larger coalition building. The center members did not fully link up with resources, such as the CSCS advocacy training programs, or fully use Advocacy Day at City Hall or the letter-writing campaigns. In this case, the "incumbents," particularly the center building's owners and landlords and the mayor's modernization plan, carried the institutional weight over a patchwork of social movement and empowerment efforts by the center members in the fight to keep the doors of the center open. The elders were working against institutions and organizations with stronger embeddedness to each other. The elders lacked the political and financial acumen of larger entities involved in the closure process. Discontented center members proved their "worthiness" and "commitment," as Giugni and colleagues' concepts suggest. But their "unity" as a collective and "commitment" to create a larger social movement were not sufficient.

Seeing how the relationship of the larger institutions and neighborhood organizations can stop the elders' efforts illustrates the role of cumulative disadvantage of these working-class, poor, immigrant, and now elderly groups. Certain institutions (such as the landlord, holding companies, DFTA, the mayor and his modernization plan) created obstacles of which there were many across the elders' life courses. Here, we get to see the consequences of being in these older persons' social positions. In the next chapter, survival strategies for existing neighborhood centers in a time of great demographic change will be explored. Possible center options for current elders and baby boomers in a time of social policy and funding changes will be addressed.

7

Reconceptualizing Centers

• •

The Baby Boomers and Their Perceived Needs

CU@SC
—Joke circulated by e-mail and on the Internet intimating that if baby boomers dared meet at a center, they would use texting shorthand for "See you at the senior center."

We live in a time when many institutions designed for older persons are undergoing great change in this country. Nursing homes, once the untoward offspring of "hospitals and poor houses" because of their clinical and hospital-like nature, now offer a more homelike environment.[1] Transformations in the culture of long-term care have incorporated such concepts as the Eden principles, which encourage elders to interact with persons of all ages and with plants and animals.[2] As such, the Eden principles have given rise to newer Green Houses, where residents live in smaller home settings, and staff and residents work together communally as true teams in shared, give-and-take relationships.[3] Such changes shift the paradigm so that institutions addressing aging are elder centered and responsive to older persons' input.

Just as their counterparts in long-term care undergo a "culture of change," so have senior center models.[4] Centers in New York City are in the midst of this "culture of change" and are becoming quite different from the first senior center, the William Hodson Center, founded in the Bronx in 1943. When asked by a reporter about the future of senior centers in the United States in 2008, John Krout, author of *Senior Centers in America* (1989), simply stated, "If they don't innovate, they will die."[5] In *Prime Time: How Baby Boomers Will Revolutionize Retirement and Transform America*, Marc Freedman predicted that centers of the future would need to undergo dramatic changes. He put his writing on the wall: "Desperately needed is an entity that could speak to these individuals, the 95 percent of the older population who find nothing of interest at the local senior center, who aren't looking for bingo or an adult day care (except for their own parents), and who are unlikely to answer to labels like 'elderly'" (1999, 235). Echoing Freedman's predictions, Scott Bass, in his "Emergence of the Third Age: Toward a Productive Aging Society," notes that "in the future, a society in which older people will have a wide array of options, and many will have the economic means to make choices, questions will arise as to the competitiveness and viability of many of the traditional, local aging organizations, such as the senior center." Even though these centers have become "a national network of community agencies," they face competition from "fitness centers, community colleges, restaurants, bookstores, and dedicated programs such as Elderhostel or lifelong learning centers" (2000, 14).

But innovation and change are not as easy as they sound, since senior centers serve very diverse groups of older persons, such as frail elders, those with disabilities, multiple cohorts of baby boomers, and identity-based groups of older persons. If neighborhood centers close and become fewer in nature, and new centers are geared toward target groups, there should be a plan to meet the needs of older persons living in neighborhoods. Many ideas have been mulled over by public and private organizations, city agencies, businesses, and researchers about potentially better center models.

The changing of center models to meet perceived boomers' needs has generated several larger questions. Why the shift in center types (from, as originally designed, a one-stop shop for all older adults to specialized centers)? Why are these newer models thought of as better? Who really benefits the most from the new models? What does the closure and rebranding of senior centers say about the future of centers and the center movement in the United States? If age- and group-segregated centers emerge, is there a societal cost? And how will all the basic functions of centers, as described in the OAA, be met by other entities in this new center landscape?

The Changing Landscape of Senior Center Models

The model familiar to most when we hear the phrase *senior center* is the multiservice senior center or typical neighborhood center. Multiservice (or multipurpose) centers were created by Title V of the 1973 Comprehensive Services Amendment of the OAA and funded beginning in 1978. Multiservice senior centers have been said to provide "the most diversified services available to the elderly" (Gelfand 2006, 145). They were designed to be a "community facility for the organization and provision of a broad spectrum of services, which shall include provision of health (including mental health), social, nutritional, and educational services and the provision of facilities for recreational activities for older individuals" (United States Congress 1965, 8–9).

In 1976, Philip Taietz found that center models were based around one of two major functions: services or social activities. The voluntary organization model had a membership based on common interest in activities. The social agency model drew members more in need of services, such as meals or utility help. Now, the multiservice center model has given way to six of what the NISC's New Models of Senior Centers Taskforce (Pardasani et al. 2009) called "emerging and innovative" center models. They are the community center, wellness, lifelong learning/arts, continuum of care, entrepreneurial, and the café program (Pardasani and Thompson 2012). More recently center models have even become "innovative" (DFTA 2011c). Yet the problem of understanding viable center models and the impetus behind such changes remains.[6]

The first emerging model,[7] the community center model, offers activities and programs for all ages. Programs have to be diverse, have a health center focus, and treat users holistically. These centers do "consistent and intensive program evaluations and needs assessments" (Pardasani et al. 2009, 36). Examples are the Fort Collins Senior Center, Colorado, with a seven-day schedule and community partnerships, and the Manzano Mesa Multi-generational Center in New Mexico, with intergenerational programs and strong community partnerships.[8] The NYC Foster Grandparent Program, begun in 1972, has four hundred grandparents who provide care to five hundred newborns and work in literacy programs with almost two thousand school-aged children in an average year (Evans and Carnegie 2009). The center used as a case study in this book also ran an intergenerational program. The center hosted a pen pal program with a local primary school where center members wrote a letter to a grammar school "pal"—a child whose first language was other than English. The children wrote back, and the final letter was accompanied by a party and picture exchange at the center among the pals.[9]

The second of the six emerging and innovative center categories is the wellness model. These centers focus on health education or improvements that can be measured. Health model centers may also work with area health providers and companies to offer classes/activities on site.[10] The 2012 Program of Excellence Award winners for Nutrition, Fitness and Health's EarthBox Giveaway Program (about container gardening) in Rancho and Lakewood Senior Centers in California and the honorable mention of a Balance and Falls program typified ways to incorporate health models into senior centers. The Via Health Fitness and Enrichment Center in Alabama is an example of a profitable health model and had received an NCOA honorable mention for fund-raising. The center offers groups the ability to market to seniors and brings in $17,968 in profit. A larger-scale health-based program of the Klein JCC Senior Center in Pennsylvania, a hands-on health program, bookstore, and media lab with five experts, including Dr. Andrew Weil, netted a fifty-five-thousand-dollar profit (NCOA 2013a).

The third model mentioned by the task force is the lifelong learning and arts model. Many lifelong learning programs and university-based models also offer services to older persons. Universities of the Third Age (U3A) and other lifelong-learning models mix younger students with older persons and center around education for both groups, improving quality of life and well-being for elders, and having elders as participants in gerontological research.

According to NISC, these centers must "focus on intellectual stimulation, personal growth, and enhance quality of life" and pay attention to "celebrating the creative self" (2009, 40). They must also have cultural and staff competences and multiple delivery sites. The New Center for Learning, in New York, cited by the 2009 NISC task force, combined well-trained instructors with a partnership with the school district for classroom space. NCOA's 2012 program of excellence mentioned several arts-based programs that could fit this bill. Centers offered a workshop with the theme "explore how to fuel a creative life out loud," a "Moving Minds" kinesthetic program, a "Passport around the World" event, and "Living Legacies" performance-based theater.

The continuum of care, or transitions, model, is the fourth of NCOA's models. This model is likely the most familiar to many, since it is the closest to a traditional, multiservice or neighborhood senior center. According to NISC, this model serves as a "focal point for aging in the community" (2009, 41). The transitional aspect refers to the way this model hooks older persons up with services they may need as they age. The center at the focus of this book would also fall under this category. NISC examples are the Avenidas Center, California; the Ann Arundel Senior Center Plus, Maryland; and St. Joseph McAuley Center and Express Care Clinic, Arkansas. These models offer a combination of daily check-in calls, transportation, activities for the frail, and community healthcare tie-ins.

Entrepreneurial centers are the NISC's fifth model as mentioned by Pardasani and Thompson (2012). According to NISC, these centers "focus on philanthropic rather than public funding." They are consumer-driven, business model–based with "strategic management tools for continuous improvement."

One example, the Senior Center Inc., Virginia, generates all its funding equally from private sources and philanthropy, so there is "no funding from the government" (2009, 45).

The café model is the final model defined by the NISC's task force on emerging models. These models of entrepreneurial cafes ("with a retail approach to programs") by private, corporate venders are cropping up. Café models are marketed as a *"proven* way to serve your community, attract more 'younger' older adults, and increase your organization's visibility and reach in your community," with marketing scripted by a well-known company to read, "From the street, a Café Plus could be any attractive and busy restaurant within a community. But look closer—it's more than a café. . . . The concept has been designed to attract active, older adults (50+) and to keep them coming back for more by providing fun, educational, and wellness programs and activities. . . . The experience starts with a cup of coffee—and from there the possibilities are endless. . . . Whether you're building a new facility or updating an existing 'senior center,' the Café Plus model can help improve the quality of service you bring to your community" (Mather LifeWays 2012).

Two model types were not included among but bridge the six emerging model categories by Pardasani and Thompson (2012)—centers without walls and the Next Chapter model. Models of centers without walls, or virtual centers, have existed for quite some time but have changed in delivery method. Using a telephone-based model, earlier centers without walls, such as the first in New York City, DOROT ("for all generations"), had community-dwelling elders picking up the telephone and joining in on live conversation topics ranging from learning language, travel, health, reminiscence, live book readings, or taking university classes. In 2010, as part of a demonstration project, the DFTA partnered with the Microsoft company, the Department of Information Technology and Telecommunications, and the Self-Help Community Services organization to provide six older adult members of the Benjamin Rosenthal Senior Center, in Queens, with touch-screen computers with interactive video technology. In their 2011 annual report, Self-Help Community Services mentions that the demonstration project has been expanded to include interactive museum tours and social visiting by Skype.

Nonprofit groups, such as the Next Chapter, listed in NISC's New Models of Senior Centers in 2009, are working to combine elements of learning, social support with all-aged-networks, and volunteerism, such as the reading-tutoring-based Experience Corps. for retirees (Civic Ventures 2012). Similar programs such as New Horizons, in Brooklyn, and the Transitions Network, in Manhattan, are two Next Chapter programs in different boroughs of New York. New Horizons offers life planning, lifelong learning, volunteering/mentoring, cultural, and recreational and fitness options, while the Transitions Network focuses on new career choices for professional women and creating positive images of women fifty years of age and over.[11]

Beyond "Modernizing": Organizations Evaluate Existing Centers and Suggest Other Ones

Around the same time that center models were winning awards, politicians in New York City were focusing on the rhetoric of decreasing center attendance. Mayor Bloomberg called 44 percent of the 329 pre-closure senior centers "substantially underutilized" and stated they were "losing popularity" in the city (Haber 2009, 288). The decline in senior center participation in New York City was attributed to several factors having to do with activities not on track with centergoers' interests or limited hours and space. Stigma associated with "senior citizens' centers" or elders distancing themselves from current "elderly" participants were also implicated in the decline. To brace for changes, some centers, such as those sponsored by the Catholic Charities and the Self-Help group, merged.[12] Remaining participants at the city's centers were typically women, over seventy, living alone, bilingual, and having higher rates of poverty, chronic health conditions, and functional impairments than nonparticipants (CSCS 2010c; NCOA 2012d; NYAM 2010).

Studies were commissioned to evaluate the state of senior centers before modernization and its changes were implemented. According to DFTA, New York City's senior centers had not being evaluated since the 1960s, and a "modernization" effort as part of Mayor Bloomberg's 2008 All Ages Project began. It initiated the process of evaluating case management, Meals on Wheels, and senior centers. Under Commissioner Méndez-Santiago, the concept of modernization was adapted from the OAA as a way to make centers more responsive to their communities' needs. But, ultimately, as envisioned by the mayor, modernization became a way to create wellness-themed centers and was viewed by many as a way to close other neighborhood centers. Centers throughout the five boroughs were reviewed to assess their level of use by community residents, and this time, about half the 325 centers "in the five boroughs [as rated by DFTA] were underutilized" (DFTA 2008b, 1). Concurrent with this evaluation process, neighborhood centers were being slated to close, and an RFP went out for "innovative models," based on a competitive-funding award process.

In the midst of the center changes, several nonprofit organizations were evaluating or contracted/partnered with DFTA to assess the state of senior centers in the city. Two major studies were conducted, one by the New York Academy of Medicine (NYAM), which issued the report *NYC Senior Centers: Visioning the Future, 2010* (NYAM 2010), and the other by the Council of Senior Center Services (CSCS), which published *21st Century Senior*

Centers: Changing the Conversation (2010c). Each offered key findings and recommendations—some of which were implemented by DFTA.

NYAM's eight findings were expressed in relation to service delivery. NYAM found that senior centers were needed to provide poor elders with links to services and benefits. Local senior centers should respond to the needs of those in their community. There was a need for greater integration of centers to prevent gaps and duplication of services. Empirical data about best practices was lacking. Multiple ways of providing core services must be investigated with center participants engaged in any changes. In terms of future recommendations, charter senior centers (for LGBT [lesbian, gay, bisexual, and transgender] elders, elders who are blind or in various cultural groups, and others) should be explored. The report also called for the development of new interest-based center models (e.g., the performing arts, books, sports, nature, and technology) and enhanced neighborhood centers ("expanding capacity, programming, sharing and coordinating resources with other centers in a geographic area"). Last, NYAM suggested that the overall "senior center image" be updated (2010, 54).

CSCS's fourteen-point blueprint for action for senior centers recommended that new charter models be based on existing strengths and weakness of current models. Existing centers would benefit from a construction and repair program and ongoing training for existing staff. DFTA must lead the effort to create networking and resource sharing among centers, and more center funding is needed. Core services (such as meals, social workers, health promotion, lifelong learning, and transportation) must be kept, while advocacy training, arts collaboration, volunteer opportunities, and intergenerational programs should be added.

Some suggestions were mentioned by both the NYAM and the CSCS report, and by the aforementioned John Krout, whose book *Senior Centers in America* (1989) is seminal in senior center research. All supported the role of neighborhood centers as points of access to public benefits. They saw the role of a neighborhood center to keep core nutrition, social activities, health and community resources and services within the center. Center participants must participate in the working of their centers, and the center staff needs training, too. There was mention of the need to differentiate center types (e.g., charter versus local neighborhood centers). All experts suggested that the variety of center options would address the needs of different elder groups. Centers, old and new, were encouraged to identify other organizations, collaborations, and linkages to promote their success and longevity as centers. Both reports called for redoing existing center models. The reports urged centers to identify the "image" of their particular center and develop that brand. The brand would be recognized publicly and could aid in securing new funding sources. Both agreed that there was a need to identify services relevant to baby boomers with some long-term planning needed to meet demographic trends over the next twenty-five years.

DFTA did follow some recommendations and develop these innovative center models from new funding streams while many neighborhood centers were in the closure process. Again, these dual processes occurring simultaneously led to the scene of some neighborhood centers struggling to keep their doors open without DFTA funding, while new center models were springing up from different funding streams. To further understand the relationship of the innovative centers to existing neighborhood ones, I asked DFTA commissioner Barrios-Paoli directly about the path from modernization, begun under a previous commissioner, to the present innovative models. She explained to me during a January 2013 phone conversation:

> What happened is that there was [a time during the previous commissioner's term when] he had tried to do an RFP. And the RFP became exceedingly controversial. Part of it was because he wanted to introduce some new programming ideas that were good. But there was no new funding on the table. And in order to fund the bigger centers that they wanted to create, they had to proceed to close a very large number of other centers. That created a lot of controversy. So the idea of the innovative centers was one that was arrived jointly by CSCS and us. Bobbie Sackman was instrumental in creating the idea. The premise of it was we knew there had to be changes in the concept of the senior center because it was something that had started roughly thirty, forty years ago and substantially had remained the same. But in order to do something like that, we needed to bring new money to the table, and how could we achieve that? So we worked hard at creating a model, and then I was very lucky that the mayor agreed to give us initial money to do that. So we were able to create the innovative centers without having to in any way affect the neighborhood centers. In order to create the new centers, we did not have to close or invalidate the neighborhood model. We sort of created something that valued both and differentiated them.

Bobbie Sackman explained to me that "the Christmas gift was that the RFP was withdrawn." As part of the campaign to modernize centers, DTFA's innovative models are heavily funded, with estimates ranging from $650,000 to $750,000.[11] Commissioner Barrios-Paoli explained her view of the relationship of the two centers models to me in a separate conversation:

> We had a number of dramatic cuts that happened to our budget. It had to do with the fiscal crisis that the country was going through and the city was going through and everybody went through. Essentially, it was in that context that we closed [neighborhood] centers. We closed about fifty-three centers serving fewer than thirty people. Centers had really bad planning issues, where they were getting flooded every time it rained, and there were some centers that had no certificate of occupancy. . . . There were issues of safety, just not good management,

of underutilization; all the centers that we closed had serious issues. . . . So one thing really had nothing to do with the other in terms of the innovative centers and [neighborhood center] closures. The big change was that to create a new model, we did not have to sacrifice people in the old model. . . . Many [neighborhood] centers did not have very creative programming because they're not appropriately funded, so the threshold for funding for the innovative centers was much higher than the average center, the neighborhood center. I think the one that has the least money is like, $650,000 a year. Most of the neighborhood centers are, hover around, two hundred thousand and three hundred thousand dollars. So it's a big difference.

The Innovative Eight

So, the innovative center concept was introduced. In addition to offering the core services required by the OAA, new RFP-funded center models must have more flexible hours, a greater catchment area, novel services, and ways to collect data to create evidence-based practices. In a 2011 article, Commissioner Barrios-Paoli outlined the two DFTA innovative center options—geographically based centers and special-population/citywide centers. Geographically based centers were defined as "enhanced centers where seniors from an extensive geographic area come for meals, services, and activities. These centers will serve as resources for the larger community of local neighborhood senior centers."[14] In comparison, special-population/citywide centers "primarily serve a special population (LGBT, seniors with hearing or vision impairments) [and] offer services similar to the geographically based innovative centers and will provide services, resources, and/or education to other innovative and neighborhood centers throughout the city" (DFTA 2011c, 51).

In October 2011, DFTA announced the first eight contracted innovative centers: two citywide, two in Manhattan, one in the Bronx, two in Queens, and one in Staten Island. The two citywide centers are New York City's first LGBT senior center and the first in the nation for blind and visually impaired older persons. Unique features of the other six include community gardening, vegetarian/organic meals, legal clinics, self-serve dinners, communication by Skype, on-site public library annexes, two-way video classes for homebound elders, special programming for the South Asian community, mental health programming, and an Olympic-sized pool and fitness center. Two additional innovative centers in Brooklyn (one in senior housing and the other using community ties) were added to the list in August 2012, making the total count ten.

To understand what it was like to be one of the first special-population/citywide centers, I spoke twice with Catherine Thurston, senior program director at the SAGE center—once before her center opened and then in person at the center after it had opened. We discussed the benefits and difficulties of the new *special-population/citywide* designation, DFTA's relationship with the center, and her advice for future centers. She spoke about the specialized category removing the requirement that a center must serve the entire elder community around the center: "That was huge, because it opened the door for organizations like SAGE and like VISIONS to apply for funding streams historically we had been shut out of. Because, in order to open a senior center, up until now, you would have to commit to serve the entire community district in which you are located." Thurston felt there was a "dialogue between DFTA and its partners" which had not existed in the past. She explained, "There is a lot of pressure on DFTA and a lot of scrutiny about these innovative centers. . . . They're bringing all these different community partners to the table to meet with all of the innovative centers to create kind of, across-the-board ideas for innovative programming. They're really, really in it. They're not just here to audit us; they're here to work in partnership with us. And I feel it and really appreciate that."

There were some issues related to being a new center type. Unlike the other initial special-population center, SAGE did not have an existing facility and purchased and renovated a new facility on the fifteenth floor of their current New York City location with DFTA funding. Just as was the case with neighborhood centers, they experienced some lags while waiting for DFTA funding to come in. Thurston called the strict budget and waits being "innovative with a reduced bottom line." Innovative centers, like neighborhood ones, must meet outcome (measures of attendance and meals), which created some concern about high quotas and "not going to meet numbers that DFTA has asked us to meet . . . because there's still that expectation positive outcome equals numbers of bodies."[15] They must also provide outreach to all other boroughs without "money for marketing."

Thurston discussed the unique challenge this center has in serving an elder LGBT community, a population that may experience both ageism and homophobia: "Now we have to reach folks that are really difficult to reach. It's not just like saying, 'Here's the senior center.' It's 'Here's the gay senior center.'" Later in the conversation, she said, "Walking through the doors of a senior center cannot be easy for anyone—even if it's their neighborhood center. But it's much more complex for people who are, in some cases, still struggling with that identity. Or people who maybe are not struggling, they come out as gay, and they're thrilled to be out, but they're not a part of the community—there is still stigma, and the stigma is not necessarily the provider, but is often on the part of the other seniors in a setting." Despite these issues, Thurston described the momentous achievement: "There were people at the opening at the launch who had been part of SAGE for ten, fifteen years who were weeping. It really was so moving." In the same breath, she was quick to recognize that "at the same time, everyone has their own experience and their own story."

Thurston offered her advice for future innovative centers around two topics: meals and budget negotiation. She spoke about the "innovation curve—they're still at the beginning end of it—is around the nutrition, because there are still so many regulations and nutritional requirements. When we were doing the design piece of this, we really were, I felt, encouraged to be revolutionary in terms of the program design. But at the end of the day, it's hard to be a revolutionary when you have sodium count and one-third RDA, and you have to write this down, and the food temperature has to be checked every day."

Thurston noted that the newness of the SAGE group in creating a center was a factor:

> In hindsight, I feel like we really were the victims of our own inexperience. Had I known how rigorous the budget negotiations were going to be, I would have done a lot more research. What ended up happening was that in that first negotiation, we were given a take-it-or-leave-it final number. We were told to go back and caucus and come back with our answer. After that I made some phone calls to colleagues and got some more information about what they were doing, how much they were charging, what their costs were. I should have done that before. I was very naive in thinking that this kind of outside-the-box innovation would go all the way through to the money. But it never really does. And that was inexperience on our part. The more prepared you could be about what you really can deliver and what you feel comfortable in terms of growth and stretching [the better].

When asked about advice for future innovative centers, Thurston talked about "aligning your aspirations with their [DFTA's] expectation": "be very realistic," and "do your homework." She gave the following instructions: "Go to centers that you admire. Find people that you think do a great job. I reached out to someone that I know has a reputation for standing up to DFTA but is still very well respected, and her centers get awarded new grants. I asked her, 'How do you do that?' And she was really helpful. I feel like it's helped me be able to push back when I need to push back in a very respectful way. But also make it clear that, our priority is not pleasing the funder, it's serving the people that it's our mission to serve."

Reflections about the First "Innovative Ten"

In January 2013, I asked Commissioner Barrios-Paoli about the state of the original ten innovative centers, since it had been some time since their awards. She replied that two centers were not running yet, one because of Hurricane Sandy. But the eight running innovative centers are "doing very, very well. Their attendance has held pretty high. There's a lot of different programming going on in all of them. So, as a whole, we're very pleased with what's going on. The next iteration is that we're going to start really measuring outcomes for the first time. So we should get a pretty good idea of whether—it's wonderful if the programming is better. But is it making a difference in the life of the seniors, is the real intent here. It's been, so far, a great experiment that actually has worked. We're very happy with it."

Barrios-Paoli spoke about an innovative center, the JCC of Staten Island, that she considered very successful because of its "Y-like setting." She elaborated: "They have a great swimming pool that's handicapped accessible and great fitness equipment. They have children's programming, so there are a lot of assets there. There's intergenerational programming. . . . I'm not entirely sure, but they have more than two thousand people on the roster; it gets filled with people the minute they open every day. They had a new building that essentially, they were not able to fill it. . . . Once they converted to a senior center—and we were doing the funding—membership exploded. This was a community willing and ready to do it but maybe couldn't afford it; the programming was totally appropriate for them. The minute that it became a senior center, it just took off."

Igal Jellinek, executive director of CSCS, also gave me his review of the innovative centers in NYC, in an interview with him and Bobbie Sackman. Jellinek explained, "If you have a strong board and you have a strong staff, you're gonna have a successful center. One of those, you do. And what's happened is over time, some of the centers have grown; infrastructures have not grown with it. So it's hard, if you look at the ten groups that are getting this [the innovative status], all have infrastructure. They've added money to the pot the city gave them. But they had to make an investment, as well, and they're all successful. They're all doing well. Some are slower start-ups. But they're successful."

The Future of Innovative Centers? Including the Boomers?

With the first round of innovative centers getting up and running, I wanted to see what future innovative centers may be like. Barrios-Paoli suggested they would continue to have creative programming and "evolve as programming hubs for seniors." Their role would be as innovators, to continually develop solid senior-relevant programs that would be directed to the neighborhood centers, as well. She sees the process as a "kind of synergy" where innovative programs "spill over to the other centers." Accreditation was a topic I brought up. I wondered whether it was part of New York City's innovative centers process. Barrios-Paoli responded that it would be DFTA, not national organizations, that would accredit innovative center models. She continued, "We're actively exploring that [accreditation] possibility right now."[16]

And where would the influx of boomers fit into the innovative center plan? Well, Barrios-Paoli felt the success of centers was matching services to the person ("senior centers are great places for seniors, but not every senior likes congregate services"). She questioned if Boomers would actually be centers' next big target audience:

> I think the boomers may or may not want to come to a senior center. Most of our centers are attended by the older seniors—seventy, seventy-five and up. Unless we create a very different kind of programming, we're not going to attract a younger senior. I'm not sure that it's important that we do so. As long as people have other options, then that's fine, they should exercise those options. We should be there for those seniors who want and need us. . . . But you have to have a hook. That's why it's important we have sort of a sense of the pulse of the community and we know what people want.[17] Not everybody's going to want to do ballroom dancing. It has to be a big variety of things and things people really want to do. So that's why I'm saying it's important we continually look at our programming, change it, and ask the seniors what it is that they want—as opposed to what we think they want.

When I asked about her view of an ideal center (without any constraints, in an ideal world), Barrios-Paoli offered a prediction: "My sense is centers will get better and better the more resources that they have. So in an ideal world, I would like to have a minimum threshold of funding for centers. Not everybody funded at $750,000, but we would have two tiers of centers. Everybody would be better funded than they presently are because a lot of the ability to be more creative is handicapped by the fact that you don't have enough resources." Her dream would include adequate funding for all, partnering with community institutions, and measurement to evaluate the programs but "not in a way that it becomes onerous and castrating to anyone." The need for future centers tracking outcomes was echoed by Jellinek. In a January 2013 interview, he also commented on the need to track data beyond the current markers: "Another thing you need to keep in mind is that DFTA, prior to this commissioner, basically was collecting data just on meals. So it wasn't measuring people who come for socialization. They weren't measuring people who were coming for activities."

If Neighborhood Centers Fail What Remains?
Limits of Aging in Place for Working-Class Elders

Let us address the false notion that we do not need centers because the push for aging in place now means elders get all needed resources within their communities. Aging in place cannot be considered a panacea. It does not serve all older persons equally well. It can even be detrimental to older persons of lower socioeconomic status. These are people living in poor neighborhoods without adequate public transportation or connections to services and programs.[18] Or they are older persons living in housing that is not compliant with the Americans with Disabilities Act or in so-called Peter Pan housing, older dwellings that were designed for occupants who would never grow old or require housing adaptations. These groups may be aging "left behind," or "stuck in place," rather than aging in place, through choices of their own. Their aging in place happens in less than optimal conditions. As center models move away from traditional OAA-like delineated centers, what existing community-based options could, possibly, pick up the slack left by the center-service loss?

Some researchers suggest that NORCs and village models present a possible framework for aging in place and picking up the slack from closing centers (Greenfield et al. 2012). You may recall that NORCs are not predesigned living spaces for older persons; rather, these are gradual concentrations of older persons developing in communities over time. These "unexpected communities" offer access to resources (healthcare, shopping, etc.) and are in close proximity to other social supports for older persons (Hochschild 1973). They allow older persons to get in touch with providers and needed services using private or public funding. Residents often prefer NORCs to more formal living options, seeing them as filling in for gaps in services. With varying definitions, in a NORC at least 40 percent of residents are over fifty-five or sixty years of age—though this percentage is usually much higher (Bedney et al. 2010; USDHHS 2004). There are fifty-four NORCs in New York State (United Hospital Fund 2005) and twenty-seven in New York City (Interboro Partners 2012), with 45,733 New York City community-dwelling older persons as part of them (Altman 2006). The majority of state NORCs are in New York City apartment buildings and receive city and state funding (to bring programs and service on site).[19]

NORCs have evolved to include Naturally Occurring Retirement Communities with Social Service Programs (NORC SSP) built into them. In terms of how a NORC SSP differs from a NORC, the U.S. Department of Health and Human Services found the SSP version offers case management, emergency or general home care, meals, transportation, and mental health and bereavement services, as well as informal supports, information and referral, nursing services, cultural events, dance or exercise classes and lectures, and health screenings (2006, 14). Since the first New York City NORC SSP, Penn South Houses, was created in 1986, NORC SSPs have had multiple, mixed-funding sources. Since the late 1990s, the state has allocated $1.2 million each year with the condition that the organization running the SSP matches 25 percent of the state grant (USDHHS 2004, 20). In 2005, this annual $1.2 million allotment was increased to $2.4 million to support new NORC model development. In 2006, New York City had twenty-seven NORC SSPs—with six in Queens (United Hospital Fund 2005).

While prior NORC models are vertical, meaning residents live in apartment-like housing complexes or "high-rises," a Neighborhood Naturally Occurring Retirement Community (NNORC) and Naturally Occurring Retirement Community without Walls (NORC WOW) are quite the opposite, horizontal in nature. Here, older persons live in clusters of single- or two-family free-standing homes. These NNORC and NORC WOW models are most common in the outer boroughs.[20] In 2006, the state legislature expanded the program to include funding for NNORCs in low-rise communities with no more than two thousand older adults, where houses were individually owned (Vladeck 2004).

In addition to elder communities that fall into place over the years, there are planned options for aging in place in the community. Ronald Manheimer (2009) describes the entire senior-designed North Carolina's Buncombes County's Livable and Senior Friendly Community. It was created using a task force model to "provide leadership in a collaborative planning process that promotes a livable and senior-friendly community" (Buncombe County Aging Planning Task Force 2007, 1). In addition to an elder-created community, the elder village model is a nonprofit, annual, fee-based collective of self-sustaining elders, at the grassroots level. They are traditionally nonprofit or privately funded. Villages are resident driven, self-governed, and designed to meet the community's specific needs. They include social activities, member referrals services, and wellness discounts. In 2011, there were 50 villages in operation and 149 at various stages of development (McDonough and Davitt 2011). Gramatan Village in Bronxville is the one and only village located in New York State.

If Neighborhood Centers Fail, What Are Funding Options for Services They Once Provided?

Home and community-based services (HCBS) were designed to allow those with Medicaid and eligible for long-term care placement to remain in their communities. In 1975, personal care services (PCS) were included so that elders could get state-based nonmedical assistance with ADLs and IADLs while at home. This waiver program, begun in the 1980s, let states get federal permission to waive federal Medicaid requirements and offer HCBS. Despite debate over their efficacy and long waiting lists, HCBS services help prevent stays in long-term care (Kane 2012). More recent additions to the program include options for Participant Directed Services (PDS) or Cash and Counsel Programs or Long-Term Care Insurance. PDS and Cash and Counsel Programs allow elders choice in how funds to keep them aging in place are allocated. For example, an elder controls whether or not he or she uses formal or informal paid caregivers. The counsel portion provides a safety net for unexpected gaps that may occur in elder planned care (such as a caregiver's absence caused by illness). In 2006, HCBS accounted for 40 percent of Medicaid expenditures, paying for respite care and daycare, with housework and meal preparation. Yet eligible elders often do not use HCBS services because they are unaware of them, believing the "services are not available" or not wanting an unknown person in their home (Casado et al. 2011).

Two current program options, Program of All-Inclusive Care for the Elderly (PACE) and Geriatric Resources for Assessment and Care of Elders (GRACE), could assist the "dual eligible" (those receiving Medicare for medical expenses and Medicaid for long-term care and in need of many services) to remain in their own neighborhoods. PACE is a person-centered drop-in program for frail elders who require the level of care provided in a skilled nursing facility. The PACE interdisciplinary team approach coordinates and integrates health care and other services through case management for elders receiving Medicare and Medicaid funding. PACE is commendable in its dual eligibility (in terms of Medicare and Medicaid recipient status), but its funding is closely tied to insurance that is policy dependent.

GRACE, a newer program, provides in-home assessment and coordination of care by a geriatric care manager and team (social worker, primary care physician, nurse practitioner). The program was designed to meet the needs of elders with low socioeconomic status, comorbid chronic conditions, and less access to—or fragmented—care. This is a group that often costs more and benefits less from traditional care that lacks comprehensive care management. Here, too, one must have Medicaid because some Medicare HMO programs may cover chronic care-related services, but traditional Medicare does not.

Discussion: Branding the "Unbrandable": Marketing to the Infamous Boomers

Senior centers are in flux—in the process of being re-created, rebranded, and reevaluated. The repackaging of senior centers began with the removal of the word *citizens* from *senior citizens centers*, which have become *centers*, as *senior* is also increasingly being removed. So, a senior center is renamed an "activity center" or reborn as a "center for living well." Congregate meal sites have become cafés, and exercise programs have become health-and-wellness centers. Bingo is out of favor, while lifelong learning via virtual centers is in.

Then enter the cohort-olatry of the baby boomers, with their numbers rising between seven thousand to ten thousand daily beginning in 2011.[21] As discussed earlier, the rise of this group has been cited as an important element in changing the senior center terrain. The problem in predicting the needs of the boomers in center models is twofold.[22] First, boomers are more heterogeneous than thought of in the literature. They have greater needs as a group than simply more opportunities for health and wellness activities or civic engagement (e.g., retirement transitions and volunteering and mentoring opportunities) than current models. In reality, many boomers do need the same services offered to contemporary older persons. Second, there is more speculation about which age-based services differing subcohorts of boomers would want than research on the subgroups themselves. Some, mostly marketing companies, are beginning to divide the boomers into four subgroups (for the year ranges of 1946–1951, 1952–1955, 1956–1959, and 1960–1964), while others divide them into the "young" boomers, born in the later part of the boom (1956–1964), and the "old" boomers, born during the first or early part (1946–1955). Unlike other age-cohort groups, the boomers' cohorts have not been named, defined, or extensively studied. For example, boomers are not subgrouped and labeled like the more recent cohort of Gen X-ers (1965–1982), who can be divided into many sub- and overlapping groups, such as Generation Y, the Net Generation, Millennials, Echo Boomers, or the Google Generation, to name a few.

The overhomogenization of baby boomers is harmful to the entire group of those who are aging. If we make false divisions between "boomers" and "existing center members," we are reifying the notion that these two groups are different and that the boomers are "successfully aging." Let me relay an example of how constructing a model of best aging hurts centergoers. A center director, who received some of the closed center's members, relayed this to me: functional status is becoming a dividing line and indicator of "success" at her center. She said, "That's a high-echelon group of your seniors. 'Because I'm still driving my car. I still have my wits about me, and I can still drive.' We have the other ones who have to come here and they take Access-a-Ride. You [also] have some people in here that should be taking Access-a-Ride, but they're too proud. So they walk. And they come here that way. Or they take a cab."

Extending dichotomies of "good" and "bad" aging implies that nonboomer groups and current centergoers have failed to age well and marginalizes these groups (see Hostetler 2011). Some argue that social class, along with the reauthorization of the OAA and its nutrition provision, is of more pressing concern than distinctions between boomer and nonboomer cohorts (Kane 2009).

Looking to the boomers as a way to rebrand centers is an example of hegemony in our culture. Antonio Gramsci's concept of hegemony, in simple terms, is the way a dominant group in society maintains control by making its values, ideals, and goals become the norm (Buttigieg 2006). These norms create power, so power is not taken by physical force. The group in power maintains this status by further reinforcing these norms. For example, who defines what worthy senior centers are like? The perceived interests of boomers are used to take over some ideas about "successful" center sites and appropriate funding. Governmental policies support the hegemonic view of health-based centers and healthy aging as the way to be. The outcome of this hegemony is to further marginalize current-day, nonboomer older persons for not meeting these constructed ideals. If the market is geared toward capturing the ideals of what the boomers want as boomers, the center is the site of conflict—where the class divide and conflict plays out. Traditional, poor elders are marginalized by the thought of a more "hip" generation. These perceptions, not the reality of this group, shape center language and influence policy.

Are New Center Models Better?

The 2009 and 2012 NCOA and NISC reports recommended six senior centers models and multiple award-winning center-based programs. Also, DFTA created two types of innovative centers models (special-population/citywide and geographically based). There are many positive elements in these models and programs. The community center model, with its intergenerational nature, brings groups together and can serve to desegregate and destigmatize or demarginalize aging. These models can create interaction and reciprocity between young and old, and all age groups, for that matter. The wellness (read, health-focused) models are thought to be the most baby boomer friendly. It is these wellness models, sometime with big-name presenters, that have brought in the most revenue. Lifelong learning/arts models are also seen as boomer-friendly.

The continuum of care/life transitions model authentically carries out the OAA mandate for services provision. It truly helps on many levels and aids in ways for older persons to age in place. The key strength of the entrepreneurial model is it brings funding—not from the government—and does ongoing process evaluation of its programs. The café model offers meals and activities and has the noncenter appeal. Just having this model recognized is a strength because, according to Igal Jellinek, "senior centers weren't seen as part of the continuum. And it's a prevention mode. And I think you really need to look at that because social—people don't want to eat alone. Most people, I won't say all people. But people want to make new friends or be with people. They don't want to be as isolated. It becomes for some people a home away from home." Innovative center models aim to support community-specific populations and improve centers work through ongoing research and formal evaluation. These models have the potential to both allow special populations to have a familiar, accepting setting and to maintain neighborhood centers in a new form. For example, Thurston, in charge of one of the first innovative centers, said, "The nice thing was that those that applied for the innovative program could tailor it the way they felt would best serve their own community." The innovative model gave centers the funding and leeway to try different programming and different settings. The future goal of empirical data collection for DFTA's innovative models and analysis will assist in making these centers and programs meet groups' needs.

My own concern about prescriptive models is that they can be limiting. They may create a "fixed" template that may limit others. Templates may be followed with the belief that this is a way to shore up or receive funding. Community center models, when intergenerational, can also resegregate elders or marginalize them if age integration does not work. Elders may feel as if they are isolated and added on to the existing setting. Coordinating intergenerational centers and projects is a huge undertaking. This is also true for arts and lifelong learning/arts models; you need a lot of collaboration with skilled instructors and buy-in from local school districts and programs. However, some (such as Formosa [2012]) have argued that these arts and lifelong learning models are elitist and favor those with access to such resources and ability to pay.

Health-and-wellness-based models reify successful aging models and activity aging theory hierarchies. They can exploit Medicaid and Medicare for health prevention and promotion services. We now have the phenomenon of adult social day centers popping up and often being associated with fraudulent Medicaid billing. Their focus is often more on recruiting participants than on real programming. If they use sponsorship or corporate endorsements for health programming, their members may become more of a "test market" than center participants. Programming can become corporate rather than member driven. This would defeat the center's goals of serving the needs and interests of their members, not clients. The continuum of care model is seen as being for "frail, dependent, poor, older people." Entrepreneurial models (or the Next Chapter ones) may place value on "doing" or "active aging."

Keeping the café model viable is tricky. As Scott Ball (2012) suggests, the café must be seen as offering inexpensive food to everyone in the community and not just elders. The entire community must buy in and become loyal customers. These cafés may still be seen, informally, as centers by some but have a higher cost of meals than a typical center. If a particular café is not profitable and leaves, what happens to the people relying on them when they close?

Yet these innovative centers, being the first of their kind, may have had high expectations placed on them without having the training and experience helpful to reach them. With their healthy budgets, sustainability without continued city/mayoral funding may be a problem. They can also create a hierarchy of centers and funding within the city. The idea that innovative centers and their ideas trickle down to neighborhood ones can imply that neighborhood centers are lacking these skills and staff (not just the enriched funding). A two-tiered system would ideally increase funding and support for both tiers (though in differing amounts), but this tiered system can also perpetuate the existing inequalities in center models as they move forward. Many of the elders in the neighborhood center with whom I spoke for this book would not feel at ease in an innovative center. While the baby boomers' motto may be "I wouldn't be caught dead at a senior center," the current centergoer's motto is "I wouldn't be caught dead in any other center them my own local, neighborhood one." We need to rethink the closure of neighborhood centers that are doing well in working-class neighborhoods and consider how the benefits of innovation are experienced by a select, smaller group, often of higher socioeconomic status.

Are NORCs, Village Models, and HCBS Feasible in a Non-Center-Based System?

NORCs are becoming of interest to funders. In 2013, Grantmakers in Aging, a funder along with Pfizer, awarded $1.3 million to "boost age friendly communities" including the call to evaluate NORC services. NORC varieties, such as NORC WOW require a lot of resident commitment and ongoing work. In a recent study of a NORC WOW in Albany, Laura Bronstein, Zvi Gellis, and Bonnie Kenaley (2011) asked residents what made this type of community successful. To make this NORC WOW work, residents suggested four main themes: a NNORC is the best model to support aging in place, informal systems of care are still heavily used in a NNORC setting, tangible support and mental health supports must be equally weighed, and collaboration between resident and service providers is necessary to make these collaborations truly work (e.g., "you need to have somebody take this by its throat and really move it" [110]). The village model offers discounted shopping options and transportation for members for a fee of around thirty-five or fifty dollars a year. While NORC models can have poor residents, historically, village models are nonprofit or privately funded, and only some village models do integrate public funding. For example, in Washington, DC, a village uses public funding to subsidize members' fees, which could expand the possibilities of membership (Poor et al. 2012). Greenfield and colleagues (2012) suggest that work needs to be done to see if NORCs and village models leave poor-to-working-class seniors in the lurch. They call for future application of their framework to explore how these living models work for elder populations of diverse social class.

Yet these living options may suffer the same fate as the center transformations—if funding is reduced for NORCs or village models. If centers and community-based service provision models are out, where is the safety net for elders in need of such services? But what about those not on Medicaid and not in a well-suited NORC or village or senior-designed setting?

Just as NORCs and village models are dependent on social policy and funding trends, HCBS, PACE, and GRACE funding options cannot be taken as a given. For example, the Community Living and Assistance Service and Supports Act (the CLASS Act of 2010), proposed under the Patient Protection and Affordable Care Act, was enacted and then quickly suspended in 2011. So it no longer was a possible funding option.

Can the Patchwork of Models and Services Meet Centers' Basic Functions?

Senior centers have six functions: health promotion/education and disease prevention, social activities, nutrition, educational opportunities, recreation, and connections to social services to meet these service needs. The provision of health education can be part of PACE or GRACE programs for the dual eligible. For those working-class elders not receiving Medicaid, village models that subsidize membership can offer older persons access to a variety of health promotion, prevention, and wellness programs. NNORC WOWs or NORC SSPs can provide meeting places for older persons to socialize within their own communities with varying levels of wealth. Senior-designed communities would also be built with social opportunities at their centers, as would village models of all socioeconomic levels—but these communities require time and financial commitment. Nonprofits, such as Next Chapter, offer volunteer opportunities and social activities with reduced membership fees based on financial need. In terms of those dual eligible (for Medicare and Medicaid), by using an HCBS waiver, older persons could receive in-home meal preparation help.

NORC SSPs would be resources for reduced-cost meal sites, while elders with additional income could find meals at a café-like setting. The cafés may offer reduced-cost meals and an elder-focused gathering space, but prices can be higher than at centers and based on a corporate model. For educational and recreational opportunities, elders may make use of Third Age learning programs. Features of purposefully designed senior communities, village models, and NORC SSPs also provide the greatest connection to social services and utility linkages, as would a PACE or GRACE program for dual-eligible persons.

Let us return to social class and a discussion of the more primary needs of older persons who use senior centers. What is the new lived reality for elders in a world with fewer centers and in which those centers that exist must meet stringent outcome measures to survive? And how can the needs of elders living in poor or working-class communities be met while the needs of multiple subcohorts of Baby Boomers are also addressed? With the passage of time, models are continually developing. There are options, such as one- or two-family house sharing for low-income elders, like the cohousing models of the Dutch. Future models are in the works that support aging in place, in community, for elders of all social classes. Social policies, such as in the Affordable Care Act and the ongoing effort beginning in 2011 to reauthorize the OAA, are also potentially changing to address the needs of the diverse groups of those aging and updating definitions of older persons in the greatest economic and social need. Let us consider how center models can be sustained nationally by social policy.

8

Beyond Rebranding

● ●

Building a Sustainable Core

> Day Centers Sprout Up, Luring Fit Elders
> and Costing Medicaid.
> —Headline of Nina Bernstein article,
> *New York Times*, spring 2013

As I write this, although we are past the sequester that began March 1, 2013, the Older Americans Act of 2011 has not been reauthorized. Despite the OAA's "expiration" in the 2011 fiscal year, Congress has allocated 19.2 percent, or $367 million, for the 2012–2013 fiscal year to Title III, supportive services—which covers senior centers. Forty-three percent, or $816.3 million, of Title III funding would go to nutrition services. About 8 percent, or $153.6 million, of Title III funding would go to the National Family Caregiver Support Program, and 1.1 percent, or $15 million, would go to disease prevention and health promotion activities (Negri 2013). While the Social Security and Medicaid programs do not foresee the same level of cuts, the National Council on Aging (NCOA) estimates that the OAA will have lost $112,015,049 across the board because of the sequester. According to some, the OAA does not have the same level of bipartisan sponsorship or support as past versions did (Sanz 2013). The Leadership Council of Aging Organizations (LCAO) urges that any cuts be weighed against the greater social good: "Any 'savings' from the sequester would pale in comparison to the added costs, resulting in premature nursing home placement for seniors who can no longer stay in their homes and communities because of reduced federal funding."[1]

The Community First Choice rule and Independence at Home demonstration projects, parts of the Patient Accountability and Affordable Care Act (ACA), are also under way. The Community First Choice, for people with disabilities, was designed to keep those needing care in a facility, from hospital to skilled nursing care facility, in their homes with community-based services and support. The federal government would match state Medicaid funding for this program. The Independence at Home demonstration projects, also under ACA, are testing ways to have physician- or nurse-led teams serve the needs of community-dwelling elders who are Medicaid recipients and suffer multiple chronic conditions and ADL/IADL limitations. These projects will end in May 2015. The potential benefit for approved providers would be incentives if they create Medicare savings. As stated in chapter 7, the Community Living and Assistance Service and Supports Act (the CLASS Act of 2010) of ACA, designed to fund community-based care, has been suspended as not cost efficient. Some may exploit the possibility for Medicaid billing and interest in community-based elder policy by the ACA, as evidenced by Nina Bernstein's April 22, 2013, *New York Times* headline that introduces this chapter. Her story tells how social day centers for older persons are on the rise, offering "clients" incentives to attend and for referring them to other friend-agencies for services. All this is billed to Medicaid, with estimates of twenty-five million dollars being inappropriately billed in the first nine months of 2012.

Boomer and Nonboomer Social Positions and Policy Planning

Boomers and their interests, whatever these are thought to be, are used as the driving force behind social policy change. Language about the rise of this group fills social policy discussion. Whether it is the rise of the "greedy geezer" or "civically engaged activist" stereotypes, this group comprises the "age wave" that will shift the demographic order of society and "bankrupt" Social Security, Medicare, Medicare, and other social programs. Boomers are accused of continuing an earlier trend of "graying the federal budget," through which about one-third of the federal budget goes to about 13 percent of the population (Torres-Gil and Villa 2000). Jacob Hacker and Ann O'Leary argue that the "framework for social protection focuses overwhelmingly on the aged, even though young adults and families with children face the greatest economic strain" (2012, 16). Frederick Lynch's *One Nation under AARP: The Fight over Medicare, Social Security, and America's Future* (2011) sees the boomers as embroiled in an ideological battle over who they are in social policy. In my opinion, this "boomer power" happens only when we, as a society, construct a common view of the group—suspending any differences in the young, middle, and older baby boomer cohorts and denying that many will be just as dependent on social policies, such as those of Social Security and Medicare, as earlier elder cohorts. So what are the trends in political ideology, or ways of thinking, that are scapegoating boomers as "entitlement users" on the heels of the current sixty-five-plus population?

This conceptualization of baby boomers (as voracious consumers—or "zoomers"—and industrious members of society) in the law hurts both boomer and nonboomer groups alike. We need to consider carefully whether and how these boomers will require policy change and altered services (Biggs et al. 2007). For that matter, will they transform what we think of as policy, care, and services for those sixty-five years of age and over? Why is there so much concern for boomers, a group many say will never visit a center? And is it the case that the poor and those in lower economic strata are left to feel the consequences?

The Political (and Moral) Economy of Aging

Social policies for older persons happen in a societal context, meaning that the way we view aging and value or devalue older people and see aging by social class is translated into the policies made for older people. Researchers such as Meredith Minkler, Carroll L. Estes, Cynthia Leedham, and Thomas Cole have called this the "political economy of aging perspective." According to their model, "The dependent position of the elderly and public policies and institutional arrangements that affect them will be seen to reflect and to reinforce the prevailing class structure in our society" (Minkler and Estes, 1984, 5). These theoretical premises have real consequences for social policy outcomes for older persons. The dominant, or hegemonic, position places elders as a group in need of care, services, and dependency—while simultaneously making all older persons the same, as one "old" class group. As Minkler and Estes put it, we "commodify the lives of the aged under the rubric of 'services' [and create] social policies that fail to reflect the existing inequalities among elders and treat the aged as one distinct class—but these class differences mean different problems exist" (33). Our social policies, developed using the rhetoric of elder dependency, reproduce the relationship of the aged and their social position. We reify and affix the "in need of services" label to older persons and deny them agency in addressing needed changes themselves.

Using this political economy model can have positive effects for elders. The model frames them as "active moral agents in the social process" to "maximize their own interests" (Hendricks and Leedham 1992, 133). Elders would not be framed in the constant state of dependency or unproductiveness and "excluded from the mainstream" or "segregated in public policy" debates (129). The moral economy model builds on the political economy model in describing the position of elders in society and social policy. A moral economy sets a price or marker or exchange value on fairness and "sensibility of social policy" for what an elder is "due in society" (Hendricks 2005). Sometimes elders, as an interest group, are given less favor than other, more powerful groups. Thus, "the aged," especially those in lower social classes, become a social problem that only larger groups, organizations, and laws can "fix."

The application to social policy of the political-economy-of-aging perspective has led to the suggestion that we expect too much from beleaguered governmental agencies. We expect a mosaic of services when our aging polices outlining those services are fragmented, at best. Researchers such as Laura Katz Olson feel that the OAA, for example, is "poorly funded service strategy that avoided challenges to the existing political structure or allocation of benefits to society" (1982, 189). She points out the rift between the great ten principal tenets of the OAA and the way each was "dwindled down" to service provision (189). For her, the OAA cannot provide needed services to the most in need. Service coordination between agencies does not happen, and programs and policies are not integrated. Even institutions that pool resources see little benefit, since all (Social Security, Medicare, food stamps, etc.) are not adequately funded. Services are market driven. So we have "haphazardly developed programs, services, and facilities that have not improved materially the quality of older peoples' lives" (213). Instead, Olson believes we focus on "safe problems" and that privatizing markets won't provide for the "welfare state."[2]

Encountering Neoliberal Ideology and Its Effect upon Current Policy

During 2012–2013, a period of coming out of the Great Recession, an ever-delayed OAA reauthorization process, and governmental sequester, federal funding is (or is in threat of) being cut.[3] Ideologically, we are experiencing a resurgence of neoliberalism in funding and policies for older adults. Neoliberalism has Malthusian roots and is a return to more of the blame-the-victim mentality, as some suggest (e.g., Hendricks and Leedham 1992; Olson 1982). This neoliberal approach focuses on individual agency rather than structure or social position when analyzing and resolving social policy issues. My use of *neoliberalism* refers to a political-economic or governmental system based on principles of competition and entrepreneurship. Neoliberalism prizes the concept of individual responsibility over that of the common good. So taking care of oneself is the concern of oneself and not the state. This belief system respects self-agency without considering real structural obstacles in society. Government services are privatized, which is frequently associated with the loss of a safety net for those without resources.

A brief history of presidential support of and public attitudes toward social aging policy starts with Lyndon B. Johnson's presidency. Building on the work of John F. Kennedy, Johnson ushered in legislation that helped elders. Subsequent presidents' support of these federal programs for older persons has varied. In the 1980s, the administration of Ronald Reagan reduced federal benefits to elders (Flynn 1984). The 1990s brought alarmist reports of the potential collapse of the Social Security system (Gil-Torres and Villa 2000). George H. W. Bush's plan focused on keeping elders in Medicare health maintenance organizations (HMOs), adjusting Medicare prescription drug coverage plans, and possibly privatizing Social Security. Bill Clinton's plans for elders revolved around prescription drug coverage, long-term home care, and of course, suggestions that Medicaid and national/state health plans be pooled (Lewin 1993). Currently, under Barack Obama, congressional groups are proposing increasing the retirement age and often raise the issue of privatizing Social Security. Legislators are advocating for federal Medicare caps, changing Medicare eligibility standards, and privatizing the program. Some want to turn Medicaid funding over to the states and generally stop the Affordable Care Act and its reforms (see Hollister and Estes 2013). While the October 2013 launch of the Affordable Care Act on the Department of Health and Human Services' website let individuals shop for plans, Medicare and Medicaid were not part of the website.[4] There was only text about covered preventative visits as part of Medicare and state-based sites for Medicaid eligibility.

Despite their political ups and downs, federal social policies for elders had some great successes. Torres-Gil and Villa highlight the role of legislation on aging as improving the situation of elders in poverty. They also quickly point out that this was accomplished in a system that has been complex, fragmented, and "vast and unwieldy" (2000, 375). It is a system of gaps and similar proportions of spending on Medicare over time. The system also lacks long-term care and often considers consolidating services for the aged and those with disabilities.

The current state of aging social policy has returned to a sense of neoliberalism and its ideals (Polivka and Estes 2009). Theorists Jason Powell and Azrini Wahidin specifically apply neoliberalism to elder policy—"There is then an ambivalence at the heart of neo-liberalism: on one hand, older people are to be 'managed' by other administrative powers such as professional experts in modernity; on the other hand, older people are left to govern themselves, a process . . . call[ed] 'action at a distance' from the State. Hence, as consumers, older people are distanced further away from the State; rather than a cause for celebration, the dystopian implications are far-reaching and include further risks the self must negotiate with the withdrawal of State" (2005, 78).

Francis Caro, in "Advancing Aging Policy as the 21st Century Begins," predicted the current disfavoring of public programs, such as the OAA, for elders.

We are in a time when "policy advocates also have to contend with reduced public enthusiasm for public-sector initiatives, generally, and federal initiatives, more specifically. In an earlier period, it was more plausible than now for policy entrepreneurs to propose federally financed benefit programs administered by a federal agency. Now, policy entrepreneurs have to emphasize less direct approaches. They are more likely to succeed at the federal level with approaches that encourage states, corporations, or private individuals to take certain specified actions" (2000, 2). Scott Bass's prophecy, in "Emergence of the Third Age: Toward a Productive Aging Society," about public programs being unable to compete with the market and the decline in political support for OAA programs, has come true. He foresaw policy changes for those elders who have lived a lifetime of cumulative disadvantage in the era of the baby boom:

> For these unfortunate elders, private charities and government-funded organizations are the best hope. Government programs become their lifeline and support. Unfortunately, funding from these programs is likely to be modest. With a potential reduction in federal anti-poverty efforts, very poor and vulnerable elderly will be dependent on the services available in their immediate communities. Some elders will go without as considerable political clout will reside with more affluent elders. As pioneers of the aging society, attention will be given to the needs of these more organized and influential elders. In all likelihood, the vulnerable elderly will be dispersed geographically throughout suburban and urban areas and, for those who have aged in place in areas without a history of services, the capacity of those communities to meet their needs will be strained (2000, 15).

Ironically, these older persons in the most need are the same individuals served by senior centers, as the language in the 1965 OAA shows. Senior centers' target audience is "older individuals (with particular attention to low-income older individuals, including low-income minority older individuals, older individuals with limited English proficiency, and older individuals residing in rural areas)."

Praxis: My Suggestions for Senior Centers Moving Forward, Beyond Blaming the Boomers and the Aging Enterprise

Ideally, there should be funding for various types of centers and a return to the original mission of the OAA with some "modernization" to add in target groups such as those recommended by Senator Bernie Sanders of Vermont, including LGBT elders, HIV-positive elders, and those with Alzheimer's disease. To me, the neighborhood center, especially in working-class or poor communities, acknowledges a sense of place and must remain a point of service.[5] In an ideal world, societal values would change so that real importance (and funding) is placed on programs, and elders are given worth. My ideal changes would naturally imply that we address early disadvantage, which becomes cumulative disadvantage in one's later years. In terms of the necessity for changes in social policy, particularly the OAA, I hark back to Scott Bass's early call: "Without these changes [updates to the OAA], the senior centers and other allied OAA activities run the risk of becoming mere shadows of what they once were" (2000, 14). Current policies will be difficult to maintain without an attitude shift. But we need to actively rethink the expert provision of services models. We need to address the issue of senior centers on several fronts. I strongly suggest we flip the service provisions script. Freedman's plan of action includes elements of flipping the later-life script. He suggests we create a "compelling new story of the benefits of civic engagement in later life" in general, in society (1999, ix). We reform organizations and create "breakthrough institutions"; we create good communities to age in. He suggests we need a Third Age (3A) Bill to help underwrite service activities (1999, 235). So, I propose, first, we revisit the original intentions of senior centers in the OAA rather than prescribe funding for centerlike or "lite" services in a fragmented (and under a conditionally funded) system.

In reality, we live in a society with a neoliberal view of public funding; so future funding is iffy, and we need to reduce dependency on it. For policy, centers must acknowledge that public funding will wax and wane, decreasing over time. But if we rely on fee-based models such as entrepreneurial centers, then we are bound by a market system, having center participants as clients or consumers of outside entities, or they are constantly sustaining their own existence through raising funds. The success of intergenerational centers, or community centers for all groups also requires further thought as this model relies on elders' space and identity being respected and maintained along with that of all other groups. The current proposal to have the Aging and Disability Resource Center (ADRC) program, called No Wrong Door or Single Entry Point by the Administration for Community Living (2013), mix age and disability services may actually double the effect of stigma, pairing the stigma of age with that of functional status. I discourage the further stigmatization and marginalization of older persons, which happens when you link senior centers only with disability centers. We must not let policy intentionally or unintentionally reflect hegemonic or stigmatizing views; instead, we need to revisit the idea of building community ties beneficial to all groups.

General Strategies Based on Social Capital Theories

Before I offer a practical to-do list, let us examine four strategies for senior centers that I have adapted from a theory of social capital and social-tie generation found in John Field's aptly titled work, *Social Capital*, about social capital–social policy linkages. These four elements underlie center growth and their movement along their own life course. My first strategy is to halt the rapid closure process and have fewer additional center closures as each reduces social capital. Each closure removes relationships and destroys the prior social networks. Some organizations, such as Catholic Charities, have merged their centers to stave off closure. In these cases, transportation was provided so that the relationships begun at one center could be literally transported to another with a similar mission statement, services, and so on. These relationships may or may not be rebuilt or survive the transfer to a new setting. A story Bobbie Sackman of the Council of Senior Centers and Services of New York City relayed to me poignantly explains the power of center-specific social capital from an elder's point of view. During a rally at City Hall, "somebody made themselves like a computer, and they were looking through the front of the box, and they said, 'Senior centers are our social network.' And it is . . . So if you're twenty, and your social network is school, and being online on Facebook—this is their Facebook—their Facebook is face to face. And that needs to be respected as you respect a twenty-, thirty-, or forty-year-old . . . and they miss each other on weekends, or in the evenings, or holidays when they can't necessarily get together."

The second strategy for senior centers as we approach the future is to focus less on stand-alone, new-center models and more on the need to create and build social capital among all center types. The linkages must be beneficial to the centers themselves. Capital generated can outlast specific funding or programmatic and staff changes. Third, there must be more grassroots, elder-driven efforts at community building with elders, nonprofits, and center staff. Building on elders' agency prevents their commodification as a group in need of services and unable to advocate for themselves. Organizations such as the National Council on Aging and its National Institute of Senior Centers (NISC) and the more local CSCS esteem elder advocacy as a key element of their mission. The advocacy component is real, with training for center participants and elders rallying around their own concerns.

The fourth and final theory-based strategy would be to create less paternalistic policies for providing funding that may not be sustainable. Theorists such as John Field (2003) and John Coleman (1990) propose that heavy state intervention alone may be counterproductive. Since social capital comes from "relationships freely engaged in by individuals," these ties will not emerge if institutions come in and replaces them (Coleman 1990, 118). It is better to build social capital through mutual aid and support. Goals are to build an engaged civil society and to construct public policy on social capital (bonds between people) over human capital (people alone). We need to foster more long-term public-private partnerships with realistic budgets. We need to prepare for a lower level of federal and state financial involvement. This holds true for centers that are not 501(c) (3) or that do not have nonprofit status and are funded heavily from a governmental entity. We must be mindful of situations as described by Igal Jellinek: "The Department for the Aging is discretionary. It's not mandated dollars. So when times are bad, that's what you can cut. So we're at their mercy—and that's a real big issue for this system, at least in New York City."

A Practical To-Do List: Taking Tangible Steps Forward

I will conclude this book with ten action steps to move forward the situation of senior centers being remodeled, rebranded, and relegislated. Although the focus will be based on recent changes in the New York City models, broader applications will be highlighted. Each step, however, may need to be adjusted when applied to a particular regional or group setting.

For the first step, we need to conduct a comprehensive needs assessment of senior centers, nationally. Regional studies, such as the NYAM and CSCS reports, enjoyed some success, but these are not consistently conducted on a larger scale. Additionally, studies of center directors and other staff are frequent but often have low response rates, around 25–35 percent (Pardasani and Goldkind 2012; Pardasani and Thompson 2012).

The second step builds on the first. I suggest we conduct a complete senior center census with full long-term, longitudinal follow-up. The census, reflecting the U.S. decennial census approach, would formally collect data from all centers nationwide. And just as the decennial census follows up on nonrespondants through in-person visits, these should be such an option in the senior center census. I recognize that there is a cost associated with this census concept, but I strongly believe that, for steps 1 and 2, this is where more funding efforts of all kinds should be placed. The evaluation process for centers should be supported in this way. Subsequent OAA reauthorizations can also help locate funding for this effort. A sampling frame, or way to begin to locate all centers nationally, exists with the National Council on Aging and its National Institute of Senior Centers.

Some longitudinal data, about particular centers and regions, exists. For example, I was told by CSCS that the NYC Department for the Aging (DFTA) is in the process of hiring a researcher to conduct a three-year longitudinal study of both neighborhood and innovative center models. Empirical longitudinal data allows us to make changes to senior centers based on data and to evaluate the impact of the changes we make. Getting such data on a national level will also allow for midcourse corrections in programs and the sharing of successes among centers, locally and nationally.[6]

Building from the longitudinal data collection and analysis, my third step is to use these data to create a list of evidence-based practices for centers in different settings. The caveat is that with this step comes a real understanding that these practices are not cookie-cutter and may not work for all centers. Also, lag time may occur as centers get up to speed, that is, choosing programs and ideas that are right for their participants and implementing them.

The fourth step is crucial: to create a clear and sustainable funding plan. Just as Social Security funding was designed as part of the often referenced three-legged stool of retirement savings (Social Security, retirement plans and pensions, and savings), senior center funding needs more than one leg or funding stream to stand on. For example, there must be more streams than just public funding. We can consider corporate sponsorship in some health models or charge for members for special events or to do service such as home repair. Medicare funding is available for some preventative services, although this funding stream has been exploited in the past. Requests for proposals (RFPs) and funding options that require specialized grant writing knowledge are risky and cannot be taken for granted as transmissible if there is staff turnover.

The fifth step encourages support for the idea that progress is slow yet happening; accreditation may be a viable option along the path. I have seen support for accreditation at the local and national levels. While NCOA supports national accreditation standards, individual agencies in specific regions, such as New York City's DFTA, may prefer their own local accreditation process. According to NISC's September 2013 list, there are 125 accredited centers, 3.2 percent (four) in New York State and 1.6 percent (two) in New York City. The process should not be seen as punitive but, rather, a way for individual centers to receive external evaluation and options for support and growth.

Steps six and seven are based upon collectivity and social network building at the micro, meso, and macro levels. In the case of the center that is the focus of this book, as well as other centers, lack of integration with other local and national organizations and institutions prevented the connections that could have served to keep the center afloat. Isolation and lack of a social network can be lethal to centers. For step six, I would suggest that centers use national and local organizations to foster bonds on all levels—from relationships with other centers in the neighborhood to national networks of centers. With these connections comes pooled knowledge and resources. These lead to my seventh step: using collective group membership and solidarity for lobbying and political action. As Manoj Pardasani and Lauri Goldkind (2012) found, senior center directors and staff are in need of advocacy training. Even though the OAA calls for agency collaboration, these researchers found that most senior center advocacy is almost always after the fact, crisis based, and local. Directors may be using written communication when web- or e-mail-based means of core building may be more appropriate. Center leaders also reported lacking knowledge of policies and fearing that their organizing activities might put off funders. Pardasani and Goldkind felt that center directors would benefit from advocacy training and leadership development. Directors should build larger advocacy-based groups and can use CSCS and NCOA materials in this effort.

I suggest that center leaders increase the scope of advocacy. They should take heart that elder-based groups have become some of the most powerful lobbying forces for issues related to older persons. Both academic and commercial presses acknowledge the power of age-based groups as lobbyists (Lichtblau 2012; Lynch 2011). In a *New York Times* article, Eric Lichtblau cited the Center for Responsive Politics, which reported that AARP "has an annual budget of about $1.4 billion and has spent more than $220 million on federal lobbying since 1998, to rank sixth among the top spenders" (2012, A12). Senior centers as a collective lobbying force would have more weight than individual centers alone. By approaching future directions of the senior center with many varied steps and directions and with great forethought and planning, we can have centers that truly reflect the interests of those older persons they serve. Diversifying funding streams will provide multiple paths to remaining in existence. Through solidarity and collaboration with other centers and entities, centers have the power to influence policy and to shape the hegemonic, or dominant, view. Centers will be seen as part of the continuum of care for aging-in-community in an aging society.

The eighth step is to change the labeling of centers as "innovative." Although this can seem a merely semantic point, this characterization implies that non-innovative centers are stale and passé and lag behind the times (for example, *activity*, in *activity center* implies that there is one successful path to take in the aging process—the innovative moniker holds the same weight). If we talk about centers using characteristics like membership size, types and numbers of meals served, types of services offered, neighborhood or community density, and so on, we can move away from the often distracting labeling process.

For the ninth step, we need to remove the "health" mandate assigned to centers as sites of health, wellness, and "healthy aging." As seen by the varieties of existing center types meeting the needs of center members, a health-only focus is reductionist. A health-dominant focus uses the biomedical view, much like that of successful-aging theories, valuing health promotion over much-needed primary services such as case management and social activities.

Tenth, we need to move beyond, and expand, the two-tiered level of center funding. Greater flexibility is needed in DFTA funding, for example. More contracted funding (which can be postevaluation or accreditation of centers) is recommended. Centers need to be made less funding dependent on RFP or

RFP-like processes alone, which favor centers whose staff can write grant proposals and understand the process of doing so.

Back to the case of the closed center, the final point of this book. With the center closed and the new tenant's programs up and running, rumors (based on members' hopes) of its reopening were finally subsiding as of this writing. News on the street had it that a new center of some kind was opening up in a storefront on the avenue, where the furniture store once was. Anita, a non-member of the closed center who went a couple of times a year, was the first to brave the trip to this new, possible senior center that opened in 2013. Her first step was to pick up the flier. It listed the name of the organization, which called itself a "social senior care center" with traditional senior center–like services and staff with an "active aging" and "holistic approach." She read that "all programs are absolutely free to qualifying participants" after first being screened in a "multilingual" "complimentary session" for full "assessment of eligibility." Since she was in her seventies and a neighborhood resident, Anita felt she met the bill and was intrigued. The next day, on her usual walk in the neighborhood, doing her morning errands, Anita went in to inquire about meal policies for nonmembers. A woman who seemed to work there said, "Breakfast is free; come and sit down and eat and have some coffee." Anita thought about getting her errands done first and asked about the times that lunch would be served. The woman responded, "For lunch you need a Medicaid card," which Anita did not have.

If we change senior center options and policies, so that we have older persons who feel "too poor" or left out of innovative centers but are considered "too rich" for Medicaid-funded social day centers, while their own neighborhood centers disappear, this group is lost without the services designated in the original OAA. This is the group the original senior center models and policy were, in the past, designed for. They survived, and more often thrived, in their own neighborhood centers. Adaptation and change are necessary, but centers need to embrace future members while keeping current centergoers in mind, so everyone has a place at the table.

Appendix A
Self-Reflection: My
Experience in the Field

Why senior centers? Senior citizens centers, as they were once called, were always a curiosity to me. My family is from a similar neighborhood setting, and several relatives attended this center in the past. My great-aunt began to attend this center, known as "the center," in the late 1970s and early 1980s after she was widowed. She would dress up to meet the "girls," and they would visit with us after the center closed for the day. I was never sure what went on at the center but knew it involved dances and "bus trips" to all sorts of locales and a lot of laughter on the part of the women who came visiting afterward. I would hear stories from my great-aunt about welcoming new center members, making weekly telephone calls to "shut-ins" as they were called, and serving on center boards. There were meals and bingo (of course), activity classes, and presentations from an ever-changing cast of characters.

My grandmother and grandfather also attended the center but less often than my aunt did. Early on, they mostly went on the trips and participated in an occasional activity. Later, my grandmother received "meals on wheels," or home-delivered meals, from the same center when she could no longer make it there in person and her dementia began to show. This same grandmother was one to organize card parties for women at a local church in the area, where older women could play bunco, win prizes, and share a Danish and coffee. There were also friends and neighbors in my childhood community who refused to go to the center and be like those "old people," not wanting to go to those "cliques of seniors" to get "government handouts"—referring to the donation of food supplies to centergoers.

I did not set out to study senior centers at all. But since the data I used for my dissertation did not define the role of social support and activities in the lives of elders from the individual's own point of view, I decided to begin doing ethnographic work to understand the places older persons visit for social support and how these places affect older persons' well-being. I chose a senior center because I was concerned with how older persons age within their own communities (aging in place). My aim was to look at how social activities and support at a center affected people's lives, authentically, and to capture their own words and thoughts, their own points of view.

So in June 2008, I began my fieldwork, focused on one particular center. I talked with frequent and less-frequent attendees, as well as staff, and even chatted with those who preferred not to go to the center. I would return to the center and "visit" many times over the next four years when, almost suddenly, the lens shifted, and I was thrown into the shuttering, or closing, of a center, the panicked calls from centergoers, and a larger picture of the center movement. It is a unique feature of this work that I, as the author, began this ethnographic project long before the closure process (initially focusing on the role of the center in individuals' daily lives) and remained embedded in the project long after the center's closure. Additionally, being familiar with and accepted by the community, I have had, and continue to have, access to the elders and remain in contact with many individuals and groups in the community.

Unlike many researchers who are seen as outsiders wanting to become embedded in a group or place, I understand the community well because of being raised and educated there. That said, leaving the community for university and an academic life, taking me to Philadelphia and Colorado, I gained another perspective. I went from native daughter to researcher and sometimes a hybrid of both. At times in this book, I note how these insider/outsider roles and identities both converge and diverge. Do you need to be from Queens to understand this "forgotten borough" and have a stance based on identity politics? No, but being from the community does grant access to a level of knowledge often absent in prior studies. This close association allowed me to gain the trust of center staff and attendees. This trust let me be privy to see the way centergoers constructed social meaning at the center. My being familiar with the setting led to ease of conversation and allowed participants to express a wide range of emotions and experiences in their narratives.

Over the course of the ethnography, my role and the way elders interacted with me changed. In the early days, the roles of interviewee and interviewer often blurred, with centergoers referring to their role in "teaching me something about being old," or letting me know "it seems like you are having a good time, too." The interviewing went through some phases of social desirability in the elders' answers ("Is this what you wanted to know?") and marginalized expression of elders' roles ("I'm taking too much of" or "wasting" "too much of your time," or "I really have nothing I can contribute"). Sometimes, once the elders "got my number," they offered overly positive self-presentations of the center: "It's like a drug," or "We're unhappy when we can't get here." In the last days before the closure, I was schooled to "tell Bloomberg [the mayor of New York] to keep this place open!"

When I returned to find the displaced center participants in 2013, I had mixed feelings. While I was always welcomed by my centergoers, some things had changed. Some groups had relocated to a new center. For example, I found Karen, who had macular degeneration, happily pushing the food cart distributing bread for lunch to her peers at a new center. There were also those who did not fare so well. At a 2013 visit to another center, a woman approached me with striking all-white hair and a walker that one could use as a seat. She had a home health aide in tow and began to show me pictures and tell me stories about her grandchildren. While she looked familiar, I just could not place her—until another centergoer told me, "That's Lily." Lily seemed to have experienced a decline in health since I'd seen her a year or so ago when she ran conversation groups at her center of origin. Also, there were those I could not locate, like Jack, who "liked to pay for the ladies' lunches." People told me he may have gotten into too many arguments at the new center, and some believed he had died. I could not find one woman, Cara. She owned her own apartment building, renting apartments out, and drove friends to and from the center. I was told the "German table" would know where she was and, when asked, they said they thought she went upstate, somewhere, with her children.

I also interviewed experts in the field, from 2012 to 2013, and spoke with many leaders in the senior center movement. They include Lilliam Barrios-Paoli, commissioner of DFTA; Paola Miceli, director of health, human services and senior services, Office of the Queens Borough President; Igal Jellinek, executive director, and Bobbie Sackman, director of public policy, at the Council of Senior Centers and Services NYC; Catherine Thurston, senior director for programs at Services and Advocacy for Gay, Lesbian, Bisexual and Transgender Elders (SAGE) in New York City; members of the local media, such as Robert Pozarycki; and center directors. I can honestly say that my conversations with the above rounded out the picture of senior center changes for me. These interviews provided more perspective about how structural elements such as law and organizations (and their ideologies) were seen and created in the field. So that the reader can get the feeling of my interviews with these leaders, I have kept some longer direct quotations from each in the text of the book.

Appendix B
Methods

The data discussed throughout the chapters of this book were a compilation of my in-depth interviews, field notes, and participant observations from 2008 to mid-2013. Those interviewed encompassed center members (of all types), older persons in the neighborhood, local center directors and staff at a couple of senior centers, local center activists, and leaders in the senior center field in New York City. My study included the collection and analysis of archival materials from the field setting (senior center newsletters, fliers, etc.). Along with work in the field, I concurrently collected media accounts (news articles, blogs, etc.) and changes in legislation and social policies about senior centers (such as the Older Americans Act) throughout the study period.

Several chapters include the results of my analysis, so I would like to talk about my process of analysis a bit more here. Major elements of my study's structure were guided by John Creswell's (2003, 2013) approach to designing qualitative work. I also found Virginia Braun and Victoria Clarke's (2006) six steps to succinctly explain the phases of thematic analysis a good way to describe my general methodological approach. First, I familiarized myself with the data collected through transcription (from its digital audio form) into typed notes and computer files. Second, after reading over all the text, I generated initial codes (for themes that arose) over all narratives to help organize all the data. Third, each code became part of a larger theme and then, fourth, I reviewed themes to create a thematic map for all the data to see how each theme fit with the others. Then, fifth, each theme was refined and made clearer so that, sixth, I could provide a rich description and text relating to my original research questions about the role of the center in older persons' lives (87).

The Process of Data Analysis

Interpretation of the Preclosure Elder Data

In the early chapters, where I have included narratives from the beginning of the six-year period, I analyzed data about the "good times" at the center from the elders' points of view using the standard thematic analysis procedures (mentioned in the prior section).

I then began to create codes or categories identifying key phrases or quotes. I used an in vivo, or open-coding, process, when creating codes, meaning that I had no preconceived codes or categories of interviewee answers set. Instead, I initially had an interview schedule of some general questions I asked the more frequent centergoers and read through and identified codes in their response text. For example, "Tell me about some of the social activities you participate in at the senior center," "How often do you participate in . . . ?" and "What do you like and dislike about participating in these activities?" But as time went on, the interviews became conversational and less "fixed." This is a true strength of the ethnographic method—the interviewer responds to the direction the interviewee pursues.

A qualitative software program, Altas.ti 7.0, allows all this thematic coding to happen as if one were writing in the margins of a document and lets free coding of text occur. Phrases, concepts, and the interviewees' own words are used to generate basic codes arising from the data. These codes then provide the elements to generate larger themes in the text. So, first, general themes or codes were identified from the first wave of narratives from the regular attendee group. With this software, codes were examined within a single document and between all the documents. I evaluated the codes in terms of their recurrence and the importance or "salience" placed on them in the narratives by the elder (see Buetow 2010). For example, how often did a theme come up in the interviews? How much time was devoted to a particular theme in one interview? A complete code list was created so the two-hundred-plus codes could be compared and combined. Themes and patterns emerged from the data (such as the center as a place of social support, "a place to be with your friends," or a place that can elevate mood "like a drug").

I employed a constant comparative method—analyzing the data as it is collected and moves forward (Glaser 1965; Merriam 2009). As part of this method, I "tried out ideas on participants" to see if the themes rang true to them (Bogdan and Biklen 2007 in Merriam 2009, 172). As recommended and preferred in qualitative research, data collection and analysis happened together as prior data collected "shaped" the next types of data to be collected (see Merriam 2009, 171). So, while coding existing narratives into categories, I also looked for differences between the narratives (that is, was there something that differed in a couple of accounts?) and made notes, or memos, of these instances. As I indexed the data, and the data collection progressed along this comparative method, increasing references were made to the "bingo" or "menu" members. To add the voice of these members to the analysis, counternarratives, or interviews with less frequently attending members, were collected. Themes were gathered from these transcripts in the same way as the regular members' transcripts and included general codes such as "quality of food or activity options declining" or "attendees not being as 'nice' as past members." Last, a couple of individuals, suggested by bingo and menu members as those rarely, if ever, attending the center, were interviewed. Themes, such as the "cliquishness of center members" or the "greater importance of outside activities/memberships," emerged.

Codes were created and merged to identify larger themes and patterns in the text. In addition to listing code counts, the Code Manager feature of Altas.ti combined individual codes via commonality of theme into code groups, or code families. This process is analogous to analytical or axial codes being moved toward selective coding—taking codes from a more general to a more specific focus. For example, forty-six subcodes for kinds of individual activities (e.g., meals for the homebound, trips, exercise, bus trips, or bookmobile) at the center were grouped together into a larger "Activities" family. The "Negative Changes in the Center" family included twenty-three codes for stopped activities, increased building construction, no trips, and others (not seniors) at the center, and so on. Direct quotes were also used to generate themes. Visually, I created word clouds of codes and code families along with code-mapping displays. I used the network view in Atlas.ti to illustrate the relationship between codes. In addition to the Altas.ti software, I used the Statistical Package for the Social Sciences (SPSS) to create summary statistics for descriptive data such as demographic or background items. Using the software while in the field, I could also reflect upon the data collection and analysis process and tie themes to larger patterns and theories.

Interpretation of Closure Elder Data

As I spent additional time in the field, data from elders' interviewers and observations during the closure process were added in to the data analysis process. These narratives that I collected during and after the closure process appear in later chapters of the book. Some of these interviews occurred at new centers or in the community (in a coffee shop or during walks with interviewees). Interviews with some new centers' staff were added to the data, as were my field notes with follow-up questions about the location of those original center members who were lost. New codes were added, such as "rapid changes in the center," "changes in the economy," increased cliquishness," "comments about the staff," "the importance of numbers," "the crowd," "director's changes," and "fear." All these codes fell under a larger theme of "new negative changes in the center."

Newspapers and Media Accounts

Along the course of the study, I also collected media accounts of events relating to the senior center that was the focal center of this book, senior centers in New York, senior centers in general, and senior center legislation. The media accounts were taken from local community-level papers (excluded from the bibliography to protect the confidentiality of elder participants), Queens (borough-based) papers, national papers such as the *New York Times*, and solely online news outlets and their related blogs about public reaction to stories. Press releases from governmental and nonprofit organizations were included in this analysis as they captured the time line of senior-center changes.

Expert Accounts and Interviews

During the years 2012 to 2013, I had a series of phone and in-person interviews with many leaders in the senior center field. These included the commissioner of the New York City Department for the Aging (DFTA); the director of health, human services and senior services, Office of the Queens Borough President; the executive director and director of public policy at the Council of Senior Centers and Services NYC; the senior director for programs at Services and Advocacy for Gay, Lesbian, Bisexual and Transgender Elders (SAGE); local center advocates; and other center directors.

The telephone interviews were digitally audio-recorded (with permission) and transcribed twice, separately, by myself and a graduate assistant. During in-person interviews, I took notes and recorded my observations after completion of the interview. Any printed materials, such as senior center directories or newsletters, were also added to the data pool. As is the ethnographic practice, I often included large sections of the leaders' direct quotes from my interview text so that the reader may interpret them, as well.

Social Policy Data

To get a sense of the impact of legislation on senior centers, I collected and reviewed documents and commentary written about senior center policies. I gathered information from center-related polices in the Older Americans Act and related law, policies, and programs, such as the Program of All-Inclusive Care for the Elderly (PACE), Geriatric Resources for Assessment and Care of Elders (GRACE), and Home and Community-Based Services (HCBS), Medicaid Waivers, and the Affordable Care Act's provisions for those sixty-five years of age and over. Official text of legislation was retrieved from the Library of Congress. Governmental policy and program data were taken from official websites, official press release statements, or search databases such as LexisNexis. After being collected, the textual data were also analyzed using content analysis and the Altas.ti data analysis software. When necessary, a peer academic with a juris doctorate was contacted for correct interpretation of the law and policy.

My Approach to Maintaining Ethnographic Rigor

Throughout the data collection process, I employed the standard ethnographic safeguards to ensure trustworthiness (that is, making sure the study at hand is valid). Specifically, rigor in qualitative studies, such as the extended case study method I used, is provided by including the four elements of trustworthiness: credibility (internal validity), transferability (external validity), dependability (reliability), and confirmability (neutrality) (Lincoln and Guba 1985; Merriam 2009).

Credibility simply means using multiple ways to collect information or having multiple sources of information about the same experience or event. Of the many ways to go about ensuring creditability, two of the best are to spend a long period of time in the field and to make repeated observations. When in the field, one collects information from multiple people and sources. Credibility can be improved by triangulation (looking at the same experience using different data sources or at different periods of time). For example, when I was writing about the heyday or closure of the center, information was triangulated or gathered from a combination of interviewing several types of center members, observational work at the senior center, my journaling, and artifacts such as the center's monthly newsletter. I followed the center members as they settled into new centers or coffee shops or left the neighborhood.

I chose interviewees who could offer differing experiences of being at the center (the regular and bingo/menu members, nonattendees, center staff, multiple center directors, and leaders in the senior center field in New York City) for at least three distinct periods of time. This variety of interviewees offering different experiences of the center act as counternarratives or discordant cases that can provide a wider range of viewpoints. I also asked some center members about my findings to double-check the "realness" or authenticity of my work (called member-checking). Using peer-debriefing, I relayed my analytical process to more academic colleagues, so they, while not directly involved in the project, could act as sounding boards.

Transferability means that a researcher must provide enough background about his or her own study so that another researcher can decide if he or she finds the current study relevant to his or her work. In other words, is the study at hand applicable to the new researcher's study? How would the present study's findings apply to another? To address transferability, I have provided rich, thick description of the elders' and experts' own narratives and their own words as direct quotations throughout the book so you may readily understand the context of my study.

To assure dependability, a researcher keeps an audit trail (about how the data were collected) and how coding decisions were made, as I did in this Appendix. In an extended case study, such as mine, the researcher acts as the instrument—recording and analyzing the data. The goal of confirmability is to make sure that what is recorded, analyzed, and found are the opinions and feeling of those in the study and not the researcher. Researchers like myself address confirmability by being aware of their own stance on an ongoing basis and being reflexive about their experience in the field. I explore the relationship between myself and the work in greater depth in appendix A.

Notes

Introduction

1. Pseudonyms are used for all elders, senior center staff, identifying locations, and organizations in the case study portion of this book. In the later chapters, discussing the future of centers, experts and leaders in the field are identified by their proper names—unless they requested and signed a pseudonym release form.
2. The quotes and description of events in this book are drawn from those interviews, my field notes, and hours spent doing field observation in the community.
3. It must be noted that this closure is one of many and that many more centers are being closed or are in danger of closing. Unfortunately, such events are becoming commonplace for senior centers.
4. The closure list was also unaffectionately called the hit list.
5. See Cabin and Fahs 2010. Additionally, they say: "Senior centers over the last two years in New York City have been criticized as costly, inefficient, and archaic" (348).
6. Companies also offer to "reword" centers' titles and create new physical structures and marketing for them. For example, Partners in Prime offers to give a center a "younger identity" to be "vibrant and fresh" with an "ageless lust for life" (2010). Picking up on the lust-for-life theme, Barbara Marshall writes about the "zoomers." Marshall describes the way this stereotype is marketed by Mireille Silcoff in *Zoomer* magazine: "[It] promotes a new kind of archetypal ideal. It is a person, say, 73, who goes footloose in five-inch Jimmy Choo stilettos. A person who can toss back a large late dinner of steak and bold Shiraz after a full, extremely hip day of dieting, ab-crunching, 'chilling,' Pilates, hardcore jogging, subtle cosmetic surgery, not looking one's age, shopping without dropping, and engaging in various non-old person modes of 'getting your game on,' including the super hot sex of one's twenties" (Marshall 2011, 403).
7. Council of Senior Centers and Services 2010; Dal Santo 2009; Krout 1994; Pardasani 2010; Salari et al. 2006; Turner 2004.
8. The focal point concept was added in a 1973 Older Americans Act revision.
9. Ashida and Heaney 2008; Farone et al. 2005; Grenier 2005; Hurd 1999; Lund and Engelsrud 2008; Michael et al. 2001; Pardasani 2010; Turner 2004; Wenger 1999.

10. Early sociological work using the extended case study approach is credited to Burawoy (1998).

11. According to the NYC Department of Planning's website, "Geographically, New York is a city with 5 boroughs, 59 community districts, and hundreds of neighborhoods" (http://www.nyc.gov/html/dcp/html/neighbor/neigh.shtml).

12. The Census Tract will be referred to as neighborhood for the purposes of this book.

13. Mayer (2009, 424) refers to what he sees as a common practice of alluding to structural forces in perpetuating inequality in elders' lives without actually including the aforementioned structural components.

14. In this case, *organizational ties* can refer to the connections between two senior centers, between a senior center and its board or management company, or between a senior center and DFTA.

15. The role of agency versus structure is discussed further in chapter 5, where I explore individual agency and power in relation to participants' complex ties to other groups at three levels of social ties (micro, meso, and macro). Each level can help or halt social capital production. The agency-versus-structure debate is revisited in chapter 8, along with the role of social class in the context of the political economy of aging theory.

16. A neighborhood adjacent to that of the case study in this book was featured in "The Best 'Hoods: Rediscover the City's Greatest Nabes" in a September 2012 issue of *Time Out New York*.

17. In the *Gerontologist* Gubrium (1992) stressed that qualitative methods are a stand-alone methodology, not pre-quantitative strategy. By 2007, qualitative work made up 18 percent of articles within the prominent gerontology journals (Oliver 2011; Schoenberg et al. 2007). Editorials have called for more qualitative articles and increased qualitative "rigor" (Schoenberg and McAuley 2007). Gerontological journal editors are providing extra space for qualitative-based writing (such as ethnography, grounded theory, and phenomenology) and adding in work from the humanities and arts (Kivnick and Pruchno 2011; Schoenberg et al. 2011).

18. There are also many ethnographies of aging in institutional care. Some, by date, include: Jaber Gubrium's *Living and Dying at Murray Manor* (1975); Jennie Keith's special issue of the *Anthropological Quarterly* (1979) featuring fieldwork with elders in a variety of settings; Gubrium and David Buckholdt's *Describing Care* (1982); Lee Bowker's *Humanizing Institutions for the Aged* (1982); Susan Sheehan's *Kate Quinton's Days* (1984); Gubrium's *The Mosaic of Care* (1991); Joel Savishinsky's *The Ends of Time* (1991); Gubrium's *Speaking of Life* (1993); Maria Vesperi and J. Neil Henderson's *The Culture of Long-Term Care* (1995); Rene Somera's *Bordered Aging* (1997); and ethnographic chapters in Janice Graham and Peter Stephenson's *Contesting Aging and Loss* (2010). There are many gerontological studies including observational work and in-depth interviewing over time, such as Gubrium's *Oldtimers and Alzheimer's* (1986). Katherine Newman's *A Different Shade of Gray* (2003) uses in-depth interviews and Allison Smith's *Ageing in Urban Neighbourhoods* (2009) includes visual neighborhood profiles.

19. An ethnographic study may take on a direction of its own. See, for example, the work of Furman (1997) on being a researcher "in the right place, at the right time" at a local beauty shop setting or that of Philippe Bourgois as he was "thrown in to crack against his will" (2002).

Chapter 1   The History of Senior Centers

1. See Council of Senior Centers 2010; Dal Santo 2009; Krout 1989.
2. Their study examined the impact of neighbors upon quality of life and found cohesion and safety were significant predictors.
3. This debate about boomers was sparked by a July 29, 2012, op-ed by Bill Keller in the *New York Times* online. Keller's article was challenged by many, leading Keller to write additional pieces under the heading "The Backlash and Boomers and Entitlements: Next Round," published in his blog in the paper's Opinion Pages. The articles received over 450 comments.
4. For example, see the Boomer Bond contracts created by the Denver Regional Council of Governments, http://www.drcog.org/index.cfm?page=BoomerBond.
5. According to Harry "Rick" Moody, cohort-olatry is "the misguided over-emphasis on cohort factors, at the expense of age and period factors. Singling out Boomers as the group at fault for public policies we don't like won't get us very far. We can, and we should, should raise questions about justice in the life-chances of different cohorts. For example, there is a genuine problem with student debt today. But that problem is not the 'fault' of Millennials or Boomers, but the result of structural factors, just as with the sub-prime mortgage disaster, which also cannot be laid at the feet of any particular cohort. Cohort language has its uses. But it also has limitations, especially when people start moralizing and generalizing" (2008a, 841).
6. This estimate varies by sex and race/ethnicity.
7. Gil-Torres and Villa's (2000) alternative read of the concept of aging in place, as being more "stuck in place" for poor elders, will be discussed in chapter 6.
8. For additional details, refer to the ElderSpirit website (http://www.elderspirit.net).
9. Council of Senior Centers and Services of New York City 2010; New York Academy of Medicine 2010. Note: this estimate does not include the fifty centers scheduled to be closed between 2010 and 2011 in the city.
10. A link to all Mayor's Management Reports is available through the archive (http://www.nyc.gov/html/ops/html/data/mmr_archives.shtml#2003).
11. Barrios-Paoli's term began on February 2, 2009.

Chapter 2   The Case of the Center before Shuttering

1. Because of confidentiality concerns as expressed by the Institutional Review Board, additional identifying characteristics of this individual center are not included. Although the focal center of this book is now closed, portions of this chapter, discussing the life of the center when it was open, are consciously written in the present tense so the reader can get the sense of what the center was like pre-closing, when the center was "alive." The themes serve as a still snapshot of what center life was like.
2. This estimate is taken from NYC Department of City Planning 2011. For the seventy-two centers listed in the fourteen community districts, the number of meals served per month range from 360 to 6,330. This center's monthly average of 3,240 falls in the middle of this range.

Chapter 3 Reconstructing Shuttering in a Larger Social Context

1. Links to all CSCS documents referred to in this chapter are available in the Reference list.
2. Prior reports (such as the Mayor's Management Reports for DFTA) do not support this claim.
3. The irony is that there were centers lost in Queens, so Assemblywomen Nolan's fears later came true.
4. In places, newspaper sources are referred to indirectly. The proper name of certain papers cannot be identified to preserve the confidentiality extended to the center participants under the conditions set forth by the IRB.
5. The article also includes a much-talked-about quote by John Krout: "'If they [centers] don't innovate,' said John A. Krout, director of the gerontology institute at Ithaca College, 'they will die'" (A14).
6. See "City Settles Sex Harassment Case at the Department of Aging" and "Sexual Harassment Claim Arises after Official Quits," both *New York Times*, December 31, 2008 (http://www.nytimes.com/2009/01/01/nyregion/01elder.html). The legal documents are posted online on a parents' advocate's website (http://www.parentadvocates.org/nicecontent/dsp_printable.cfm?articleID=7503).
7. See http://www.linkedin.com/pub/edwin-m%C3%A9ndez-santiago-lcsw/22/35a/bb3.
8. The report discussed the potential loss of forty-one centers in NYC low-income housing units, leaving elder residents without access to food and services.
9. The center studied in this book is not on this list or on the leaked *New York Times* list.
10. A list of the affected centers was included; the center discussed in this book is not on the list. It has not been on any closure list to date.

Chapter 4 The Case of the Center as It Is Shuttered

1. Scout felt that this one official gets the majority of allocated funding for many community-based programs because of his pull and influence with local boards. There is support from Nicole Marwell's book *Bargaining for Brooklyn* (2007) that some political figures, named directly by Scout, "apply political pressure to the elected officials who control key elements of the contacting process" (97). Scout called this process ballot stuffing.
2. As stated in the prior chapter, newspaper sources are referred to indirectly. The proper names of certain papers, new stories, or reporters are not identified to preserve the confidentiality extended to the center participants under the conditions set forth by the IRB. Some of these items may be omitted from the bibliography as well.

Chapter 5 The Organizational Embeddedness of Capital

1. In writing about "social capital as a societal resource," gerontologists Dawn Carr and Jon Hendricks (2011) want to clear up some common misconceptions about older persons and social capital. They caution that traditional social capital theory (which may focus on younger persons) often does not consider the ways social capital may be accumulated throughout life, ultimately affecting the capital that elders may be able to give back to others.
2. Small is referring to childcare centers as opposed to senior centers.
3. Here, I am referring to C. Wright Mills's concepts, with *personal troubles* referring

to issues at the level of the individual and *public issues* referring to issues facing larger groups in society.

4. Robert Putnam's *Bowling Alone* (2000) renewed interest in these types of brokered relationships. Putnam describes ties as bonding or bridging. Bonding capital acts like insider brokerage and links individuals inward as "sociological Superglue." Bridging capital is "outward looking" and "sociological W-D 40." He argues that bridging capital is more difficult to cultivate and maintain than the bonding kind.

5. My use of the term *outsider advantage* varies from but includes the common usage of Burt and others. Thomas Ng and Daniel Feldman's work (2010) supports the idea that once an individual is embedded in an organization, his or her ability to generate future social capital may be hampered.

6. Adam Kleinbaum (2012) has developed the term "organizational misfits" to reflect someone in an organization who has an untypical path that harms his or her advancement. I have expanded the term to include matches that are good, bad, or indifferent.

7. After the center was shuttered, the mayor, along with a famous actor, visited another center in the community for a holiday meal in 2011.

8. Later, this relationship turned negative; in 2011, the building was on the market for $1.8 million.

9. The full citation for this *IBO Web Blog* is not included here because it directly identifies the focal center of this book.

10. See Lee 2008.

Chapter 6   Poor Centers

1. Fullilove's concept was developed to describe the removal of African American residents in the waves of "urban renewal" in cities. Petrovic (2007) originally applied this term to elders.

2. Realtors and real estate exchanges played a large role in the center. One of the center board's directors was a realtor. And there were rumors among the displaced center participants that one center director ended up working for a local realtor once the center closed.

3. Martín Sánchez-Jankowski, in *Cracks in the Pavement: Social Change and Resilience in Poor Neighborhoods* (2008), discusses the way institutions are looked to as caretakers in poor neighborhoods.

Chapter 7   Reconceptualizing Centers

1. As described by Bill Thomas: "A hospital and a poor house got together, and they had a baby, and the baby was a nursing home. And you know, it's a little bit like its mama and a little bit like its papa. And at its deepest heart, it's an institution, and that is just not any way to live a life." "A Nursing Home Alternative," *The News Hour with Jim Lehrer* (http://www.pbs.org/newshour/bb/health/jan-june02/eden_2–27 .html#). This website is now defunct.

2. For a description of all ten Eden principles, see http://www.edenalt.org/our-10 -principles.

3. A Green House is formally defined as "an intentional community for elders built into residential scale and devoted to the pursuit of the most positive elderhood possible. The value of clinical services is recognized and is then made part of a

habilitative social framework that gives primacy to human development in later life"
(Thomas 2004, 226).

4. For example, the Colorado Culture Change in Action plan's principles are based
on person-centered care with the elder deciding the rhythm of daily life from social
contact to meal times (http://www.coculturechange.org/about.html).

5. See Gross 2008.

6. A recent survey by Pardasani and Thompson (2012) had response rates from center
staff below 25 percent.

7. This is based on an overview of six types of models discussed by Manoj Pardasani
and Peter Thompson (2012). They adapted their models directly from an earlier
source, the 2009 NISC's New Models of Senior Centers Taskforce's study. The
NISC report states aspects of these models may overlap, and other models may
exist. I have also recategorized and placed some of the 2012 NCOA's Programs of
Excellence Award winners into the current six center categories discussed here.

8. Benefits of intergenerational programs for volunteers and children have long been
known within the field of gerontology (Aday et al. 1991). Stephanie Davidson and
Beverly Boals-Gilbert stress the commonality of the experiences of children and
older persons in terms of "changes in development, a need for companionship, and
the desire to be understood" (2010, 23). Programs based on choice of partner, flexible roles, and an inviting setting can set the stage for strong reciprocal relationships
to form (Larkin and Kaplan 2010).

9. A local center director, who took in some of the displaced members of the center
focused on in this book, gave her view of intergenerational programs: "You have
to have a network of different ages. You got to have some young people; you got to
have some people your age. You can have a few maybe older than you. But if you
have that mix going on, you're going live a nice, healthy life. But if you just stick
with just your age group, you're going to have a lot of loss, until you get to the point
where there's only one friend left."

10. The three examples in the 2009 NISC report were Baltimore County Senior Centers (in Maryland), the OPC Center (in Michigan), and the Center in the Park (in
Pennsylvania).

11. Beyond the five boroughs, Intergenerational Strategies on Long Island, the Renaissance Network in Westchester County, and 55-Plus Yonkers Connection offer
volunteering, learning, and mentoring opportunities.

12. Personal correspondence with Paola Miceli, December 2012.

13. Bobbi Sackman described her thought processes when developing the charter
center model: "Why don't we have charter senior centers like charter schools,
where you give them more money, flexibility, not all the paperwork and the
restrictions, the regulatory restrictions. You let them build on what they already
know how to do and do well but also give them a chance to experiment and do
different things."

14. Centers appeal to diverse groups. Robbyn Wacker and Karen Roberto (2014)
describe the two models: the open and targeted and closed and targeted kinds.
Open targeted models are open to the community while providing outreach to
diverse groups. The closed and targeted models refer to centers exclusive to a particular target group.

15. When I visited this center after it opened, the numbers of members were up, and
that evening they were hosting a black-tie gala fund-raiser.

16. Barrios-Paoli also remarked, "There are centers that are doing exceedingly good

work and are not yet called innovative centers. And we're trying to figure out if there's a way of accrediting them as innovative centers. But there are ten or twelve more that are doing . . . pretty much the same thing as innovative centers and have great facilities. And people are using them in very creative ways."

17. She relays a story of a staff member's relative finding a place at a neighborhood center through contact with a center's dance program.

18. To address the lack of transportation by bus and subway, a taxi smart card program was created by DFTA and the Mayor's Office on Disability. Launched in January 2013, it was designed to give "disabled residents" in Astoria, Queens, and Canarsie, Brooklyn, taxi or livery cab funding. The program provides $87.50 to an elder's $12.50 charge on the card. To supplement services of Access-a-Ride, the program offsets transportation costs to doctors' appointments, shopping, or visiting. For further information, see http://www.ahrcnyc.org/news/?p=2107.

19. For additional description and characteristics of NORCs, see Vladeck and Segel 2010.

20. According to the Northeast Queens Jewish Community Council (2004) press release, the original NORC WOW model was located in northeast Queens.

21. Moody (2008a) calls the obsessive focus on the baby boomer cohort "cohort-olatry" and suggests that this focus neglects the role of many other social forces. He also sees the great marketability of this group (2008b).

22. Baby boomers have dropped the *baby* portion of their label.

Chapter 8   Beyond Rebranding

1. For LCAO's full analysis of the sequester, probable cuts, and its recommendations, see LCAO 2013.

2. Olson suggests that federal and local organizations designed to protect and advocate for older persons were never given the power to do more than provide fragmented services for them. These entities do not have power within the infra-structure to complete their mission. For example, the Area Agencies on Aging are lacking power and their resulting service becomes fragmented and not intercon-nected. Agencies are left fighting for autonomy in smaller arenas (see Olson 1982). National organizations working on elder policy and on elders' behalf are moving and changing their positions within the governmental structure. For example, as of April 16, 2012, the Administration on Aging has fallen under the Administra-tion for Community Living (ACL) (Administration for Community Living 2013). The ACL houses the Administration on Aging, the Office on Disability, and the Administration on Developmental Disabilities, placing all these groups together in many aspects.

3. While Social Security, Medicare, and Medicaid are codified entitlement programs and do not need reauthorization, the OAA is not an entitlement program. It needs to be reauthorized, which allows changes to be made to it. Although the OAA is often lumped together with these programs, it is different. Entitlement-based pro-grams, such as Medicare and Medicaid, are most frequently cited in the media and culture as the culprits in increased government spending (see Gorin 2010).

4. See https://www.healthcare.gov/.

5. My definition of *praxis*, a term found in the heading for this section, involves using knowledge and theory for some action rather than theorizing alone. Praxis centers around using more academic information to change the way we do things. Through

praxis, we can influence the way things are done by organizations and seen in social policies. As Carroll Estes and colleagues (2013) suggest, all critical gerontologists use praxis, or "linking theory and research to action and social change" (360). For my own reflections on my views throughout the process of this study, see appendix A.

6. As a given, these data need to come from studies with acceptable response rates, ones that do not lose elders to follow-up or attrition.

References

ABC Eyewitness News. 2012. "Innovative Senior Centers Offer More to the Elderly." http://abclocal.go.com/wabc/story?section=news/local/new_york&id=8660337.

Aday, Ronald H., Gayle C. Kehoe, and Lori A. Farney. 2006. "Impact of Senior Center Friendships on Aging Women Who Live Alone." *Journal of Women and Aging* 18 (1): 57–73.

Aday, Ronald H., Cyndee Rice Sims, and Emilie Evans. 1991. "Intergenerational Partners Project: A Model Linking Elementary Students with Senior Center Volunteers." *Gerontologist* 31 (2): 263–266.

Administration for Community Living. 2013. "Aging and Disability Resource Centers Program." http://acl.gov/Programs/CDAP/OIP/ADRC/index.aspx.

Administration on Aging. 2012a. "Older Americans Act Reauthorization." http://aoa.gov/AoARoot/AoA_Programs/OAA/Reauthorization/.

———. 2012b. *A Profile of Older Americans: 2011*. Washington, DC: U.S. Department of Health and Human Services.

Altman, Anita. 2006. "The New York NORC–Supportive Service Program." *Journal of Jewish Communal Service* 81:195–200.

Angrosino, Michael V. 2007. *Doing Ethnographic and Observational Research*. Los Angeles: SAGE.

Ashida, Sato, and Catherine Heaney. 2008. "Social Networks and Participation in Social Activities at a New Senior Center: Reaching Out to Older Adults Who Could Benefit the Most." *Activities, Adaptation and Aging* 32:40–58.

Baker, Dean, and David Rosnick. 2010. "The Impact of the Housing Crash on the Wealth of the Baby Boom Cohorts." Center for Economic and Policy Research. http://www.cepr.net/index.php/publications/reports/the-impact-of-the-housing-crash-on-the-wealth-of-the-baby-boom-cohorts.

Baker, Dorothy, Margaret Gottschalk, and Luann Bianco. 2007. "Step by Step: Integrating Evidence-Based Fall-Risk Management into Senior Centers." *Gerontologist* 47 (4): 548–554.

Ball, Scott, and Ebooks Corporation. 2012. *Livable Communities for Aging Populations: Urban Design for Longevity*. Hoboken, NJ: John Wiley and Sons.

Barbaro, Michael. 2008. "Bloomberg Retreats on Overhaul of Senior Centers." *New York Times*, May 8.

Bass, Scott. 2000. "Emergence of the Third Age: Toward a Productive Aging Society." *Journal of Aging and Social Policy* 11 (2–3): 7–17.

Baum, Stephanie. 2012. "Five Ways Healthcare Innovators Are Helping Old People." *MedCity News*, August 8. http://medcitynews.com/2012/08/5-ways-healthcare-entrepreneurs-are-helping-old-people/.

Bedney, Barbara, Robert Goldberg, and Kate Josephson. 2010. "Aging in Place in Naturally Occurring Retirement Communities: Transforming Aging through Supportive Service Programs." *Journal of Housing for the Elderly* 24:304–321.

Bencin, T. 1996. *Gottschee: A History of a German Community in Slovenia from the Fourteenth to the Twentieth Century*. Louisville, CO: Gottscheer Heritage and Genealogy Association.

Berland, Penn Schoen. 2012. "The United States of Aging Survey." National Council on Aging, June 8. http://www.ncoa.org/improve-health/community-education/united-states-of-aging/united-states-of-aging.html.

Bernstein, Nina. 2013. "Day Centers Sprout Up, Luring Fit Elders and Costing Medicaid." *New York Times*. April 22, A1.

Biggs, Simon, Chris Phillipson, Rebecca Leach, and Annemarie Money. 2007. "Baby Boomers and Adult Ageing: Issues for Social and Public Policy." *Quality in Ageing—Policy, Practice and Research* 8 (3): 32–40.

Bogdan, Robert, and Sari Knopp Biklen. 2007. *Qualitative Research for Education: An Introduction to Theory and Methods*. Boston: Pearson.

Bourdieu, Pierre. 1986. "The Forms of Capital." In *The Handbook of Theory and Research for the Sociology of Education*, ed. J. G. Richardson, 241–258. New York: Greenwood.

Bourgois, Philippe. 2003. *In Search of Respect: Selling Crack in El Barrio*. Cambridge, UK: Cambridge University Press.

Bowker, Lee H. 1982. *Humanizing Institutions for the Aged*. Lexington, MA: Lexington Books.

Braun, Virginia, and Victoria Clarke. 2006. "Using Thematic Analysis in Psychology." *Qualitative Research in Psychology* 3 (2): 77–101.

Bronstein, Laura, Zvi Gellis, and Bonnie Kenaley. 2011. "A Neighborhood Naturally Occurring Retirement Community: Views from Providers and Residents." *Journal of Applied Gerontology* 30 (1): 104–112.

Buetow, Stephen. 2010. "Thematic Analysis and Its Reconceptualization as 'Saliency Analysis.'" *Journal of Health Services Research and Policy* 15 (2): 123–125.

Buncombe County Aging Planning Task Force. 2007. "Framework for a Livable and Senior-Friendly Community." http://www.ncdhhs.gov/aging/demograpic/AttachmentD_1of3_LocalAgingLeadershipTeams_BuncombeCounty.pdf.

Burawoy, Michael. 1998. "The Extended Case Method." *Sociological Theory* 16 (1): 4–33.

Burns, Victoria F., Jean-Pierre Lavoie, and Damaris Rose. 2011. "Revisiting the Role of Neighbourhood Change in Social Exclusion and Inclusion of Older People." *Journal of Aging Research* 2012:1–2.

Burt, Ronald S. 2010. *Neighborhood Networks: Competitive Advantage Local and Personal*. New York: Oxford University Press.

Buttigieg, Joseph. 2006. "The Prison Notebooks: Antonio Gramsci's Work in Progress." *Rethinking Marxism* 18 (1): 37–42.

Cabin, William D., and Marianne C. Fahs. 2010. "Eyes Wide Open or Not: Developing a Model for Predicting Depression among Older Americans." *Home Health Care Management and Practice* 23:342–355.

Callahan, James J. 1992. "Aging in Place." *Generations* 16 (2): 5–6.

Caro, Francis, ed. 2000. "Advancing Aging Policy as the 21st Century Begins." *Journal of Aging and Social Policy* 11 (2–3): 1–210.

Carr, Dawn C., and Jon Hendricks. 2011. "Relevance of Social Capital and Lifestyle for the Third Age." In *Gerontology in the Era of the Third Age: Implications and Future Steps*, ed. Dawn C. Carr and Katherine Komp, 207–223. New York: Springer.

Casado, Banghwa Lee, Kimberly S. van Vulpen, and Stacey L. Davis. 2011. "Unmet Needs for Home and Community-Based Services among Frail Older Americans and Their Caregivers." *Journal of Aging and Health* 23 (3): 529–553.

CBS. 2012. "Superstorm Sandy Slams Northeast, Triggers Massive Blackouts and Flooding." October 30. http://www.cbsnews.com/8301-201-162-57542273/superstorm-sandy-slams-northeast-triggers-massive-blackouts-and-flooding/.

CBS New York. 2011. "New Yorkers Continue to Fight to Keep Senior Centers Open." March 18. http://newyork.cbslocal.com/2011/03/18/new-yorkers-continue-fight-to-keep-senior-centers-open/.

CCAL. n.d. "PCL Overview." http://www.ccal.org//?s=PCL+Overview.

Chan, Sewell, and David W. Chen. 2008. "Bloomberg Names Commissioner for Aging." *New York Times*, December 17.

Chen, David W. 2010a. "At Least 50 of City's Senior Centers Expected to Close to Save Money." *New York Times*, April 30, A15.

———. 2010b. "City Selects 50 Senior Centers to Close." *New York Times City Room* (blog), May 10. http://cityroom.blogs.nytimes.com/2010/05/10/city-selects-fifty-senior-centers-to-close/comment-page-1/?_php=true&_type=blogs&_r=0.

Chen, David W., and Fernanda Santos. 2008. "Quinn Vehemently Denounces Bloomberg's Plans." *New York Times*, November 14.

City and State. 2012. "New York City Power 100." December 5.

Civic Ventures. 2012. "Blueprint for the Next Chapter." http://www.civicventures.org/publications/booklets/blueprint.pdf.

Cohen, Deborah, Amber Sehgal, Stephanie Williamson, Terry Marsh, Daniela Golinelli, and Thomas L. McKenzie. 2009. "New Recreational Facilities for the Young and the Old in Los Angeles: Policy and Programming Implications." *Journal of Public Health Policy* 30:S248–S263.

Cohen-Mansfield, Jiska, and Perla Werner. 1998. "Predictors of Aggressive Behaviors: A Longitudinal Study in Senior Day Care Centers." *Journal of Gerontology: Psychological Sciences* 53B:P300–P310.

Coleman, James. 1990. *Foundations of Social Theory*. Cambridge, MA: Harvard University Press.

Committee on Quality of Health Care in America, Institute of Medicine. 2001. *Crossing the Quality Chasm: A New Health System for the 21st Century*. Washington, DC: National Academies Press.

Copquin, Claudia Gryvatz. 2007. *The Neighborhoods of Queens*. New York: Citizens Committee for New York City; New Haven: Yale University Press.

Costella, AnnMarie. 2010. "Ten Senior Centers in Queens May Close." *Queens Chronicle*, May 13.

Council of Senior Centers and Services of New York City (CSCS). 2004a. *Elimination of ESL Classes at Senior Centers*. February. http://cscs-ny.org/advocacy/reports/elssurvey04.php.

———. 2004b. *30 Ways Seniors Benefit from Senior Centers*. October 21. http://cscs-ny.org/advocacy/files/30waysbenefit.php.

———. 2006. *Growing Old in New York City: The Age Revolution.* February. http://cscs-ny
.org/advocacy/files/GrowingOld_FEB2006.pdf.

———. 2007. *Hunger Hurts.* December. http://cscs-ny.org/advocacy/files/2007CSCS
HUNGERSTUDYFinalReport.pdf.

———. 2009. *Charter Senior Center Concept.* August 17. http://cscs-ny.org/files/
chartersrconcept.pdf.

———. 2010a. *More with Less Is Impossible.* April. http://cscs-ny.org/files/More-with-Less-is
-Impossible-2010.pdf.

———. 2010b. "The Shoe Drops." Action alert. April 26. http://www.cscs-ny.org/advocacy/
action-alerts/2010-04-26-action-alert.php.

———. 2010c. *21st Century Senior Centers: Changing the Conversation; A Study of New York
City's Senior Centers.* http://cscs-ny.org/files/FINAL-WHOLE-REPORT.pdf.

———. 2013. *The Power of Aging: The Intersection of Health and Social Services.* Brochure for
Twenty-fourth annual Conference on Aging and Vendor Expo. January 24.http://cscs-ny
.org/events/conference/2013ConferenceBrochure.pdf.

———. n.d.a. "How Age-Friendly Is NYC?" http://www.cscs-ny.org/files/infographic-cuts
.pdf. Infographic.

———. n.d.b. "Under-enrollment of Older New Yorkers (60+) in the SNAP/Food Stamps
Program by NYC Community Districts by Percent." Map with tables.

Counihan, Beth. 2008. "When I Wake Up in the Morning, It All Depends What I Want to
Do: Ethnography of Leisure in the Lives of Elderly Women." *Journal of Aging, Humanities and the Arts* (2): 25–35.

Creswell, John W. 2003. *Research Design: Qualitative, Quantitative, and Mixed Methods
Approaches.* Thousand Oaks, CA: Sage.

———. 2013. *Qualitative Inquiry and Research Design: Choosing Among Five Approaches.*
Thousand Oaks, CA: Sage.

Crouse-Dick, Christine. 2010. Review of *Unanticipated Gains: Origins of Network Inequality
in Everyday Life*, by Mario Luis Small. *Women's Studies in Communication* 33 (1): 74–76.

Crystal, Stephen, and Pearl Beck. 1992. "A Room of One's Own: The SRO and the Single
Elderly." *Gerontologist* 32 (5): 684–692.

Dal Santo, Teresa S. 2009. *Senior Center Literature Review: Reflecting and Responding to
Community Needs.* Sacramento: California Commission on Aging.

Dannefer, Dale. 2003. "Cumulative Advantage/Disadvantage and the Life Course: Cross-
Fertilizing Age and Social Science Theory." *Journals of Gerontology, Series A, Biological
Sciences and Medical Sciences* 58A (11): S327–S337.

———. 2012. "Enriching the Tapestry: Expanding the Scope of Life Course Concepts." *Journals of Gerontology, Series B, Psychological Sciences and Social Sciences* 67 (2): 221–225.

Davidson, Stephanie, and Beverly Boals Gilbert. 2010. "What Age Gap? Building Intergenerational Relationships." *Dimensions of Early Childhood* 38 (2): 23–29.

Davis, Pete. 2010. "Seniors Suffer: Nine Senior Citizens Centers Shut Down." *Queens Courier*, July 13. http://queenscourier.com/2010/seniors-sufferbr-br-nine-senior-citizen
-centers-close-1793/.

Dawsey, Josh. 2012. "Hospitals Eye Big Changes after Sandy." *Wall Street Journal*, February 1.
http://online.wsj.com/article/SB10001424127887324900204578282131232611070.html.

Denver Regional Council of Governments (DRCOG). 2013. "Boomer Bond Contracts."
http://www.drcog.org/index.cfm?page=BoomerBond.

Duncan, David F., Thomas Nicholson, John B. White, Dana Burr Bradley, and John Bonaguro. 2010. "The Baby Boomer Effect: Changing Patterns of Substance Abuse among
Adults Ages 55 and Older." *Journal of Aging and Social Policy* 22 (3): 237–248.

Eaton, Jacqueline, and Sonia Salari. 2005. "Environments for Lifelong Learning in Senior Centers." *Educational Gerontology* 31(6): 461–480.

Eckert, J. Kevin. 1980. *The Unseen Elderly: A Study of Marginally Subsistent Hotel Dwellers.* San Diego: Campanile Press, San Diego State University.

Eckert, J. Kevin, Paula Carder, Leslie A. Morgan, Ann Christine Frankowski, and Erin Roth. 2009. *Inside Assisted Living: The Search for Home.* Baltimore: Johns Hopkins University Press.

Elder, Glen H. 1974. *Children of the Great Depression: Social Change in Life Experience.* Chicago: University of Chicago Press.

———. 1994. "Time, Human Agency, and Social Change: Perspectives on the Life Course." *Social Psychology Quarterly* 57 (1): 4–15.

Estes, Carroll, Susan A. Chapman, Catherine Dodd, Brooke Hollister, and Eva Williams, eds. 2013. *Health Policy: Crisis and Reform.* Portland, MA: Jones & Bartlett Learning.

Evans, Gail, and Lynna Carnegie. 2009. "New York City's Foster Grandparent Program: A Model of Older Volunteer Management." *Case Management Journals* 10 (3): 115–120.

Fahs, Mimi. 2012. "Healthy Aging: A Public Health Challenge for the 21st Century." Brookdale Center for Health Aging and Longevity. www.brookdale.org.

Farone, Diane Weis, Tanya R. Fitzpatrick, and Thanh V. Tran. 2005. "Use of Senior Centers as a Moderator of Stress-Related Distress among Latino Elders." *Journal of Gerontological Social Work* 46:65–83.

Federal Interagency Forum on Aging-Related Statistics. 2010. *Older Americans 2010: Key Indicators of Well-Being.* Washington, DC: Government Printing Office.

Ferraro, Kenneth F., Tetyana Pylypiv Shippee, and Markus H. Schafer. 2009. "Cumulative Inequality Theory for Research on Aging and the Life Course." In *Handbook of Theories of Aging*, 2nd ed., ed. V. L. Bengtson, D. Gans, N. M. Putney, and M. Silverstein, 413–435. New York: Springer.

Field, John. 2003. *Social Capital.* New York: Routledge.

Fingerman, Karen L., Karl A. Pillemer, Merril Silverstein, and J. Jill Suitor. 2012. "The Baby Boomers' Intergenerational Relationships." *Gerontologist* 52 (2): 199–209.

Finkelstein, Emily S., M. Carrington Reid, Alison Kleppinger, Karl Pillemer, and Julie Robison. 2012. "Are Baby Boomers Who Care for Their Older Parents Planning for Their Own Future Long-Term Care Needs?" *Journal of Aging and Social Policy* 24 (1): 29–45.

Finkelstein, Ruth, Ana Garcia, Julie Netherland, and Jessica Walker. 2008. *Towards An Age-Friendly New York City: A Findings Report.* New York: New York Academy of Medicine.

Fitzpatrick, Tanya R., Richard J. Gitelson, Kathleen L. Andereck, and Ellen Sue Mesbur. 2005. "Social Support Factors and Health among a Senior Center Population in Southern Ontario, Canada." *Social Work in Health Care* 40 (3): 15–37.

Fitzpatrick, Tanya R., and James McCabe. 2008. "Future Challenges for Senior Center Programming to Serve Younger and More Active Baby Boomers." *Activities, Adaptation, and Aging* 32 (3): 198–213.

Fligstein, Neil, and Doug McAdam. 2011. "Toward a General Theory of Strategic Action Fields." *Sociological Theory* 29 (1): 1–26.

Flynn, Raymond. 1984. "Reagan Cutbacks Hurt the Elderly, Says Flynn." *Boston Globe*, July 29. http://0-search.proquest.com.source.unco.edu/docview/294199493?accountid=12832.

Fogel, Barry S. 1992. "Psychological Aspects of Staying at Home." *Generations* 16 (2): 15–19.

Formosa, Marvin. 2012. "Education and Older Adults at the University of the Third Age." *Educational Gerontology* 38 (2): 114–126.

Frankel, Bruce. 2012. "How Generous Are Baby Boomers?" *Next Avenue*, August 6. http://www.nextavenue.org/article/2012-07/how-generous-are-baby-boomers.

Freedman, Marc. 1999. *Prime Time: How Baby Boomers Will Revolutionize Retirement and Transform America.* New York: Public Affairs.

Freudenheim, Ellen. 2006. *Queens: What to Do, Where to Go (and How Not to Get Lost) in New York's Undiscovered Borough.* New York: St. Martin's Griffin Press.

Frey, William. 2010. "Baby Boomers and the New Demographics of American Seniors." *Generations* 34 (3): 28–37.

Friedman, Dana, Nina S. Parikh, Nancy Giunta, Marianne C. Fahs, and William T. Gallo. 2012. "The Influence of Neighborhood Factors on the Quality of Life of Older Adults Attending New York City Senior Centers: Results from the Health Indicators Project." *Quality of Life Research: An International Journal of Quality of Life Aspects of Treatment, Care, and Rehabilitation* 21 (1): 123–131.

Fullilove, Mindy Thompson. 2001. "Root Shock: The Consequences of African American Dispossession." *Journal of Urban Health: Bulletin of the New York Academy of Medicine* 78 (1): 72–80.

Furman, Frida Kerner. 1997. *Facing the Mirror: Older Women and Beauty Shop Culture.* New York: Routledge.

Gans, Herbert J. 1974. "Gans on Granovetter's 'Strength of Weak Ties.'" *American Journal of Sociology* 80 (2): 524–527.

Gelfand, Donald. 2006. *The Aging Network: Programs and Services.* New York: Springer.

Gianoulis, Tina. 2013. "Hipsters." In *St. James Encyclopedia of Popular Culture,* ed. Thomas Riggs, 675–676. Detroit: St. James Press.

Gillibrand, Kirsten. 2012. "FY 2011 Transportation, Housing and Urban Development, and Related Agencies Federal Funding Requests." Link available at "Federal Funding Requests." http://www.gillibrand.senate.gov/services/federal_funding/.

Gitlin, Laura N. 2003. "Conducting Research on Home Environments: Lessons Learned and New Directions." *Gerontologist* 43 (5): 628–637.

Giugni, Marco, Doug McAdam, and Charles Tilly. 1999. *How Social Movements Matter.* Minneapolis: University of Minnesota Press.

Glaser, Barney G. 1965. "The Constant Comparative Method of Qualitative Analysis." *Social Problems* 12 (4): 436–445.

Glass, Anne P. 2009. "Aging in a Community of Mutual Support: The Emergence of an Elder Intentional Cohousing Community in the United States." *Journal of Housing for the Elderly* 23 (4): 283–303.

Glass, Ruth. 1965. *London's Housing Needs: Statement of Evidence to the Committee on Housing in Greater London.* London: Committee on Housing in Greater London.

Glendinning, Amy. 2012. "Stand Up for Old Folks." *M.E.N.,* November 7, 21.

Gluckman, Max. 1961. "Ethnographic Data in British Social Anthropology." *Sociological Review* 9 (1): 5–17.

Golant, Stephen M. 2003. "Conceptualizing Time and Behavior in Environmental Gerontology: A Pair of Old Issues Deserving New Thought." *Gerontologist* 43 (5): 638–648.

———. 2008. "Commentary: Irrational Exuberance for the Aging in Place of Vulnerable Low-Income Older Homeowners." *Journal of Aging and Social Policy* 20 (4): 379–397.

Gorin, Stephen. 2010. "Health Care Reform and Older Adults." *Health and Social Work* 35 (1): 3–6.

Graham, Janice E. 2010. "'Them' Are 'Us': Building Appropriate Policies from Fieldwork to Practice." In *Contesting Aging and Loss,* ed. Janice E. Graham and Peter H. Stephenson, 177–190. Toronto, Ontario, Canada: University of Toronto Press.

Graham, Janice E., and Peter H. Stephenson, eds. 2010. *Contesting Aging and Loss.* New York: University of Toronto Press.

Granovetter, Mark. 1973. "The Strength of Weak Ties." *American Journal of Sociology* 78:1360–1380.

Grant, Geraldine S. 1981a. *New Immigrants and Ethnicity: A Preliminary Research Report on Immigrants in Queens.* Ethnic Studies Project, City University of New York, Flushing, NY. Microfilm.

———. 1981b. *Six Immigrant Groups in Queens: A Pilot Study.* Ethnic Studies Project, City University of New York, Flushing, NY. Microfilm.

Grantmakers in Aging. 2013. *Age-Friendly Communities: The Movement to Create Great Places to Grow Up and Grow Old in America; An Introduction for Private and Public Funders.* New York: Community AGEnda and Pfizer Foundation.

Greenfield, Emily, Scharlach, Andrew, Lehning, John and Joan Davitt. 2012. "A Conceptual Framework for Examining the Promise of the NORC Program and Village Models to Promote Aging in Place." *Journal of Aging Studies* 26 (3): 273–284.

Gregory, Steven. 1998. *Black Corona: Race and the Politics of Place in an Urban Community.* Princeton, NJ: Princeton University Press.

Greif, Mark. 2010. "What Was the Hipster?" *New York Magazine*, October 24. http://nymag .com/news/features/69129/.

Grenier, Amanda M. 2005. "The Contextual and Social Locations of Older Women's Experiences of Disability and Decline." *Journal of Aging Studies* 19:131–146.

Gross, Jane. 2008. "Its Appeal Slipping, the Senior Center Steps Livelier." *New York Times*, March 25. http://www.nytimes.com/2008/03/25/us/25cafe.html.

Gubrium, Jaber F. 1975. *Living and Dying at Murray Manor.* New York: St. Martin's Press.

———. 1986. *Oldtimers and Alzheimer's: The Descriptive Organization of Senility.* Greenwich, CT: JAI Press.

———. 1988. *Analyzing Field Reality.* Newbury Park, CA: Sage.

———. 1991. *The Mosaic of Care: Frail Elderly and Their Families in the Real World.* New York: Springer.

———. 1992. "Editorials: Qualitative Research Comes of Age in Gerontology." *Gerontologist* 32 (5): 581–582.

———. 1993. *Speaking of Life: Horizons of Meaning for Nursing Home Residents.* New York: Aldine de Gruyter.

Gubrium, Jaber F., and David R. Buckholdt. 1982. *Describing Care: Image and Practice in Rehabilitation.* Cambridge, MA: Gunn and Hain.

Gubrium, Jaber F., and James Holstein, 1993. "Family Discourse, Organizational Embeddedness, and Local Enactment." *Journal of Family Issues* 14 (1): 66–82.

———. 2012. "Theoretical Validity and Empirical Utility of a Constructionist Analytics." *Sociological Quarterly* 53 (3): 341–359.

Gubrium, Jaber F., and Andrea Sankar. 1990. *The Home Care Experience: Ethnography and Policy.* Newbury Park, CA: Sage.

———. 1994. *Qualitative Methods in Aging Research.* Thousand Oaks, CA: Sage.

Haber, David. 2009. "Gerontology: Adding an Empowerment Paradigm." *Journal of Applied Gerontology* 28:283–297.

Hacker, Jacob S., and Ann O'Leary. 2012. *Shared Responsibility, Shared Risk: Government, Markets, and Social Policy in The Twenty-First Century.* New York: Oxford University Press.

Hae, Laam. 2011. "Dilemmas of the Nightlife Fix: Post-Industrialization and the Gentrification of Nightlife in New York City." *Urban Studies* 48 (16): 3449–3465.

Hannon, Kerry. 2012. "Bye-Bye Snowbird: Fewer Boomers Expect to Move to Another State in Retirement." *Forbes*, July 29. http://www.forbes.com/sites/kerryhannon/2012/07/29/ bye-bye-snowbird-fewer-boomers-expect-to-move-to-another-state-in-retirement/.

Harris, Neil, and John Grootjans. 2012. "The Application of Ecological Thinking to Better Understand the Needs of Communities of Older People." *Australasian Journal on Ageing* 31 (1): 17–21.

Heavens, Alan. 2002. "Visitability Made Viable Using Universal Design Concept, Builders Are Making Homes More Accessible for Strollers as Well as Wheelchairs." *Pittsburgh Post*, July 7. www.post-gazette.com.

Henchoz, Karine, Stefano Cavalli, and Myriam Girardin. 2008. "Health Perception and Health Status in Advanced Old Age: A Paradox of Association." *Journal of Aging Studies* 22 (3): 282–290.

Henderson, J. Neil. 1994. "Ethnic and Racial Issues." In *Qualitative Methods in Aging Research*, ed. Jaber F. Gubrium and Andrea Sankar, 33–50. Thousand Oaks, CA: Sage.

Hendricks, Jon. 2005. *Moral Economy and Ageing*. Cambridge, UK: Cambridge University Press.

———. 2012. "Considering Life Course Concepts." *Journals of Gerontology, Series B, Psychological Sciences and Social Sciences* 67 (2): 226–231.

Hendricks, Jon, and Cynthia Leedham. 1992. "Toward a Political and Moral Economy of Aging: An Alternative Perspective." *International Journal of Health Services: Planning, Administration, Evaluation* 22 (1): 125–137.

Hochschild, Arlie. 1973. *The Unexpected Community*. Englewood Cliffs, NJ: Prentice-Hall.

Hollister, Brooke, and Carroll Estes. 2013. "Local Long-Term Care Ombudsman Program Effectiveness and the Measurement of Program Resources." *Journal of Applied Gerontology* 32 (6): 708–728.

Hostetler, Andrew J. 2011. "Senior Centers in the Era of the 'Third Age': Country Clubs, Community Centers, or Something Else?" *Journal of Aging Studies* 25 (2): 166–176.

Hung, William, Joseph Ross, Kenneth Boockvar, and Albert Siu. 2011. "Recent Trends in Chronic Disease, Impairment, and Disability among Older Adults in the United States." *BMC Geriatrics* 11(1): 1–12.

Hurd, Laura C. 1999. "'We're Not Old!' Older Women's Negation of Aging and Oldness." *Journal of Aging Studies* 13:419–439.

Interboro Partners. 2012. "NORCs in NYC." http://urbanomnibus.net/2010/03/norcs-in -nyc/.

Jacobs, Jerry. 1974. *Fun City: An Ethnographic Study of a Retirement Community*. New York: Holt, Rinehart and Winston.

Jaworski, Margaret. 2011. "Who Loves You, Baby Boomer? Senior Emergency Departments Deliver Best Care for Older Americans." *Geriatric Nursing* 32 (3): 228–229.

Kahana, Eva, Loren Lovegreen, Boaz Kahana, and Michael Kahana. 2003. "Person, Environment, and Person-Environment Fit as Influences on Residential Satisfaction of Elders." *Environment and Behavior* 35 (3): 434–453.

Kane, Rosalie. 2009. "Empowerment of Seniors and Paradigm Change: A Commentary on Haber's Empowerment Paradigm." *Journal of Applied Gerontology* 28 (3): 298–303.

———. 2012. "30 Years of HCBS: Moving Care Closer to Home." *Generations* 36 (1) 6–13.

Keith, Jennie. 1979. "The Ethnography of Old Age: Introduction." *Anthropological Quarterly* 52 (1): 1–6.

Keller, Bill. 2012. "The Entitled Generation." *New York Times*, July 29, Op-Ed, A19.

Kendig, Hal. 2003. "Directions in Environmental Gerontology: A Multidisciplinary Field." *Gerontologist* 43 (5): 611–615.

Khan, Bilal. 2012. "Hipsters Reveal Innermost Thoughts on Gentrification." *Curbed NY*, March 18. http://ny.curbed.com/archives/2012/03/18/hipsters_reveal_innermost _thoughts_on_gentrification.php.

Kim, Hyun-Shik, Kazuhiro Harada, Masashi Miyashita, Eun-A Lee, Jin-Kee Park, and Yoshio Nakamura. 2011. "Use of Senior Center and the Health-Related Quality of Life in Korean Older Adults." *Journal of Preventive Medicine and Public Health* 44 (4): 149–156.

Kivnick, Helen Q., and Rachel Pruchno. 2011. "Bridges and Boundaries: Humanities and Arts Enhance Gerontology." *Gerontologist* 51 (2): 142–144.

Kleinbaum, Adam M. 2012. "Organizational Misfits and the Origins of Brokerage in Intrafirm Networks." *Administrative Science Quarterly* 57 (3): 407–452.

Klinenberg, Eric. 2002. *Heat Wave: A Social Autopsy of Disaster in Chicago*. Chicago: University of Chicago Press.

Koren, Mary Jane. 2010. "Person-Centered Care for Nursing Home Residents: The Culture-Change Movement." *Health Affairs* 29 (2): 312–317.

Kroger, Jane, and Vivienne Adair. 2008. "Symbolic Meanings of Valued Personal Objects in Identity Transitions of Late Adulthood." *Identity: An International Journal of Theory and Research* 8:5–24.

Krout, John. 1987. "Rural Versus Urban Differences in Senior Center Activities and Services." *Gerontologist* 2 (1): 92–97.

———. 1989. *Senior Centers in America*. New York: Greenwood Press.

———. 1994. "Changes in Senior Center Participant Characteristics during the 1980s." *Journal of Gerontological Social Work* 22:41–60.

Krout, John, Stephen J. Cutler, and Raymond Coward. 1990. "Correlates of Senior Center Participation: A National Analysis." *Gerontologist* 30 (1): 72–79.

Kuczmarski, Marie Fanelli, and Nancy Cotugna. 2009. "Outcome Evaluation of a 3-Year Senior Health and Wellness Initiative." *Journal of Community Health* 34:33–39.

Laditka, James, Sarah B. Laditka, and Kathryn B. Lowe. 2012. "Promoting Cognitive Health: A Web Site Review of Health Systems, Public Health Departments, and Senior Centers." *American Journal of Alzheimer's Disease and Other Dementias* 27 (8): 600–608.

La Gory, Mark, Russell Ward, and Susan Sherman. 1985. "The Ecology of Aging: Neighborhood Satisfaction in Older Populations." *Sociological Quarterly* 26 (3): 405–418.

Larkin, Elizabeth, and Matthew Kaplan. 2010. "Intergenerational Relationships at the Center: Finding Shared Meaning from Programs in the U.S. and Japan." *Young Children* 65 (3): 88–94.

Lawton, M. Powell. 1982. "Competence, Environmental Press, and the Adaptation of Older People." In *Aging and the Environment*, ed. M. P. Lawton, P. G. Windley, and T. Byerts, 233–259. New York: Springer.

———. 1990. "Aging and Performance of Home Tasks." *Human Factors* 32 (5): 527–536.

Lawton, M. Powell, and Lucille Nahemow. 1973. "Ecology and the Aging Process." In *The Psychology of Adult Development and Aging*, ed. C. Eisdorfer and M. P. Lawton, 619–674. Washington, DC: American Psychological Association.

Leadership Council of Aging Organizations (LCAO). 2013. "Sequestration Issue Brief with Federal Budget Principles." http://www.lcao.org/lcao-sequestration-issue-brief-oct2012/.

Lee, Susan. 2002. "Best of Senior Centers 2002." *Queens Tribune*. http://queenstribune .com/best2002/seniorscenters-best2002.htm.

Lee, Trymaine. 2008. "City Settles Sex Harassment Case at Department for Aging." *New York Times*, January 1. http://www.nytimes.com/2009/01/01/nyregion/01elder.html?r =0.

Lehning, Amanda J., Richard J. Smith, and Ruth E. Dunkle. 2013. "Do Age-Friendly Characteristics Influence the Expectation to Age in Place? A Comparison of Low-Income and Higher Income Detroit Elders." *Journal of Applied Gerontology*. http://jag.sagepub.com/ content/early/2013/03/21/0733464813483210.full.

Lestch, Corinne. 2011. "Senior Thrilled to Get Thanksgiving Meals Delivered by Actress Kathleen Turner and Mayor Bloomberg." *New York Daily News*, November 24.

Lewin, Tamar. 1993. "Clinton's Health Plan; Elderly with Large Health Care Bills See Special Boon in Clinton Proposal: The Clinton Prescription." *New York Times*, September 27, A14.

Lichtblau, Eric. 2012. "With a Major Push, AARP Returns to a Hard Line against Cuts in Benefits." *New York Times*, December 14, A12.

Lincoln, Yvonna S., and Egon G. Guba. 1985. *Naturalistic Inquiry*. Beverly Hills, CA: Sage.

Loe, Meika. 2011. *Aging Our Way: Lessons for Living from 85 and Beyond*. New York: Oxford University Press.

Love, Karen, and Annette Kelly. 2011. "Person-Centered Care: Changing with the Times." *Geriatric Nursing* 32 (2): 125–129.

Lucadamo, Kathleen. 2011. "City Unveils Senior-Center Hit List—Budget Cuts Force 105 Centers to Close at Month's End." *Daily News*, March 4. http://www.nydailynews.com/new-york/city-unveils-senior-center-hit-list-budget-cuts-force-105-centers-close-month-article-1.116731#ixzz2URYldXdf.

Lund, Anne, and Gunn Engelsrud. 2008. "I Am Not That Old: Inter-personal Experiences of Thriving and Threats at a Senior Center." *Ageing and Society* 28:675–692.

Lynch, Frederick. 2011. *One Nation under AARP: The Fight over Medicare, Social Security, and America's Future*. Berkeley: University of California Press.

Maltz, Jerry, and Christine Hunter. 2012. "Aging in Place: There's No Place Like Home." *Oculus*. http://www.nxtbook.com/nxtbooks/naylor/ARCQ0113/index.php?startid=28.

Manheimer, Ronald. 2009. "Creating Meaningful Senior-Friendly Spaces." *Generations* 33 (2): 60–65.

Marcum, Christopher Steven. 2010. "Unanticipated Gains: The Origins of Network Inequality in Everyday Life." *Washington: American Sociological Association* 39 (3): 348–349.

Marshall, Barbara. 2011. "The Graying of 'Sexual Health': A Critical Research Agenda." *Canadian Review of Sociology* 48 (4): 390–413.

Martin, Linda G., Robert F. Schoeni, and Patricia M. Andreski. 2010. "Trends in Health of Older Adults in the United States: Past, Present, Future." *Demography* 47:S17–S40.

Marwell, Nicole. 2007. *Bargaining for Brooklyn: Community Organizations in the Entrepreneurial City*. Chicago: University of Chicago Press.

Mather LifeWays. 2012. "Café Plus." http://www.matherlifeways.com/iyc_cafereplication.asp.

Mayer, Karl Ulrich. 2009. "New Trends in Life Course Research." *Annual Review of Sociology* 35:493–514.

Mayer, Karl Ulrich, and Urs Schoepflin. 1989. "The State and the Life Course." *Annual Review of Sociology* 15 (1): 187–209.

McAdam, Doug, and Sidney G. Tarrow. 2010. "Ballots and Barricades: On the Reciprocal Relationship between Elections and Social Movements." *Perspectives on Politics* 8 (2): 529–542.

McClintock, Pamela. 2012. "Old People, Old Stars: Hollywood's New Hot Demo Is Saving the Box Office." *Hollywood Reporter*, August 22. http://www.hollywoodreporter.com/news/meryl-streep-arnold-schwarzenegger-sylvester-stallone-364548.

McDonough, Kathryn, and Joan Davitt. 2011. "It Takes a Village: Community Practice, Social Work, and Aging-in-Place." *Journal of Gerontological Social Work* 54 (5): 528–541.

Merriam, Sharan B. 2009. *Qualitative Research: A Guide to Design and Implementation*. San Francisco: Jossey-Bass.

Merrill, John, and Michael E. Hunt. 1990. "Aging in Place: A Dilemma for Retirement Housing Administrators." *Journal of Applied Gerontology: The Official Journal of the Southern Gerontological Society* 9 (1): 60–76.

Meyer, David S. 2003. "How Social Movements Matter." *Contexts* 2 (4): 30–35.

Michael, Yvonne, Lisa F. Berkman, Graham A. Colditz, and Ichiro Kawachi. 2001. "Living Arrangements, Social Integration, and Change in Health Status." *American Journal of Epidemiology* 153:123–131.

Microsoft. 2010. "Virtual Senior Center Connects Homebound Seniors to Community and Family." http://www.microsoft.com/en-us/news/press/2010/mar10/03-10VSCPR.aspx.

Miller, Baila, Richard T. Campbell, Lucille Davis, Sylvia Furner, Aida Giachello, Thomas Prohaska, Julie E. Kaufman, Min Li, and Carmen Perez. 1996. "Minority Use of Community Long-Term Care Services: A Comparative Analysis." *Journals of Gerontology, Series B, Psychological Sciences and Social Sciences* 51B (2): S70–S81.

Milligan, Christine. 2009. *There's No Place Like Home: Place and Care in an Ageing Society.* Burlington, VT: Ashgate.

Miner, Sonia, John R. Logan, and Glenna Spitze. 1993. "Predicting the Frequency of Senior Center Attendance." *Gerontologist* 33 (5): 650–657.

Minkler, Meredith, and Carroll Estes. 1984. *Readings in the Political Economy of Aging.* New York: Baywood.

Moody, Harry "Rick." 2006. "The White House Conference on Aging 2015: The Shape of Things to Come." *Public Policy and Aging Report* 16 (1): 24–27.

———. 2008a. "Aging America and the Boomer War." *Gerontologist* 48 (6): 839–844.

———. 2008b. "The New Aging Enterprise." *AARP Academic Affairs Occasional Papers*, no. 4, AARP Academic Affairs, Washington, DC.

Myerhoff, Barbara G. 1979. *Number Our Days.* New York: Dutton.

Myers, Phyllis. 1982. *Aging in Place: Strategies to Help the Elderly Stay in Revitalizing Neighborhoods.* Washington, DC: Conservation Foundation and Urban Institute.

National Council on Aging (NCOA). 2012a. "Accredited Senior Centers: A Snapshot." November. http://www.ncoa.org/national-institute-of-senior-centers/standards -accreditation/accredited-senior-centers-a.html.

———. 2012b. "Older Americans Act Reauthorization." Issue brief. http://www.ncoa.org/ public-policy-action/older-americans-act/.

———. 2012c. *Building Excellence: National Council on Aging/National Institute of Senior Center—the National Senior Center Self-Assessment Process.* (NISC's national accreditation manual.) http://www.ncoa.org/assets/files/pdf/nisc/Building-Excellence-Intro.pdf.

———. 2012d. "Senior Centers: Fact Sheet." October. http://www.ncoa.org/press-room/fact -sheets/senior-centers-fact-sheet.html.

———. 2012e. "What You Don't Know about Your Local Senior Center." September. http:// www.ncoa.org/national-institute-of-senior-centers/nisc-news/what-you-dont-know -about.html.

———. 2013a. "NCOA's 2012 Programs of Excellence Awards." March. http://www.ncoa .org/calendar-of-events/nisc-2012-programs-of.html.

———. 2013b. "Senior Centers Reach the Hard-to-Reach." March 11. http://www.ncoa.org/ national-institute-of-senior-centers/nisc-news/senior-centers-reach-the.html.

———. n.d. *NCOA Public Policy Priorities for the 113th Congress (2013–2014).* http://www.ncoa .org/assets/files/pdf/public-policy--action/Public-Policy-Priorities-113th-Congress.pdf.

National Council on Aging and National Institute of Senior Centers. 2011. "Older Americans Act Reauthorization: Multipurpose Senior Centers for Positive Aging." Issue brief. September. http://www.ncoa.org/assets/files/pdf/OAA-Reauthorization-Senior-Center -Issue-Brief-Sept-2011.pdf.

National Health Policy Forum. 2009. *The Basics: Older Americans Act.* Washington, DC: George Washington University.

Negri, Kathleen. 2013. "The Older Americans Act: What Every Elder Law Attorney Needs to Know." *Colorado Lawyer* 42 (5): 41–56.

Newman, Katherine S. 2003. *A Different Shade of Gray: Midlife and Beyond in the Inner City.* New York: New Press/W. W. Norton.

New York Academy of Medicine (NYAM). 2009. *Age-Friendly NYC: Enhancing Our City's Livability for Older New Yorkers.* http://www.nyam.org/agefriendlynyc/initiatives/current/city-government.html.

———. 2010. *NYC Senior Centers: Visioning the Future.* http://www.nyam.org/news/publications/research-and-reports/hp-1.html.

New York Beat. 2011. "NYC Seniors Come Together to Protest the Closing of Senior Centers." June 2. http://thenewyorkbeat.com/nyc-seniors-come-together-to-protest-the-closing-of-senior-centers.

New York City Council. 2009. *New York City Council Budget Report: Analysis of the Fiscal 2010 Preliminary Budget and Fiscal 2009 Preliminary Mayor's Management Report for the Department for the Aging.* New York: City Council. http://council.nyc.gov/downloads/pdf/budget/fy2010_budget_report_aging_3_09.pdf.

———. 2010a. "City Council and Senior Advocates Launch 'Save Our Centers' Campaign." March 9. http://council.nyc.gov/html/pr/aging_03_09_10.shtml.

———. 2010b. *Hearing on the Mayor's Fiscal Year 2011 Preliminary Budget for the Department for the Aging.* New York: City Council. March 9. http://council.nyc.gov/downloads/pdf/budget/2011/pbr_dfta_2011.pdf.

———. 2011a. *Council's Response to the Mayor's FY 2012 Preliminary Budget and Preliminary Management Report.* April 8. http://council.nyc.gov/downloads/pdf/budget/2012/budget_response_fy_2012.pdf.

———. 2011b. *Hearing on the Mayor's Fiscal Year 2012 Preliminary Budget and the Fiscal Year 2011 Preliminary Mayor's Management Report.* March 14. http://council.nyc.gov/downloads/pdf/budget/2012/dfta_125.pdf.

———. 2012. *Hearing on the Mayor's Fiscal 2013 Preliminary Budget and the Fiscal 2012 Preliminary Mayor's Management Report for the Department for the Aging.* March 12. http://council.nyc.gov/downloads/pdf/budget/2013/125%20Aging%20%28DFTA%29.pdf.

New York City Department for the Aging (DFTA). 2007. *Critical Factors in the Successful Utilization of Senior Center Meals.* New York.

———. 2008a. "Getting Fresh: Seniors Board Yellow School Buses Headed to Green Markets." Press release. October 13. http://www.nyc.gov/html/dfta/downloads/pdf/press_release/yellow_buses.pdf.

——— 2008b. "DFTA Launches Aging Services Modernization to Address Senior Needs of Today and Tomorrow—Effort Examines the Department's Three Core Services: Case Management, Home Delivered Meals, and Senior Centers." Press release. January 22.

———. 2008c. *Promoting Positive Aging, 2005–2007.* New York City Department for the Aging.

———. 2010. *Profile of Older New Yorkers.* http://www.nyc.gov/html/dfta/downloads/pdf/demographic/profile_olderNYRS_0911_newsummaries_update.pdf.

———. 2011a. "The City of New York Receives Our Town Grant from the National Endowment for the Arts." Press release. July 12. http://www.nyc.gov/html/dcla/downloads/pdf/Our_Town-Space_for_Art_%2007132011.pdf.

———. 2011b. "NYC Service and Aging in New York Fund Hold 'The Great Exchange' the Largest Time Banking Event Ever." Press release. June 12. http://www.nyc.gov/html/dfta/downloads/pdf/press_release/timebank.pdf.

———. 2011c. "Innovative Senior Centers." *Care Management Journals* 12 (2): 50–53.

———. 2012. *NYC Department for the Aging Annual Plan Summary, April 1, 2013–March 31, 2014*. September. http://www.nyc.gov/html/dfta/downloads/pdf/publications/annual_plan_summary_1314.pdf.

———. n.d. "Senior Centers." http://www.nyc.gov/html/dfta/html/services/centers.shtml.

New York City Department of City Planning. 2008. *Community District Needs: Queens; Fiscal Year 2010.* http://www.nyc.gov/html/dcp/pdf/pub/qnneeds_2010.pdf.

———. 2011a. *Community District Needs for Fiscal Year 2012.* http://www.nyc.gov/html/dcp/html/pub/cdnd12.shtml.

———. 2011b. "Community District Profiles." http://www.nyc.gov/html/dcp/html/lucds/cdstart.shtml.

———. 2013. *NYC: A City of Neighborhoods.* http://www.nyc.gov/html/dcp/html/neighbor/neigh.shtml.

New York City Department of Health and Mental Hygiene. 2006. *New York City Community Health Profiles: New York City.* 2nd ed. http://www.nyc.gov/html/doh/html/data/nyc-health-profiles.shtml.

New York City Mayor's Office. 2003. *The Mayor's Management Report Fiscal 2003.* https://partner.hpdnyc.org/whalecom81b846a8d7ea6a1bb1b6bf/whalecom0/html/ops/downloads/pdf/mmr/0903_mmr.pdf.

———. 2004. *The Mayor's Management Report Fiscal 2004.* http://www.nyc.gov/html/ops/downloads/pdf/mmr/0904_mmr.pdf.

———. 2005. *The Mayor's Management Report Fiscal 2005.* http://www.nyc.gov/html/ops/downloads/pdf/mmr/0905_mmr.pdf.

———. 2007. *The Mayor's Management Report Fiscal 2007.* http://www.nyc.gov/html/ops/downloads/pdf/mmr/0907_mmr.pdf.

———. 2009a. "Initiatives Fulfill 2008 State of the City Promise and Follow Guidelines to Become a World Health Organization Age-Friendly City." Press release. August 25. http://www.nyc.gov/portal/site/nycgov/menuitem.c0935b9a57bb4ef3daf2f1c701c789a0/index.jsp?pageID=mayor_press_release&catID=1194&doc_name=http%3A%2F%2Fwww.nyc.gov%2Fhtml%2Fom%2Fhtml%2F2009b%2Fpr386-09.html&cc=unused1978&rc=1194&ndi=1.

———. 2009b. "Mayor Bloomberg, Speaker Quinn and the New York Academy of Medicine Unveil Blueprint to Enhance City's Livability for Older New Yorkers." Press release. Mayor's Office, New York. http://www.nyc.gov/html/dfta/downloads/pdf/press_release/all_ages_intiatives.pdf.

———. 2009c. *Preliminary Mayor's Management Report for the Department for the Aging.* New York: Mayor's Office. http://council.nyc.gov/downloads/pdf/budget/fy2010_budget_report_aging_3_09.pdf.

———. 2011. "Mayor Bloomberg Announces Eight Providers Selected to Develop the City's First Innovative Senior Centers." Press release. October 19. http://www.nyc.gov/html/dfta/downloads/pdf/press_release/innovative_senior_center.pdf.

New York Nonprofit Press. 2010a. "DFTA Lists 50 Senior Centers to Close June 30." May 12. http://nynp.biz/index.php/breaking-news/2486-dfta-lists-50-senior-centers-to-close-june-30-.

———. 2010b. "Future Is Soon! DFTA Previews New Senior Center Model, New Contracting Process." August 17. http://www.nynp.biz/index.php/breaking-news/3280-the-future-is-soon-dfta-previews-new-senior-center-model-new-contracting-process.

———. 2010c. "NYC Providers Face over $200 Million in Cuts." June 17. http://www.nynp.biz/index.php/breaking-news/2683-nyc-providers-face-over-200-million-in-cuts.

New York State Assembly. 2008. "Assemblywoman Catherine Nolan Advocates for Queens Seniors." February 28. http://assembly.state.ny.us/mem/Catherine-Nolan/story/26201/.

———. 2010. "Senior Centers: Funding, Challenges, and Value to the Community." Notice of public hearing by the Assembly Standing Committee on Aging [and] Assembly Standing Committee on Children and Families, November 6. http://assembly.state.ny.us/comm/Aging/20101006/.

New York State Office for the Aging. 2003. *Project 2015 State Agencies Prepare for the Impact of an Aging New York.* New York: State University of New York. https://www.suny.edu/provost/project2015.cfm.

———. 2008. "Michael Burgess' Hearing Testimony: Ensuring That Senior Centers Retain Access to Essential Supports during the Aging Services Modernization Initiative in NYC." En-De Reporting Services, New York.

Ng, Thomas W. H., and Daniel C. Feldman. 2010. "The Effects of Organizational Embeddedness on Development of Social Capital and Human Capital." *Journal of Applied Psychology* 95 (4): 696–712.

Nielson and BoomAgers. 2012. "Introducing Boomers: Marketing's Most Valuable Generation (MVG)." http://www.nielsen.com/us/en/insights/reports-downloads/2012/introducing-boomers—marketing-s-most-valuable-generation.html.

Northeast Queens Jewish Community Council. 2004. "NORC WOW Opens Office to Help Seniors Stay in Community." Press release. October 12.

Nyden, Phyllis, Emily Edlynn, and Julie Davis. 2006. *The Differential Impact of Gentrification on Communities in Chicago.* Chicago: Loyola University, Chicago Center for Urban Research and Learning.

NY1. 2011a. "City Council Members Blast Proposed Senior Center Closures." March 11. http://www.ny1.com/content/politics/political_news/135380/city-council-members-blast-proposed-senior-center-closures.

———. 2011b. "105 Senior Centers Slated to Close." *The Call* (blog), March 4. http://www.ny1.com/content/news/134943/105-senior-centers-slated-to-close/.

———. 2011c. "Senior Center Closures off the Table." October 20. http://www.ny1.com/content/politics/political_news/149333/senior-center-closures-off-the-table--agency-says.

Oliver, Debra Parker. 2011. "Rigor in Qualitative Research." *Research on Aging* 33 (4): 359–360.

Olson, Laura Katz. 1982. *The Political Economy of Aging: The State, Private Powers, and Social Welfare.* New York: Columbia University Press.

O'Rand, Angela M. 2012. "Plus ça la Change, Plus C'est la Même Chose: Latest Words on 'Life Words.'" *Journals of Gerontology, Series B, Psychological Sciences and Social Sciences* 67 (2): 235–237.

Oswald, Frank, Daniela Jopp, Christoph Rott, and Hans-Werner Wahl. 2011. "Is Aging in Place a Resource for or Risk to Life Satisfaction?" *Gerontologist* 51 (2): 238–250.

Owens, Ann. 2012. "Neighborhoods on the Rise: A Typology of Neighborhoods Experiencing Socioeconomic Ascent." *City and Community* 11 (4): 345–369.

Pardasani, Manoj. 2010. "Senior Centers: Characteristics of Participants and Nonparticipants." *Activities, Adaptation, and Aging* 34:48–70.

Pardasani, Manoj, and Lauri Goldkind. 2012. "Senior Centers and Policy Advocacy: Changing Public Perceptions." *Educational Gerontology* 38 (6): 375–390.

Pardasani Manoj, Kathy Sporre, and Peter Thompson. 2009. *New Models Taskforce: Final Report.* Washington, DC: National Institute of Senior Centers.

Pardasani, Manoj, and Peter Thompson. 2012. "Senior Centers: Innovative and Emerging Models." *Journal of Applied Gerontology* 31 (1): 52–77.

Partners in Prime. 2010. "Senior Center/Community Center." Presentation at the National Council on Aging and American Society on Aging's "Aging in America" conference, New Orleans, LA, March 15–19.

Petrovic, Ana. 2007. "The Elderly Facing Gentrification: Neglect, Invisibility, Entrapment, and Loss." *Elder Law Journal* 15 (2): 533–607.

Phillips, Judith, Nigel Walford, and Ann Hockey. 2012. "How Do Unfamiliar Environments Convey Meaning to Older People? Urban Dimensions of Placelessness and Attachment." *International Journal of Ageing and Later Life* 6 (2): 73–102.

Polivka, Larry, and Carroll Estes. 2009. "The Economic Meltdown and Old Age Politics." *Generations* 33 (3): 56–62.

Poor, Susan, Candace Baldwin, and Judy Willet. 2012. "The Village Movement Empowers Older Adults to Stay Connected to Home and Community." *Generations* 36 (1): 112–117.

Powell, Jason, and Azrini Wahidin. 2005. "Ageing in the 'Risk Society.'" *International Journal of Sociology and Social Policy* 25 (8): 70–83.

Putnam, Robert D. 2000. *Bowling Alone: The Collapse and Revival of American Community.* New York: Simon & Schuster.

Pynoos, Jon, Christy Nishita, Caroline Cicero, and Rachel Caraviello. 2008. "Aging in Place, Housing, and the Law." *Elder Law Journal* 16 (1): 1–34.

Ralston, Penny A. 1991. "Senior Centers and Minority Elders: A Critical Review." *Gerontologist* 31 (3): 325–331.

Reaney, Patricia. 2012. "Older Americans Upbeat about Aging, Future: Survey." *Reuters*, August 7.

Reinharz, Shulemit. 1994. "Qualitative Evaluation and Policy." In *Qualitative Methods in Aging Research*, ed. Jaber F. Gubrium and Andrea Sankar, 263–267. Thousand Oaks, CA: Sage.

Rodwin, Victor, and Michael K. Gusmano. 2006. *Growing Older in World Cities.* Nashville, TN: Vanderbilt University Press.

Rogerson, Peter A., and Daejong Kim. 2012. "Population Distribution and Redistribution of the Baby Boom Cohort in the United States: Recent Trends and Implications." In *Population and Society: Essential Readings*, ed. Frank Trovato, 323–332. Ontario: Oxford University Press.

Rootshock.org. 2012. Homepage. http://www.rootshock.org/Home.

Rose, Miriam, Farida Ejaz, Linda Noelker, and Melissa Castora-Binkley. 2010. "Recent Findings on Home and Community-Based Services across the States." *Public Policy and Aging Report* 20 (1): 10–15.

Rosel, Natalie. 2003. "Aging in Place: Knowing Where You Are." *International Journal of Aging and Human Development* 57 (1): 77–90.

Rosenberg, Buck C. 2013. "Social Spaces for Seniors: Exploring Seniors' Centers and Clubs in Australia." *Journal of Sociology.* http://0-jos.sagepub.com.source.unco.edu/content/early/2013/01/24/1440783312474083.

Roth, Erin G., Lynn Keimig, Robert L. Rubinstein, Leslie Morgan, Kevin J. Eckert, Susan Goldman, and Amanda D. Peeples. 2012. "Baby Boomers in an Active Adult Retirement Community: Comity Interrupted." *Gerontologist* 52 (2): 189–198.

Rowles, Graham D. 1978. *Prisoners of Space? Exploring the Geographical Experience of Older People.* Boulder, CO: Westview Press.

———. 1993. "Evolving Images of Place in Aging and 'Aging in Place.'" *Generations* 17 (2): 65–70.

Rowles, Graham D., and Linda Manning 2011. *Experiencing the Third Age: The Practice of Qualitative Inquiry.* New York: Springer.

Rubenstein, Robert. 1989. "The Home Environments of Older People: Description of the Psychosocial Processes Linking Person to Place." *Journal of Gerontology: Social Sciences* 44 (2): S45–S53.

Sabia, Joseph J. 2008. "There's No Place like Home: A Hazard Model Analysis of Aging in Place among Older Homeowners in the PSID." *Research on Aging* 30 (1): 3–35.

Sackman, Bobbie. 2008. "Aging in a New Era." *Gotham Gazette*, March 17. http://www.gothamgazette.com/index.php/social-services/3914-aging-in-a-new-era-.

Salari, Sonia, Barbara Brown, and Jacqueline Eaton. 2006. "Conflicts, Friendships Cliques, and Territorial Displays in Senior Center Environments." *Journal of Aging Studies* 20:237–252.

Salas, Nashla, and Doug Turetsky. 2011. "Senior Centers Come, Senior Centers Go." *IBO Web Blog*, December 8. http://ibo.nyc.ny.us/cgi-park/?p=411.

Samuels, Tanyanika. 2012. "City Creates 'Aging Improvement District' in North-East Bronx to Help Improve Daily Lives of Seniors." *New York Daily News*, October 9.

Sánchez-Jankowski, Martín. 2008. *Cracks in the Pavement: Social Change and Resilience in Poor Neighborhoods.* Berkeley: University of California Press.

Sanders, Bernie. 2012. "Older Americans Act 2011 Amendments." http://www.sanders.senate.gov/imo/media/doc/OAA-fact-sheet.pdf.

Sanjek, Roger. 2000. "Color-Full before Color Blind: The Emergence of Multiracial Neighborhood Politics in Queens, New York City." *American Anthropologist* 102:762–772.

Sanz, Marilina. 2013. "Older Americans Act Reauthorization Bill Introduced in Senate by Sanders." http://www.naco.org/newsroom/countynews/Current%20Issue/6-3-2013/Pages/Older-Americans-Act-reauthorization-bill-introduced-in-Senate-by-Sanders.aspx.

Savishinsky, Joel S. 1991. *The Ends of Time: Life and Work in a Nursing Home.* New York: Bergin and Garvey.

Schafer, Markus H., Kenneth F. Ferraro, and Sarah A. Mustillo. 2011. "Children of Misfortune: Early Adversity and Cumulative Inequality in Perceived Life Trajectories." *American Journal of Sociology* 116 (4): 1053–1091.

Scharlach, Andrew E. 2009. "Creating Aging-Friendly Communities." *Generations* 33 (2): 5–11.

Schoenberg, Nancy, and William McAuley. 2007. "Promoting Qualitative Research." *Gerontologist* 47 (5): 576–577.

Schoenberg, Nancy, Edward Miller, and Rachel Pruchno. 2011. "The Qualitative Portfolio at the Gerontologist: Strong and Getting Stronger." *Gerontologist* 51 (3): 281–284.

Schoenberg, Nancy, Dina Shenk, and Cary Kart. 2007. "Food for Thought: Nourishing the Publication of Qualitative Research." *Journal of Applied Gerontology* 26 (1): 4–16.

Seewer, John. 2012. "Aging Baby Boomers Face Home Health Care Challenges." *Associated Press*, August 5. http://www.businessweek.com/ap/2012-08-05/aging-baby-boomers-face-home-health-care-challenge.

Settersten, Richard, and Molly Trauten. 2009. "The New Terrain of Old Age: Hallmarks, Freedom, and Risks." In *Handbook of Theories of Aging*, ed. Vern Bengtson et al., 455–469. New York: Springer.

Sheehan, Susan. 1984. *Kate Quinton's Days.* Boston: Houghton Mifflin.

Silcoff, Mireille. 2010. "Against Zoomerism: Reaching 65 Was Once Enough to Put You Beyond the Petty Youth-centric Hype Machine, but Sadly That's No Longer True." *National Post*, April 24.

Slater, Tom. 2008. "A Literal Necessity to be Re-placed: A Rejoinder to the Gentrification Debate." *International Journal of Urban and Regional Research* 32 (1): 212–223.

Small, Mario Luis. 2009. *Unanticipated Gains: Origins of Network Inequality in Everyday Life.* New York: Oxford University Press.

Smith, Allison E. 2009. *Ageing in Urban Neighbourhoods: Place Attachment and Social Exclusion.* Portland, OR: Polity.

Smithers, Janice A. 1985. *Determined Survivors: Community Life among the Urban Elderly.* New Brunswick, NJ: Rutgers University Press.

Solimeo, Samantha. 2009. *With Shaking Hands: Aging with Parkinson's Disease in America's Heartland.* New Brunswick, NJ: Rutgers University Press.

Somera, Rene. 1997. *Bordered Aging: Ethnography of Daily Life in a Filipino Home for the Aged.* Manila: De La Salle University Press.

Sperazza, Lynda J., and Priya Banerjee. 2010. "Baby Boomers and Seniors: Understanding Their Leisure Values Enhances Programs." *Activities, Adaptation, and Aging* 34 (3): 196–215.

Spradley, James P. 1979. *The Ethnographic Interview.* Belmont, CA: Wasdworth.

Stafford, Philip B. 2009. *Elderburbia: Aging with a Sense of Place in America.* Santa Barbara, CA: Praeger.

Stanley, Jennifer Tehan, and Fredda Blanchard-Fields. 2010. "Beliefs about Behavior Account for Age Differences in the Correspondence Bias." *Journal of Gerontology B: Psychological and Social Science* 66B (2): 169–176.

State Society on Aging of New York. 2008. State Society on Aging (SSA) Bulletin, October 25, http://ssany.org/pdf/winter08_newsletter.pdf.

Steinberg, Nicole. 2011. *Forgotten Borough: Writers Come to Terms with Queens.* Albany: State University of New York Press.

Stephens, Robert, and Helen Kwah. 2009. "Critical Factors in the Successful Utilization of Senior Center Meals." *Care Management Journals* 10 (4): 163–175.

Stovel, Katherine, and Lynette Shaw. 2012. "Brokerage." *Annual Review of Sociology* 38 (1): 139–158.

Sullivan, Mercer L. 2002. "Exploring Layers: Extended Case Method as a Tool for Multilevel Analysis of School Violence." *Sociological Methods and Research* 31 (2): 255–285.

Taietz, Philip. 1976. "Two Conceptual Models of the Senior Center." *Journal of Gerontology* 31 (2): 219–222.

Tang, Fengyan, and Yeonjung Lee. 2010. "Home- and Community-Based Services Utilization and Aging in Place." *Home Health Care Services Quarterly* 29 (3): 138–154.

———. 2011. "Social Support Networks and Expectations for Aging in Place and Moving." *Research on Aging* 33:444–464.

Tang, Fenyang, and Joseph Pickard. 2008. "Aging in Place or Relocation: Perceived Awareness of Community-Based Long-Term Care and Services." *Journal of Housing for the Elderly* 22 (4): 404–422.

Thomas, William. 2004. *What Are Old People For? How Elders Will Save the World.* New York: Vanderwyk and Burnham.

Thompson, Peter. 2009. New Models of Senior Centers Webinar, October 15. http://vimeo .com/21700253.

Tillotson, Kristin. 2012. "Website Targets 'Tween' Seniors: Developed at TPT in St. Paul, Next Avenue Features a Wide Range of Topics Geared toward Aging Baby Boomers." *Minneapolis Star Tribune*, March 15, E1.

Torres, Stacy. 2010. "Bloomberg Shuttering Lifesaving Senior Centers." *Huffington Post*, May 14. http://www.huffingtonpost.com/stacy-torres/bloomberg-shuttering-life_b _576507.html.

Torres-Gil, Fernando, and Brian Hofland. 2012. "Vulnerable Populations." In *Independent for Life: Homes and Neighborhoods for an Aging America*, ed. Henry Cisneros, Margaret Dyer-Chamberlain, and Jane Hickie, 221–232. Austin: University of Texas Press.

Torres-Gil, Fernando, and Diana Lam. 2010. "Aging in Place: The Nature of Limited Choice" (graphic). Reproduced in "Vulnerable Populations," by Fernando Torres-Gil and Brian Hofland, in *Independent for Life: Homes and Neighborhoods for an Aging America*, ed. Henry Cisneros, Margaret Dyer-Chamberlain, and Jane Hickie, 221–232. Austin: University of Texas Press, 2012.

———. 2011. "America Is at the Nexus of Aging and Multiculturalism." *Aging Today* 32 (2): 1–2.

Torres-Gil, Fernando, and Valentine Villa. 2000. "Social Policy and Aging." In *The Handbook of Social Policy*, ed. J. Midgley, M. Tracy, and M. Livermore, 209–220. Thousand Oaks, CA: Sage.

Transportation Alternatives. 2010. *Walk the Walk: Connecting Senior Pedestrian Safety to Seniors in New York City, Safe Routes for Seniors*. Report. New York. http://transalt.org/files/news/reports/2009/walk_the_walk.pdf.

Turner, K. Whisnant. 2004. "Senior Citizens Centers: What They Offer, Who Participates, and What They Gain." *Journal of Gerontological Social Work* 43:37–47.

Tuttle, Brad. 2012. "Psychology of Money: Baby Boomers Like Discounts—Just Not the 'Senior Discount.'" *Time's Moneyland*, July 27. http://moneyland.time.com/2012/07/27/baby-boomers-like-discounts-just-not-the-senior-discount/.

United Health Foundation. 2013. America's Health Rankings Senior Report.

United Hospital Fund. 2005. *A Directory of NORC Supportive Service Programs in New York City*. New York: Aging in Place Initiative.

United States Census. 2009. *Census 2000 Demographic Profile*. http://www.americanfactfinder.gov.

———. 2010. Census *Census 2010 Demographic Profile*. http://www.americanfactfinder.gov.

United States Congress. 1965. *Older Americans Act Amendments of 1965*. Washington, DC: Government Printing Office.

———. 2011. *Senator Sanders' Older Americans Act 2012 Amendments. S. S2037*.

United States Department of Health and Human Services (USDHHS). 2004. *Supportive Services Programs in Naturally Occurring Retirement Communities*. New York: Urban Institute.

———. 2012. "HHS Announces New Affordable Care Act Options for Community-Based Care Medicaid and Medicare Introduce Greater Flexibility for Beneficiaries to Receive Care at Home or in Settings of Their Choice." http://www.hhs.gov/news/press/2012pres/04/20120426a.html.

Van den Hoonaard, Deborah Kestin. 2005. "Am I Doing It Right? Older Widows as Interview Participants in Qualitative Research." *Journal of Aging Studies* 19:393–406.

Van Ryzin, Jean. 2010. "Tomorrow's Senior Center: Dynamic, Accessible, and Perhaps Not Even Called Senior." National Council on Aging. http://www.ncoa.org/strengthening-community-organizations/senior-centers/nisc/tomorrows-senior-center.html.

van Velsen, Jaap. 1967. "The Extended-Case Method and Situational Analysis." In *The Craft of Social Anthropology*, ed. A. L. Epstein, 129–149. London: Tavistock.

Venugopal, Arun. 2009. "A New Center for Indian Seniors." *WNYC News*. WNYC, March 29. http://www.wnyc.org/articles/wnyc-news/2009/mar/29/a-new-center-for-indian-seniors/.

Vesperi, Maria D. 1985. *City of Green Benches: Growing Old in a New Downtown*. Ithaca, NY: Cornell University Press.

Vesperi, Maria D., and J. Neil Henderson. 1995. *The Culture of Long-Term Care: Nursing Home Ethnography*. Westport, CT: Bergin and Garvey.

Vladeck, Fredda. 2004. *A Good Place to Grow Old New York's Model for NORC Supportive Service Programs*. New York: United Hospital Fund.

Vladeck, Fredda, and Rebecca Segel. 2010. "Identifying Risks to Healthy Aging in New York City's Varied NORCs." *Journal of Housing for the Elderly* 24 (3–4): 356–372.

Wacker, Robbyn R., and Karen A. Roberto. 2014. *Community Resources for Older Adults: Programs and Services in an Era of Change*. New York: SAGE.

Wagner, Donna. 1995. *Senior Center Research in America: An Overview of What We Know*. Washington, DC: National Council on the Aging.

Wahl, Hans-Werner, and Gerald D. Weisman. 2003. "Environmental Gerontology at the Beginning of the New Millennium: Reflections on Its Historical, Empirical, and Theoretical Development." *Gerontologist* 43 (5): 616–627.

Walker, Jan, Carol Bisbee, Russell Porter, and Joanne Flanders. 2004. "Increasing Practitioners' Knowledge of Participation among Elderly Adults in Senior Center Activities." *Educational Gerontology* 30 (5): 353–366.

Wenger, G. Clare. 1999. "Advantages Gained by Combining Qualitative and Quantitative Data in a Longitudinal Study." *Journal of Aging Studies* 13:369–376.

White House Conference on Aging. 2005. "The Booming Dynamics of Aging: From Awareness to Action." Washington, DC.

Whyte, William H. 1988. *City: Rediscovering the Center*. New York: Doubleday.

———. (1980) 2000. *The Social Life of Small Urban Spaces*. New York: Project for Public Spaces.

Wiles, Janine L., Annette Leibing, Nancy Guberman, Jeanee Reeve, and Ruth E. S. Allen. 2012. "The Meaning of 'Aging in Place' to Older People." *Gerontologist* 52 (3): 357–366.

Wilson, Basil. 2009. "Caribbean Immigrants in New York City and the Rise of a Black Middle Class in Southeast Queens." *Wadabagei: A Journal of the Caribbean and Its Diasporas* 12:33–45.

World Health Organization. 2007. *Global Age-Friendly Cities: A Guide*. New York: United Nations.

Yearwood, Ann. W., and Paula L. Dressel. 1983. "Interracial Dynamics in a Southern Rural Senior Center." *Gerontologist* 23 (5): 512–517.

Zimmerman, Sheryl, and Lauren W. Cohen. 2010. "Evidence behind the Green House and Similar Models of Nursing Home Care." *Aging Health* 6 (6): 717–737.

Zukin, Sharon. 1995. *The Cultures of Cities*. Cambridge, MA: Blackwell.

———. 2009. "Changing Landscapes of Power: Opulence and the Urge for Authenticity." *International Journal of Urban and Regional Research* 33 (2): 543–553.

———. 2010. *Naked City: The Death and Life of Authentic Urban Places*. New York: Oxford University Press.

———. 2011. "Reconstructing the Authenticity of Place." *Theory and Society* 40 (2): 161–165.

Index

TimeBankNYC program, 75
Title III funding, 152
Title XX funding, 68–69, 72, 113, 114, 116
Torres, Stacey, 71
Torres-Gil, Fernando, 120, 156, 177n7
Trailview Development Corporation, 37
transferability, 173
Transitions Network, 135
transportation, 47, 50, 122; Access-a-Ride,
      84, 147, 181n18; aging in place and,
      144; for centergoers to merged centers,
      159; commuting and, 8; taxi smart card
      program for, 181n18
Transportation Alternative, 66
trips/outings, 46, 57
trustworthiness, 173
Turner, Kathleen, 98
*21st Century Senior Centers: Changing the
      Conversation; A Study of NYC's Senior
      Centers* (CSCS report), 68, 112, 136, 137

UJA Federation of New York, 69
underutilization of centers, 64, 65, 66, 136.
      See also attendance of centers
unemployment, 8, 10
United Healthcare Foundation, 29
"United States of Aging, The" (2012 tele-
      phone survey), 29
Universities of the Third Age (U3A), 134
Upper West Side (Manhattan), 78
urban neighborhoods, 6
USA Today, 29
U.S. Census, 10, 120
U.S. Congress, 4, 79, 94, 152
U.S. Department of Energy, 111
U.S. Department of Health and Human
      Services, 144, 156; Health and Human
      Services education appropriation, 78
U.S. Department of Housing and Urban
      Development, 33
utilization of centers' services, 38–41

Van den Hoonaard, Deborah Kestin, 58
van Velsen, Jaap, 16

Vesperi, Maria, *City of Green Benches*, 17
Via Health Fitness and Enrichment Center
      (AL), 134
Victoria (regular), 2, 49, 51–52, 53, 84, 85, 106
Villa, Valentine, 156, 177n7
Visions Center at Selis Manor, 41, 75
visitability, 37
volunteering, 2, 38, 46, 106, 151

Wahidin, Azrini, 156
Walford, Nigel, 121
Walker, Jan, 28, 59
*Walk the Walk: Connecting Senior Pedestrian
      Safety to Seniors in NYC* (Transporta-
      tion Alternative), 66
Wall Street Journal, 80
Ward, Russell, 121
Weil, Andrew, 134
wellness centers. *See* health and wellness centers
West Community Center expansion, 96
Westside Senior-Supported Agriculture
      Food Bag Program, 80
"What's in a Name? Perspectives on the
      Sociology of Age, Aging, and the Life
      Course" (panel), 35
White House Conference on Aging (1961), 26
White House Conference on Aging (2005), 62
Wiles, Janine, 33
William Hodson Center (Bronx), 25, 132
Williamsburg, Brooklyn, 15, 126
women, 1–3; friendship support for, 59;
      honor awards for, at Queens senior
      center, 89
working class people, 10, 123
Works Progress Administration, 9
World Health Organization (WHO), 32, 67

YM/YWHA of Washington Heights and
      Inwood (Manhattan), 41, 75
youth. *See* intergenerational centers

Zimmerman, Sheryl, 37
Zukin, Sharon, 15, 23, 119, 124–125, 126

About the Author

Joyce Weil, PhD, MPH, is an assistant professor of gerontology at the University of Northern Colorado. Her articles have appeared in *Journal of Aging, Humanities, and Arts*; *Journal of Loss and Trauma*; *Social Forces*; *International Journal of Aging and Society*; and *Research on Aging*. She is the coeditor, with Diditi Mitra, of *Race and the Lifecourse: Readings from the Intersection of Race, Ethnicity and Age*.

CPSIA information can be obtained at www.ICGtesting.com
Printed in the USA
LVOW11s1726210215

427833LV00001B/13/P